Moon, Sun, and Rising Signs

An Essential Guide to Star Sign Astrology, Personality Types, and Psychic Development

© Copyright 2023 - All rights reserved.

The content contained within this book may not be reproduced, duplicated, or transmitted without direct written permission from the author or the publisher.

Under no circumstances will any blame or legal responsibility be held against the publisher, or author, for any damages, reparation, or monetary loss due to the information contained within this book, either directly or indirectly.

Legal Notice:

This book is copyright protected. It is only for personal use. You cannot amend, distribute, sell, use, quote, or paraphrase any part, or the content within this book, without the consent of the author or publisher.

Disclaimer Notice:

Please note the information contained within this document is for educational and entertainment purposes only. All effort has been executed to present accurate, up-to-date, reliable, and complete information. No warranties of any kind are declared or implied. Readers acknowledge that the author is not engaging in the rendering of legal, financial, medical, or professional advice. The content within this book has been derived from various sources. Please consult a licensed professional before attempting any techniques outlined in this book.

By reading this document, the reader agrees that under no circumstances is the author responsible for any losses, direct or indirect, that are incurred as a result of the use of the information contained within this document, including, but not limited to, errors, omissions, or inaccuracies.

Free Bonus from Silvia Hill available for limited time

Hi Spirituality Lovers!

My name is Silvia Hill, and first off, I want to THANK YOU for reading my book.

Now you have a chance to join my exclusive spirituality email list so you can get the ebooks below for free as well as the potential to get more spirituality ebooks for free! Simply click the link below to join.

P.S. Remember that it's 100% free to join the list.

~~$27~~ **FREE BONUSES**

- 9 Types of Spirit Guides and How to Connect to Them
- How to Develop Your Intuition: 7 Secrets for Psychic Development and Tarot Reading
- Tarot Reading Secrets for Love, Career, and General Messages

Access your free bonuses here
https://livetolearn.lpages.co/moon-sun-and-rising-signs-paperback/

Table of Contents

PART 1: MOON SIGNS 1
    INTRODUCTION 2
    CHAPTER 1: WHAT ARE MOON SIGNS? 4
    CHAPTER 2: THE FOUR PSYCHIC POWERS 13
    CHAPTER 3: YOUR MOON SIGN DETERMINES YOUR PSYCHIC POWERS 23
    CHAPTER 4: BOLD MOONS: ARIES, LEO, AND SAGITTARIUS 30
    CHAPTER 5: THOUGHTFUL MOONS: LIBRA, AQUARIUS, AND GEMINI 41
    CHAPTER 6: GROUNDED MOONS: TAURUS, VIRGO, AND CAPRICORN 53
    CHAPTER 7: EMOTIONAL MOONS: PISCES, SCORPIO, AND CANCER 65
    CHAPTER 8: GETTING TO KNOW YOUR PSYCHIC POWERS 76
    CHAPTER 9: TAPPING INTO THE FOUR CLAIRS 86
    CHAPTER 10: TURNING YOUR PSYCHIC POWERS ON AND OFF 94
    CONCLUSION 100
PART 2: SUN SIGNS 102
    INTRODUCTION 103
    CHAPTER 1: INTRODUCING ASTROLOGY 105
    CHAPTER 2: PLANETS: THE SOURCE OF ENERGY 116

CHAPTER 3: ZODIAC SIGNS: THE TYPE OF ENERGY 127
CHAPTER 4: THE HOUSES: WHERE THE ENERGY
MANIFESTS 139
CHAPTER 5: DISCOVERING YOUR SUN SIGN 147
CHAPTER 6: IDENTIFYING YOUR MOON SIGN 170
CHAPTER 7: SUN-MOON COMBINATIONS I - EARTH-
SUN SIGNS 193
CHAPTER 8: SUN-MOON COMBINATIONS II: AIR SUN
SIGNS 205
CHAPTER 9: SUN-MOON COMBINATIONS ILL: WATER
SUN SIGNS 216
CHAPTER 10: SUN-MOON COMBINATIONS IV: FIRE
SUN SIGNS 229
CONCLUSION 240

PART 3: RISING SIGNS 242
INTRODUCTION 243
CHAPTER 1: INTRODUCING THE RISING SIGN 245
CHAPTER 2: IDENTIFYING YOUR RISING SIGN 254
CHAPTER 3: UNDERSTANDING YOUR RISING SIGN 266
CHAPTER 4: ARIES RISING AND TAURUS RISING 278
CHAPTER 5: GEMINI RISING AND CANCER RISING 288
CHAPTER 6: LEO RISING AND VIRGO RISING 298
CHAPTER 7: LIBRA RISING AND SCORPIO RISING 307
CHAPTER 8: SAGITTARIUS RISING AND CAPRICORN
RISING 317
CHAPTER 9: AQUARIUS RISING AND PISCES RISING 326
CHAPTER 10: A GUIDE TO EMBRACE YOUR RISING
SIGN 335
CONCLUSION 345

HERE'S ANOTHER BOOK BY SILVIA HILL THAT YOU
MIGHT LIKE 347
FREE BONUS FROM SILVIA HILL AVAILABLE FOR
LIMITED TIME 348
REFERENCES 349

Part 1: Moon Signs

Secrets to Tapping into Your Psychic Abilities and More According to Your Moon Sign

Introduction

Why are some people more intuitive than others? How do they seem to have a "sixth sense" that allows them to predict the future or read other people's thoughts? The answer may lie in your moon sign.

Your moon sign is the astrological sign corresponding to the moon's position at the time of your birth. Just as sun signs represent your overall personality, your moon sign represents your inner self - your emotions, intuition, and your subconscious mind. Moon signs can be used to predict everything from your emotional response to certain situations to how strong the likelihood is of you developing psychic abilities. This book will explore the connection between your moon sign and your psychic powers. We'll also look at how you can use your moon sign to unlock your psychic abilities.

The book is divided into three parts. Part One will introduce you to the basics of moon sign astrology and psychic powers. In Part Two, you will learn how your moon sign affects your psychic abilities, and in Part Three, you will learn how to develop and use your psychic powers. At the end of this book, you'll have better insight into your psychic abilities and how to use them to your advantage.

Chapter 1 will introduce you to the basics of moon signs. You'll learn what they are and how they're used in astrology. Chapter 2 will explore the four psychic powers: Clairvoyance, Clairsentience, Claircognizance, and clairaudience. You'll learn how each of these powers works and how they can be used to your advantage. Chapter 3 will show you how your moon sign determines your psychic powers.

In Part Two, you will learn about the different types of moon signs and how they affect your psychic abilities. Chapter 4 will explore the bold moons - Aries, Leo, and Sagittarius. You'll learn how these signs are more likely to develop psychic abilities and how they can use their powers to their advantage. Chapter 5 will examine the thoughtful moons — Libra, Aquarius, and Gemini. You'll learn how these signs are more likely to be in tune with their intuition and how they can use their psychic abilities to make better decisions.

Chapter 6 will explore the grounded moons — Taurus, Virgo, and Capricorn. You'll learn how these signs are more likely to have practical psychic abilities and how they can use their powers to their advantage. Chapter 7 will examine the emotional moons — Pisces, Scorpio, and Cancer. You'll learn how these signs are more likely to be in touch with their emotions and how they can use their psychic abilities to better understand the emotions of others.

In Part Three, you will learn how to develop and use your psychic abilities. Chapter 8 will help you to understand how to get to know your psychic abilities. Chapter 9 will take a deeper look at the four main types of psychic abilities described above: Clairvoyance, Clairsentience, Claircognizance, and Clairaudience. You'll learn how to develop each of these abilities and how to use them to your advantage. Finally, Chapter 10 teaches you how to turn your psychic abilities on and off.

By the end of this book, you will better understand your psychic abilities and how to use them to your advantage. So, let's get started!

Chapter 1: What Are Moon Signs?

"There is a moon inside every human being. Learn to be companions with it."

- Rumi

Many people are familiar with the 12 Sun signs, which mark the sun's position at the time of our birth. However, Moon signs are just as influential in astrology and can reveal plenty of information about our personalities and private thoughts. The Moon changes sign every two to three days, so your Moon sign is likely to be different from your Sun sign.

While Sun signs show how we present ourselves to the world, Moon signs represent our innermost selves. They tell us what we need to feel emotionally secure and what drives our deepest desires. If you're curious about your Moon sign, this chapter will explain everything you need to know. We'll start by discussing what Moon signs are and then give an overview of the 12 signs. Using your birth chart, you'll learn how to identify your own Moon sign. Finally, we'll explore their importance and teach you how understanding them can lead to a more fulfilling life.

Moon Signs

A Moon sign is, in fact, the sign of the zodiac the moon was in at the time of your birth. The moon moves through all twelve zodiac signs every month, spending about two and a half days in each sign. It's associated with our emotions, so our Moon sign reveals how we deal with them. It shows us what makes us feel emotionally secure and what kind of environment we need to feel comfortable in. Moon signs also reveal our innermost desires, the things we need to feel fulfilled.

A moon sign represents a person's core identity and the aspect of themselves that others may not see. It is the inner child, the emotional inner world, or the mushy center. The moon sign is often called the "emotional operating system." It is the part of us that responds emotionally to the events and experiences of our lives. The moon sign is the soul of our identity, the part of us that we may keep hidden from others.

The Twelve Moon Signs

There are twelve signs of the zodiac, and each one is associated with a different set of qualities. These can be divided into four elements: fire, earth, air, and water. The elements are used to describe the fundamental nature of each sign. Fire signs are passionate and bold, while earth signs are practical and down-to-earth. Air signs are intellectual and quick-witted, while water signs are emotional and compassionate.

Each element is also associated with a modality or way of being. The three modalities are cardinal, fixed, and mutable. Cardinal signs are the leaders of the zodiac, while fixed signs are the stabilizers. Mutable signs are adaptable and able to change and flow with the ebbs and tides of life.

1. **Aries: Fire, Cardinal**

As the first sign of the zodiac, Aries is associated with new beginnings and initiative. Those born under this sign are typically energetic and enthusiastic, with a natural ability to take charge. Aries is a fire sign; those who fall under this astrological influence tend to be passionate, impulsive, and sometimes hot-headed.

However, Aries is also a cardinal sign, meaning that those born under its influence are often natural leaders. They are driven and determined, always looking for new ways to prove themselves. Whether it's in their career or personal life, Aries is always up for a challenge.

2. Taurus: Earth, Fixed

Taurus is an earth sign. People born under this sign tend to be practical and down-to-earth. They are often very reliable and hardworking and take their commitments seriously. Taureans also have a strong sense of stability and security and value tradition and maintaining the status quo. However, this can also mean that Taureans can be inflexible and resistant to change.

People born under the sign of Taurus are usually patient and sensual and enjoy life's simple pleasures. They often have a strong appreciation for nature, music, and art. Taureans are loyal friends and partners, and they build lasting relationships. If you are looking for someone reliable, a Taurean makes a great friend or partner.

3. Gemini: Air, Mutable

Gemini is an air sign, and those born under this sign are known for their quick thinking, adaptability, and curiosity. Gemini is also a mutable sign, meaning its natives are characterized by their flexible nature and ability to change with the times. These qualities make Gemini some excellent communicators, as they can quickly adapt their message to suit their audience.

Gemini is also known for its dual nature, which can be both a strength and a weakness. On the positive side, this duality allows Gemini to see both sides of every issue. However, it can also make Gemini seem unpredictable or superficial. Ultimately, those born under this sign are intelligent, adaptable people who are always interesting to be around.

4. Cancer: Water, Cardinal

Water signs are highly emotional and intuitive. They are known for their compassionate nature and their ability to build strong emotional bonds. Water signs are also very nurturing, and they often put the needs of others before their own needs. Cancer is a water sign, and it is ruled by the planet Mercury. The element of water is associated with emotions, and Cancer is the sign that is most in touch with their feelings.

Cancerians are known for their domesticity and often create warm, inviting homes full of love and laughter. They are loyal friends and family members and will do anything to protect those they love. However, Cancerians can also be moody and insecure and may withdraw from those they love when they feel hurt or rejected. If you have a Cancer friend or family member, tell them that you support and care for them, no matter what.

5. Leo: Fire, Fixed

The fifth sign of the zodiac, Leo, is associated with the element of fire. Those born under this sign are fiercely loyal and can persevere through difficult times. Leos are also natural leaders who often take on a central role in their social groups. Although they can be strong-willed and stubborn, they also have a big heart and are always willing to help those in need.

Regarding relationships, Leos are looking for a partner who can keep up with their high energy level. They want someone exciting and adventurous but who is also reliable and loyal. The perfect partner for a Leo is someone who can make them feel like the center of attention. If you are in a relationship with a Leo, be prepared for a wild ride!

6. Virgo: Earth, Mutable

Virgo is an earth sign, which means that people born under this sign are practical and down-to-earth, are often interested in health and fitness, and have a strong sense of duty. They are also often very detail-oriented and strongly need security and stability. Virgos tend to be levelheaded and logical, but they can also be worriers who are sometimes overly critical of themselves and others.

As a mutable sign, Virgo is adaptable and flexible but can sometimes be indecisive. Virgos are usually good at communication and have the knack for seeing both sides of every issue. Overall, Virgos are hardworking, diligent people who strive for perfection in everything they do. The perfect partner for a Virgo is patient and understanding and who can help them relax and enjoy life.

7. Libra: Air, Cardinal

Libra is an air sign, and its element is air. Libra is also a cardinal sign. These two traits combine to create a sign that is communicative, social, and always on the move. Libras are natural diplomats, and they excel at mediating conflicts. Their airy nature gives them a lightness of being that is both charming and refreshing.

Libras are also highly adaptable and able to change course instantly if they feel it is necessary. This flexibility can be both a strength and a weakness, as Libras sometimes has difficulty making decisions. However, their ability to see both sides of every issue ensures that Libras are always fair-minded and just.

8. Scorpio: Water, Fixed

Scorpio is one of the three water signs of the zodiac, along with Cancer and Pisces. Like all water signs, Scorpio is highly emotional and intuitive. They are also incredibly loyal and passionate, making them quite intense. Regarding relationships, Scorpios are looking for a partner who can match their intensity and passion. They want someone honest and trustworthy and who will never betray their trust.

Scorpio is a fixed sign, meaning they are very stubborn and tenacious. They are also natural leaders who are not afraid to take risks. In many ways, Scorpio is the most extreme of all the signs. They can be both incredibly loving and fiercely protective, but they can also be jealous and vengeful. Nonetheless, Scorpio is a sign that is always worth getting to know.

9. Sagittarius: Fire, Mutable

As one of the fire signs, Sagittarius is associated with energy, enthusiasm, and a zest for life. Those born under this sign are optimistic, outgoing, and have a natural talent for taking risks. In addition, Sagittarius is a mutable sign, which means that those born under this sign are adaptable and flexible.

Sagittarians can often roll with the punches and make the best of any situation. However, this same trait can also make them prone to scattered thinking and impulsiveness. But overall, fire signs like Sagittarius are known for their passion, courage, and ability to light up a room - literally and figuratively.

10. Capricorn: Earth, Cardinal

Capricorn is an earth sign, meaning those who identify with this astrological sign are grounded, practical, and down-to-earth. Capricorns are also Cardinal signs, meaning that they are natural leaders. Those who fall under the Capricorn sign tend to be ambitious and driven. They know what they want, and they go after it with determination.

Capricorns tend to be patient and level-headed but can also be quite stubborn. They are reliable and trustworthy, but they can also be skeptics. Those who fall under the Capricorn sign are complex individuals who embody positive and negative traits. However, their strong work ethic, practical nature, and leadership abilities make them well-suited for success in any endeavor.

11. Aquarius: Air, Fixed

Aquarius is associated with the element of air. Aquarius is a fixed sign, meaning that it is associated with stability and perseverance. People born under this sign are often seen as independent and original thinkers. They are often very humanitarian in their outlook and are known for their ability to see both sides of every issue.

Aquarius is a popular sign, as it is often seen as an optimistic influence. Aquarius-born people are often passionate about making the world a better place. If you know someone with an Aquarius sun sign, you can be sure that they are always up for a good discussion!

12. Pisces: Water, Mutable

Pisces is represented by the symbol of two fish echoing the Latin stem of its name. It's a water sign, meaning emotions play a significant role in their lives. Pisces is also considered to be a mutable sign, which means they are adaptable and can flow with change. Pisces are known for their compassionate and nurturing nature, and they often put the needs of others before their own needs.

Pisces is also highly intuitive and have a great connection to the spiritual world. Regarding relationships, Pisces are often drawn to creative and sensitive people. Pisces needs a partner who understands their deep emotions and can provide them with the stability they need. The Pisces sign is often misunderstood, but if you take the time to get to know Pisces, you will find they are one of the most compassionate and caring signs of the zodiac.

How to Identify Your Moon Sign

In astrology, your moon sign is just as important as your sun sign. So, if you're interested in getting a fuller picture of yourself, it's worth taking the time to find your moon sign. But how exactly do you do that? Luckily, it's not as complicated as it sounds. Here's a step-by-step guide:

First, you'll need to know your birth date and time. Armed with that information, head over to an online astrology calculator (there are plenty of free ones available). Enter your birth date into the calculator, and it will generate a birth chart showing the position of the planets at the time of your birth. Look at the planet listed next to your sign in the "Moon" column - that is your moon sign. For example, if you're a Gemini with a Cancer moon, it means that at the time of your birth, the moon was in the sign of Cancer.

Remember that your moon sign can give clues about your inner emotional life - so don't be afraid to explore what it says about you!

How Understanding Moon Signs Can Improve Your Life

Moon signs represent your emotions and moods and can give you valuable insights into your innermost self. Unlike your sun sign, which remains the same throughout your life, your moon sign changes frequently. This means that it's essential to keep track of it to understand how it's affecting your current mood and outlook on life.

Paying attention to your moon sign can also help you better understand the people around you. By understanding their emotional needs and triggers, you can develop more empathy and compassion for them. In short, paying attention to your moon sign is a crucial way to gain a deeper understanding of yourself and those around you. Here are some of the benefits of understanding your moon sign:

1. **More Self-Awareness**

Understanding your Moon sign can help you become more self-aware and better understand your moods and reactions. For example, suppose you have a Cancer Moon sign. In that case, you may find yourself feeling more sensitive and emotional than other signs. This can be both a blessing and a curse, but it's essential to be aware of your tendencies to adjust accordingly. If you're feeling especially down or anxious, it may help to connect with loved ones or nature. Understanding your Moon sign can also help you to make more informed decisions in all areas of life, from relationships to career choices.

2. **Greater Compassion for Yourself and Others**

If you've ever read your daily horoscope and felt like it was speaking directly to you, there's a good chance that you have a solid connection to your moon sign. Moon signs represent our emotional selves - the part of us that is instinctively reactive and feeling-oriented. By understanding our own moon sign, we can gain greater insight into our emotional triggers and learn how to deal with the ups and downs of life. In turn, this can lead to greater compassion for us and others.

3. **Improved Relationships**

Another benefit of understanding your moon sign is that you can better understand your emotional needs and how they influence your behavior. This can be helpful in all kinds of relationships, from friendships to romantic partnerships. After all, if you know what makes you tick, it's easier to find someone who appreciates and understands you. In fact, one of the best ways to find true compatibility is to look for someone with a complementary moon sign.

4. **Deeper Connection to Intuition**

Have you ever felt like you just "know" something, even though you can't explain how you know it? This is your intuition talking. And according to astrology, your moon sign is the key to understanding and harnessing your intuition. By understanding your moon sign, you can learn to trust your intuition and tap into your inner wisdom more easily. You can develop a deeper connection to your intuition and use it to guide you through life's challenges.

5. **Better Decision Making**

Making decisions can be challenging. Whether you're choosing what to wear or whether to take a new job, it's not always easy to know what the right choice is. That's where understanding your moon sign can come in handy. By knowing your moon sign, you can better understand your emotional needs and make decisions that align with how you're feeling.

6. **Greater Clarity and Focus**

Finding clarity and focus in a constantly moving and changing world can be tricky. But according to astrology, your moon sign can help you to tap into your inner wisdom and find the clarity and focus you need. By understanding your moon sign, you can learn to trust your intuition and make decisions that align with your deepest desires. In turn, this can lead to a greater sense of clarity and focus in all areas of your life.

For example, suppose you're a person who tends to operate from a place of logic. In that case, you may find that your moon sign helps you connect with your emotions and make more balanced decisions. Alternatively, if you're someone who lets their emotions rule their decision-making, understanding your sign can help you to bring some logic into the mix and avoid making impulsive decisions that you may later regret. In short, understanding your moon sign can help you to make better decisions in all areas of your life.

Moon signs play an important role in astrology and can provide valuable insights into our lives. The moon's position at our time of birth can reveal our emotional needs and how we react to the ups and downs of life. By understanding our moon sign, we can gain greater self-awareness and compassion, improve our relationships, connect more deeply with our intuition, and make better decisions. All of these things can lead to a more fulfilling and satisfying life. So, if you're curious about astrology and want to learn more about yourself, check out your moon sign. It just might be the key to a happier, more fulfilling life.

Chapter 2: The Four Psychic Powers

"Psychic power is the ability to download information directly from the Universe."

- Lada Ray

Have you ever felt that you knew something, even though you couldn't know it? Many people believe these experiences are evidence of psychic power or an ability to tap into a hidden source of knowledge. According to this view, not everyone can connect to the information in the Universe, and psychic power is the power to access this information.

Some people believe everyone possesses psychic abilities, but most people are unaware or don't trust their abilities. Whether or not you believe in psychic power, it's fascinating to consider the possibility that we may all have the ability to connect with a hidden source of knowledge. And who knows what secrets the Universe may hold?

This chapter will explore the four main types of psychic abilities, also known as the "Clairs." These are Clairaudience (clear hearing), Clairvoyance (clear seeing), Clairsentience (clear feeling), and Claircognizance (clear knowing). We will also discuss how you can strengthen your psychic powers. So, if you've ever wondered whether you have psychic abilities, read on to find out more!

What Are Psychic Abilities?

Psychic abilities are special talents that allow someone to sense or perceive things that the five physical senses cannot detect. Although the term "psychic ability" is often used to refer to extraordinary feats of mind-reading or divination, there is no one definitive answer to that question. Some people believe that we all have latent psychic abilities and that developing them through training and practice is possible. Others maintain psychic ability is an innate talent that cannot be learned. Still, others believe that psychic ability is a supernatural power that defies explanation.

Whatever your beliefs, there is no denying that some people seem to possess an uncanny ability to intuit information or foresee events. Whether these abilities can be scientifically proven remains a matter of debate, but the stories of those who have had paranormal experiences are sure to fascinate and intrigue. One thing is for sure - the study of psychic ability is a fascinating journey into the unknown!

Clairaudience: The Power of Clear Hearing

Clairaudience is described as the ability to hear clearly. It is a psychic ability through which people receive information via auditory means. It can include hearing voices or sounds that are not audible to the average person. Clairaudience is a form of extrasensory perception or ESP. People with this ability can tap into a higher audio frequency than the average person, giving them access to information beyond the realm of normal human hearing.

Clairaudience is often associated with other psychic abilities, such as Clairvoyance and Clairsentience. People who have Clairaudience may also be able to receive messages from spirit guides, angels, and other higher beings. This ability can be used for guidance, healing, and personal growth. If you think you may have Clairaudience, there are several ways to develop and strengthen your ability. One way is to meditate and visualize yourself receiving clear messages. You can also try keeping a journal of your experiences. As you become more attuned to your abilities, you will likely find that Clairaudience becomes more reliable and accurate.

Benefits of Clairaudience

Having the gift of Clairaudience often means that you can hear things from the past and future. Some people use Clairaudience to receive guidance from their higher selves or Spirit Guides. Others use it to receive messages from loved ones who have passed away. Clairaudience can be a valuable tool for anyone seeking guidance or information.

When used correctly, it can give you insights that would otherwise be unavailable. Tuning into a higher frequency and having the ability to hear all these messages can give you a greater sense of peace and well-being. If you are open to the possibility of hearing things beyond the range of human hearing, Clairaudience may be something worth exploring.

Other benefits of this psychic ability include:

- It can be used for guidance in making decisions.
- It can be used to communicate with loved ones who have passed away.
- It can provide warnings about potential dangers.
- It can be used to help heal oneself or others.

How Clairaudience Is Used

Clairaudience is one of the main ways the Spirit communicates with Mediums during a reading. Clairaudience can manifest in different ways. Some people may hear an inner voice, while others may hear actual words spoken. Some people may even hear music or other sounds not of this world.

There is no wrong way to experience Clairaudience, and it is one of the easiest forms of mediumship to develop. The best way to start developing your Clairaudience is to simply pay deep attention to your inner thoughts and feelings. If you frequently have intuitive hunches or sudden insights, you may be starting to tap into your clairaudient abilities. Trust your gut and see where it takes you!

True Tales of Clairaudience

There are many stories concerning Clairaudience which have been passed down through the ages. Some of these stories are about famous figures such as Nostradamus, while others are about people with more personal experiences.

Nostradamus was perhaps the most famous clairaudient of all time. He was a 16th-century French doctor who was best known for his predictions. Nostradamus allegedly used Clairaudience to receive his visions of the future. He would reportedly go into a trance and then record what he heard. Many of his predictions have come true, and he is considered one of the most accurate psychics in history.

Another famous clairaudient is Edgar Cayce, an American born in 1877. He was a self-educated man with no formal training in the psychic arts; still, he is considered one of the most gifted psychics. Cayce allegedly used Clairaudience to receive healing messages from the other side. He would go into a trance and then pass on the information he received to whoever had asked for it. Cayce's work has helped to change many people's lives, and he is still revered as a psychic giant.

Clairvoyance: The Power of Clear Seeing

Clairvoyance is the ability to see clearly. It is not just seeing with the physical eyes but also the inner eye. Clairvoyance is about having a clear understanding of something. When you are clairvoyant, you can see beyond the physical world and into the spiritual realm, and you can see the truth that is hidden from most people.

Clairvoyance is a powerful ability that can be used for good or evil. A clairvoyant person can use their power to help others, or they can use it to control and manipulate them. It all depends on the intent of the clairvoyant person. It is, however, a rare ability that few people have. If you think you might be clairvoyant, it is crucial to learn how to use your power wisely.

Benefits of Clairvoyance

Being able to see beyond natural physical sight means a clairvoyant person can see places, people, and events that are not physically present at the time. For example, a clairvoyant person may be able to see a loved one who has passed away or an event that has not yet happened. It can also be used to see into the future and gain insight into upcoming events; however, before you get too excited, it doesn't mean a clairvoyant can give you the winning numbers for the lottery!

While some people dismiss Clairvoyance as being too far-fetched, there are many benefits to having this ability. For one, it can comfort those who have lost loved ones. Seeing them again, even if only in spirit form, can help ease the pain of grief and impart a sense of peace to the bereaved. Additionally, Clairvoyance can also be used as a tool for making decisions.

By seeing into the future, a person with this ability can avoid potential pitfalls and make choices that will lead to positive outcomes. In summary, there are many benefits to being clairvoyant. While some might view it as a supernatural ability, its benefits are very real and practical. It can provide comfort in times of grief, help people make better choices, and even give them a glimpse into the future.

Other benefits of this psychic ability include:

- It can help you connect with loved ones who have passed away.
- It can provide comfort and peace during times of grief.
- It can help you make better decisions by seeing into the future.
- It can give you a glimpse into other realms and dimensions.

How Clairvoyance Is Used

Clairvoyance may be either external, involving the perception of objects or events outside the body, or internal, involving the perception of thoughts and feelings within the mind. It's often used for purposes such as divination, prophecy, and healing. Divination is the practice of using Clairvoyance to gain insights into future events. Prophecy is the act of using Clairvoyance to interpret or predict future events. Healing is the use of Clairvoyance to diagnose and treat illness.

Clairvoyance can also be used simply to obtain information that would otherwise be inaccessible. For example, a clairvoyant may be able to see a hidden object or receive messages from people who have died. Clairvoyance is a controversial ability, with some people claiming to have it and others dismissing it as superstition. However, there are many documented cases of Clairvoyance being used successfully. Whether or not Clairvoyance is real, it remains an intriguing phenomenon.

True Tales of Clairvoyance

Clairvoyance is a fascinating art that has been shrouded in mystery for centuries. There are many stories and accounts of Clairvoyance throughout history. Here are just a few examples:

In the early 1900s, a woman named Frieda Harrison claimed to have clairvoyant abilities. She was tested by the Society for Psychical Research and was found to be genuine. In the 1970s, a man named Ingo Swann gained notoriety for his clairvoyant abilities. He could accurately describe objects and events taking place in other parts of the world. In 2001, a man named Uri Geller made headlines when he correctly predicted the 9/11 terrorist attack. He had previously gained fame for his ability to bend spoons with his mind.

Clairsentience: The Power of Clear Feeling

Clairsentience is the psychic ability to feel or sense things that are not physically present. It's often described as a "gut feeling" or "sixth sense." Clairsentience can manifest in many ways, from sensing the presence of ghosts or spirits to knowing when someone is lying. Intuition is a form of clairsentience. For example, you may strongly feel you should take a different route to work, even though there's no logical reason to do so. Later, you may find out that there was an accident on your usual route.

Some lucky people are born with strong clairsentient abilities, while others develop them through meditation or other spiritual practices. Clairsentience is a valuable tool to check into, especially when big decisions have to be made, but you can also use it for smaller decisions. The ability to sense when something is "off" can help you avoid danger or make the best choice in a difficult situation. Clairsentience can also be used for healing. By sensing imbalances in the body, a clairsentient person can help to restore health and well-being. The next time you get a gut feeling about something, trust it to show you a way you might not have considered.

Benefits of Clairsentience

Although some people view clairsentience as a mere parlor trick, there are a lot of positives that come with being clairsentient.

For one, clairsentients can often sense when something is about to happen, whether it's a natural disaster or an accident. This means they can sound the alarm and potentially save lives. It can also help you make up your mind about issues or choices, as clairsentients often sense which choice is the best. Clairsentients often have a deep connection to the spiritual realm and can serve as mediums between the living and the dead. This can bring closure and peace of mind to those who are grieving and battling to come to terms with losing a loved one. Finally, clairsentients often have keen insights into the human condition and can offer guidance and wisdom to those who seek it. In short, there are many advantages to being clairsentient. Those who are blessed with this gift should not take it for granted.

Other benefits of this psychic ability include:
- It can help you connect with the spiritual realm.
- It can provide guidance and wisdom.
- It can help you sense when something is about to happen.
- It can give you insights into the human condition.

How Clairsentience Is Used

Clairsentient people often report feeling a physical sensation when a spirit is present, such as a tingling in their hair or a chill down their spine. Some people also report seeing flashes of light or colorful images when spirits are nearby. Clairsentience can be used to communicate with spirits, angels, and other supernatural beings. It can also be used to detect the presence of ghosts and poltergeists.

Clairsentient people often have a solid intuitive understanding of the world around them. They may be able to sense when something is about to happen, even if they do not know what that event will be. Clairsentience is a natural ability that can be developed with practice. Many books and resources are available to help people develop their clairsentient abilities.

True Tales of Clairsentience

Throughout history, there have been many reports of clairsentient experiences. One famous example comes from the Bible. In the Book of Acts, chapter 16, Paul and Timothy are traveling to the city of Philippi. As they approach the city, they sense that there is danger ahead. Paul has a vision of a man begging him to come to Macedonia, so they change their plans and go there instead. It is believed that Paul's clairsentience saved them from danger.

Another popular story comes from the life of Abraham Lincoln. In 1862, Lincoln was presented with two options for military strategy: send troops to Virginia or Tennessee. He had a dream where he saw soldiers marching and fighting in a wheat field - and chose Virginia. The next day, he learned that troops in Virginia had been victorious in the Battle of Antietam. Lincoln attributed his decision to his clairsentient dream and later said, "I believe it was God's will that I should be the instrument, under Providence, of saving the Union."

Claircognizance: The Power of Clear Knowing

Also known as clear knowing or inner knowing, Clair cognizance is considered one of the most potent forms of intuition. People who have this ability often know things without being able to explain how they know them. For example, they may suddenly feel strongly that something is about to happen, even though they have no prior knowledge of the event.

Claircognizance can also manifest as a sudden understanding of something previously unidentified. This inner knowing often comes from a higher power or intelligence, which is why it is sometimes referred to as a "sixth sense." While everyone has some degree of Claircognizance, some people are more attuned to this form of intuition than others. By developing their psychic ability, individuals can learn to trust their inner knowing and use it for guidance in their lives.

Benefits of Claircognizance

Claircognizance is often associated with the third eye, which is located in the center of the forehead just above the eyebrows; this third eye is known as the *Ajna chakra* in yoga and meditation practices. Claircognizance can be used for practical purposes such as making better decisions, determining career paths, or improving relationships. It can also be used for personal growth and self-awareness.

You can develop and strengthen this ability through meditation, visualization, and other spiritual practices. Many claircognizant people are also empathic, meaning they can feel the emotions of others. Claircognizance is a valuable ability that can be used to improve your life in many ways. Other benefits of this psychic ability include:

- Greater clarity and understanding.
- Increased self-awareness.
- The ability to see through the deception.
- Improved decision-making skills.
- Greater creativity and intuition.

How Is Claircognizance Used?

There are different ways that Claircognizance can manifest. For some people, it's a sudden understanding or realization of something. For others, Claircognizance may show up as a gut feeling or intuition about a situation. Psychics and mediums often use Claircognizance during readings. It can also be helpful in day-to-day life. For example, if you're trying to decide whether to take a new job, you can use Claircognizance to see whether it's the right fit for you.

The ability to know things without knowing how you know them is a powerful gift. Claircognizance can be used for personal growth and transformation. It can also help you make sense of and understand the world around you. Many resources are available to help you on your journey if you'd like to develop your claircognizant abilities.

True Tales of Claircognizance

One woman shared how Clairs cognizance saved her from a potentially dangerous situation. Jenna was out for a walk one day when she suddenly had the urge to go home. She strongly felt something was wrong, so she decided to listen to her intuition and head home. When she arrived, she found that her house had been broken into and her belongings were scattered everywhere. She was thankful that she had listened to her intuition and gone home when she did.

The four psychic abilities, Clairvoyance, Clairsentience, Claircognizance, and Clairaudience, are each unique in their own way. While some people may be more attuned to one ability than another, we all have the potential to develop all four abilities. By honing our psychic skills, we can learn to trust our intuition and use it for guidance in our lives.

This chapter covered the basics of the four psychic abilities. You will have learned that Clairvoyance is the ability to see things using psychic powers, while Clairsentience is the ability to feel or sense energy, Claircognizance is the ability to know things without knowing how you know them, and Clairaudience is the ability to hear psychic information. We also explored the different ways these abilities can manifest and the benefits of developing each. In the next chapter, we'll see how your Moon Sign determines your psychic ability.

Chapter 3: Your Moon Sign Determines Your Psychic Powers

If you've ever wondered what your most potent psychic power might be, the answer could lie in the stars. According to astrology, your moon sign represents your innermost self and can offer clues about your natural gifts and abilities. For example, suppose you have a Cancer moon sign. In that case, you may be intuitive and compassionate, with a solid ability to read people's emotions. If you have a Leo moon sign, on the other hand, you may be confident and outgoing, with a natural talent for manipulation.

This chapter will explore the connection between the moon and psychic powers and how your moon sign can determine your most robust psychic ability. We'll also look at the fundamentals of astrology and how the moon is said to influence our lives. So, if you're ready to discover your hidden gifts, read on!

The Moon and Psychic Powers

The moon has long been associated with magic and the supernatural. In many cultures, the moon is seen as a powerful force with the supernatural ability to influence our emotions, our behavior, and even the tides. The moon is also linked to the divine feminine and is said to represent our unconscious mind. According to astrology, the moon's energy can also be used to tap into our psychic abilities.

For centuries, people have looked to the night sky for answers to life's mysteries and have long associated the moon with psychic powers and intuition. Some believe that the moon's energy can be harnessed and used to heighten one's psychic abilities. There is no scientific evidence to support this claim, but many intuitively swear by it.

If you are interested in exploring your psychic side, you may want to try meditating or doing energy work under the light of the full moon. You may also want to keep a journal of your dreams and intuitive insights during this time. Who knows what you might discover?

The Fundamentals

To understand how the moon can influence our psychic powers, it is first crucial to understand the basic connection between the planets and our human experience. In astrology, the planets are said to represent different sides of our personalities. For example, the planet Mars is said to represent our aggression, while the planet Venus is said to represent our love and relationships.

Similarly, the moon is said to represent our emotions, our intuition, and our subconscious mind. The moon is also said to be connected to the divine feminine and is often seen as a symbol of fertility and creativity. In astrology, the moon's energy is believed to be very powerful and often unpredictable. It is said that the moon can influence our moods, our behavior, and even the tides.

The Moon and Divination

For centuries, the Moon has been a source of fascination for humanity. Early cultures looked to the night sky and saw a reflection of their beliefs and mythology. The Moon was often seen as a god or goddess, and it was believed that its changes dictated the course of human events. In some cultures, the Moon was also associated with divination, the art of predicting the future. It was thought that the phases of the Moon could provide clues about what was to come.

Divination is the practice of using tools to gain insight into the future. There are many different forms of divination, each using a different method to divine information. Some common forms of divination include tarot cards, crystal balls, tea leaves, and bones. The Moon is thought to be connected to the art of divination, and many believe that its energy can be used to enhance your psychic abilities.

Today, divination is often seen as a superstitious practice, but there is still a deep connection between the Moon and our sense of intuition. Just as the Moon reflects the light of the Sun, our intuition allows us to tap into our inner wisdom. We can gain insight into what lies ahead when we listen to our intuition. This is why many believe that the Moon can be a powerful ally in our journey to develop our psychic abilities.

The Moon and Meditation

Meditation is connected to the Moon's energy.
https://www.pexels.com/photo/woman-meditating-in-bedroom-3772612/

Meditation is another practice that is said to be connected to the energy of the Moon. Meditation is a process of clearing the mind and focusing on the present moment. When we meditate, we can quieten the world's noise and connect with our inner voice. This inner voice is called our intuition and thought to be our connection to the divine.

We can focus on our breath and connect with our power during meditation. We can also use visualization to connect with the moon's energy. When we visualize under the light of the full moon, we can tap into our psychic abilities and receive insights into our lives. We open ourselves to psychic energies that can give us guidance and direction.

The full moon is also a time for release, and by visualizing under its light, we can let go of negative patterns and behaviors that are no longer serving us. If you are seeking guidance or clarity in your life, spend some time visualizing under the light of the full moon. You may be surprised at the insights you receive.

The Moon and Feminine Power

Throughout history, the Moon has been associated with feminine power. In many cultures, the Moon is worshipped the same way one worships a goddess, and its cycles are seen as a metaphor for the phases of womanhood. The waxing and waning of the Moon are often seen as representations of the ebb and flow of life, and its light is said to symbolize hope and guidance.

The Moon is also a symbol of fertility, and its energy is said to be creative and nurturing. When we connect with the energy of the Moon, we can tap into our feminine power and creativity. We can also use its energy to help us manifest our desires. The Moon is a powerful ally for anyone seeking to create positive change in their lives.

For many women, the Moon is a source of strength and inspiration. Its presence in the night sky reminds us that we are all connected to the rhythms of nature. Even on the darkest of nights, the Moon reminds us that there is always light to be found. It symbolizes hope and guidance; its energy can help us tap into our psychic abilities.

The Moon and Ancient Wisdom

Humans have looked to the night sky for guidance and inspiration for centuries. The stars and planets have been used to navigate the seas, predict the weather, and even tell time. However, of all the celestial bodies, none has had a more significant impact on human civilization than the Moon. The Moon's regular waxing and waning cycles have long served as a marker of the passing of time, helping our ancestors track the seasons and plan their activities accordingly.

Many of our modern calendars are based on the lunar cycle. The Moon's eerie glow has also been a source of fascination and superstition throughout history. For some cultures, the Moon is seen as a benevolent deity, while others view it as a harbinger of death and destruction. Regardless of how it is regarded, there is no denying the Moon has a significant place in human history.

The rhythms of the Moon helped our ancestors to track the passage of time, and they used this knowledge to plant crops, hunt games, and predict the weather. Today, we may not look to the Moon with the same reverence as our ancestors did, but it still has the power to inspire us. As we gaze at its ever-changing face, we cannot help but be reminded of our place in the life cycle.

How Your Moon Sign Determines Your Psychic Powers

While astrology can't predict the future with 100% accuracy, there is a lot of truth to the idea that our birth sign reveals certain personality traits. For example, those born under the sign of Cancer are often said to be highly intuitive. Coincidentally, many of history's most famous psychics were born under this sign. If you're wondering whether you have psychic abilities, it may be worth looking into your moon sign.

Like your sun sign, your moon sign is determined by the date and time of your birth. However, while your sun sign represents your outward personality, your moon sign represents your innermost emotions. Those with a strong moon sign are often in touch with their intuition and are highly sensitive to the energy around them. This section will explain how one´s psychic power is linked to one´s moon sign.

The Connection between Moon Signs and Psychic Powers

Many people believe there is a connection between the moon's phases and psychic powers. After all, the moon has long been associated with magic and mystery. The word "lunatic" comes from the Latin word for moon, and many cultures believed that the full moon could cause madness. The moon's changing phases have also been used for centuries to predict the future.

Some claim that the waxing and waning of the moon affect our moods and change our energy levels, making us more or less susceptible to psychic activity. Whether or not there is a scientific basis for these claims, there is no doubt that the moon has a powerful hold over our imaginations. For those who believe in the supernatural, the moon is a reminder that anything is possible.

How Your Moon Sign Reveals Your Psychic Powers

Firstly, it's important to understand that everyone has psychic powers. However, some people are more in touch with their abilities than others. And your moon sign can play a role in how strong your psychic powers are.

If you're a Scorpio, you're likely to be very intuitive and have strong Clairvoyant abilities. If you're a Pisces, you're probably very compassionate and have a strong connection to your emotions - which can be a powerful tool for reading people. And, if you're an Aries, you're probably quick-thinking and always on the lookout for adventure - which can make you a natural when it comes to precognition.

So, what does all this mean for you? Well, it simply means that it's worth considering your moon sign if you want to develop your psychic abilities. After all, understanding your natural strengths can help you focus your efforts in the right direction. Who knows - with a little bit of practice, you could be the next big thing in the psychic world!

Psychic Powers and the 12 Moon Signs

If you believe in psychic powers, you may be interested to know that each of the 12 moon signs is associated with a different psychic ability. For example, those born under the sign of Aries are said to be gifted at Clairvoyance or the ability to see things that are not visible to the naked eye. Those born under the sign of Taurus are said to be adept at Clairaudience, or the ability to hear spirits.

Gemini subjects are associated with precognition, or the ability to see into the future, while Cancer is linked with psychometry, or the ability to read the history of an object simply by touching it. Whether you believe in psychic powers or not, it can be fun to explore what each sign is said to represent. Who knows, you might just discover that you have a hidden talent!

When it comes to psychic abilities, there is said to be a link between these powers and moon signs. Different moon signs have different strengths when it comes to psychic abilities. This chapter explained how your moon sign may just give you a little insight into your psychic abilities.

Regardless of your moon sign, there is a connection between this astronomical phenomenon and your psychic abilities. If you're looking to develop your skills, it's worth considering your natural strengths and weaknesses. According to astrology, each zodiac sign is associated with a different psychic power. So, if you want to develop your abilities, look toward your moon sign.

Chapter 4: Bold Moons: Aries, Leo, and Sagittarius

It's time to continue your delve into the world of moon signs! Part Two of this book will explain each moon sign and elaborate on it. We'll see each sign's strengths, weaknesses, and what it means when this is your moon sign. You'll also get a taste of the strongest psychic powers for individuals with these signs. Finally, we'll finish with a fitting affirmation for each sign. This chapter will focus on the bold moons - Aries, Leo, and Sagittarius. These fire signs are known for their passion and zest for life. So, let's get started!

Bold Moons

Have you ever felt drawn to someone because they seemed to have an aura of excitement and adventure about them? If so, they may very well be one of the three zodiac signs ruled by the fire element; Aries, Leo, or Sagittarius. Also known as bold moons or fire moons, these signs are known for their fiery, passionate natures. They are natural leaders and often have a strong sense of identity.

Fire moons are especially powerful during the month of their associated sun sign. So, if you were born under a Leo fire moon, your power period would be during August. Pay attention to your intuition during these times and follow your heart. It's also a good time to take risks and experiment with new things. Trust your gut, and let your inner fire guide you. Let's take a closer look at each of these three bold moons.

Aries - The Fireball

Aries Symbol.
Denis Moskowitz, CC BY-SA 4.0 <https://creativecommons.org/licenses/by-sa/4.0>, via Wikimedia Commons: https://commons.wikimedia.org/wiki/File:Aries_symbol_(Moskowitz,_variable_width).svg

People born under the Aries fire moon are natural leaders with a strong sense of identity. They are also known for their explosive reactions and ability to get things done quickly. However, they can also be impulsive and may not think things through before acting. When this is your moon sign, you are likely to be happiest when taking risks and pushing yourself to your limits.

When it comes to relationships, Aries moon signs crave adventure. They need a partner who keeps up with their energetic nature and will never try to hold them back. If you have an Aries moon sign, remember to stay true to yourself and never give up on your dreams. Learning to control your temper is also crucial, as your explosive reactions can sometimes lead to problems.

Zodiac Symbol - The Ram

The Ram is the symbol of the zodiac sign Aries, and it is no surprise that this fiery creature would be associated with such an energetic and passionate sign. After all, Rams are known for their strength, determination, and ability to overcome any obstacle in their path. It is also said that Rams are always first to charge into battle, fearless and unafraid of what may lie ahead.

In many ways, the Ram embodies the spirit of Aries perfectly - bold, impulsive, and always ready for a challenge. So, if you happen to be an Aries yourself, or if you know someone who is, keep an eye out for this courageous creature - it may just have a few lessons to teach you about living life to the fullest.

Strengths - Passionate, Driven, Creative

Aries is one of the most passionate signs of the Zodiac. When they set their sights on something, they go after it with everything they've got. This determination can be a great strength but can also result in impulsive decisions and a tendency to burn out quickly.

Aries also has a lot of creative flair. They're always coming up with new ideas and are always ready to try something new. This makes them very adaptable, but it can also mean they lack focus. Aries must learn to channel their boundless energy into productive outlets, or they'll quickly become overwhelmed. But when they do channel that energy correctly, there's no limit to what they can achieve.

Weaknesses - Impulsive, Short Tempered, Impatient

Aries, the first sign of the Zodiac, are known for their fiery personality. They are confident and determined and often lead by example. However, Aries can also be impulsive and short-tempered and may have difficulty finishing what they start. They may also be impatient with others, especially if they feel like they are not being heard.

Though these qualities can be seen as weaknesses, they can also be strengths. Aries are natural leaders, and their impulsivity and determination can help them to achieve their goals. They are also highly creative and always up for a challenge. So, while Aries may have some weaknesses, they also have many strengths that make them unique and special.

Traits of Those with This Moon Sign - Adventurous, Bravery, Independence

Adventurous at heart, Aries people are always up for a challenge and love nothing more than to be in charge. Aries are also incredibly brave, willing to take risks that others wouldn't even dream of. This combination of qualities makes them ideal candidates for any high-pressure job. Regarding their personal lives, Aries value their independence above all else.

They're fiercely independent and hate feeling tied down. This can sometimes make them seem aloof or uninterested, but it's because they like to keep their options open. So, if you're looking for an exciting new adventure or someone to take charge and lead the way, look no further than an Aries.

Psychic Power - Claircognizance

Aries people are known for their psychic ability of Claircognizance, which is the ability to know things without being told. This can manifest in many ways but is often seen as a gut feeling or intuition. Aries people often trust their instincts and are not afraid to act on them. This ability can be a great strength but can also lead to impulsive decisions. Aries need to learn to listen to their intuition but also to use their head as well. They will be unstoppable if they can find a balance between the two.

Affirmation - "I am Fearlessly Brave"

No challenge is too great for Aries, and they will always face their fears head-on. This fearless nature can sometimes lead to impulsive decisions, making them natural leaders. When Aries sets their mind to something, they will stop at nothing to achieve it. So, if you're an Aries, remember that you are fearlessly brave. Embrace your inner fire and let it guide you to success.

This affirmation will help Aries to remember their courage and bravery and to use it to achieve their goals. It will also remind them to listen to their intuition and to use it to make decisions. By affirming their ability to be brave and to lead, Aries will be able to reach their full potential. It also reminds them that they are independent and need not rely on others to achieve their goals.

Leo - The Golden One

Leo Zodiac Symbol.
Google, Apache License 2.0 <http://www.apache.org/licenses/LICENSE-2.0>, via Wikimedia Commons: https://commons.wikimedia.org/wiki/File:Green_Leo_emoji.svg

There's a reason why people born under the Leo moon sign are known as the "golden ones." Leos are warm, welcoming, and full of life. They bring sunshine wherever they go, and their infectious positive attitude is impossible to resist. But there's more to Leo than just their sunny disposition.

These celestial lions are also fiercely loyal, protective, and generous. They will go above and beyond for the people they love and always be there when you need them. So, consider yourself truly blessed if you're lucky enough to know a Leo. You've found a rare treasure indeed.

Zodiac Symbol - The Lion

The Lion is the symbol of the Leo zodiac sign. The Lion is a proud and regal animal, and like Leo, it is known for its strength, courage, and nobility. The Lion is also a symbol of good luck, and many people believe that having a Lion as their zodiac sign can bring them success in life. Leo is a Fixed Fire sign, and because of this, it is associated with the element of fire. Fire signs are known for their passion and determination, and Leo is no exception. Those born under this sign are often natural leaders who dare to follow their dreams. Leo is a loyal friend and an affectionate lover, and those lucky enough to have a Lion in their lives will never forget the experience.

Strengths - Generous, Warmhearted, Playful

Anyone who knows a Leo will likely attest to their generous, warmhearted, and playful nature. Leos are some of the most fun-loving people you'll ever meet, and they're always up for a good time. They're also incredibly generous, always willing to lend a helping hand or share what they have with others. And their warmth and kindness are evident in everything they do, from how they interact with friends and family to how they treat strangers. If you're looking for someone who will make you laugh, lift your spirits, and brighten your day, look no further than a Leo.

Weaknesses - Arrogant, Domineering, Stubborn

Although Leos are known for their regal bearing and commanding presence, this zodiac sign also has its weaknesses. One of most common Leo's weaknesses is arrogance. Leos are often so sure of themselves that they fail to see other points of view. This can make them seem domineering and overbearing to those around them. In addition, Leos tend to be quite stubborn.

Once they have set their minds on something, it can be difficult to change their course. However, these same qualities can also be seen as strengths. After all, confidence and determination are essential qualities in any leader. Ultimately, it is up to each Leo to strike the right balance between their positive and negative qualities.

Traits of Those with This Moon Sign - Confidence, Enthusiasm, Loyalty

Leo is one of the most easily recognizable signs of the Zodiac. People born under this sign are often natural leaders who have a strong sense of self. They are confident and enthusiastic and have no trouble lending their support to a cause they believe in. Leo is also a loyal friend; they will stick by you through thick and thin. If you're looking for someone to help you achieve your goals, a Leo is a person you want on your team. So, if you know a Leo, tell them how much you appreciate them. After all, Leo is the sign of the lion, and there's nothing more powerful than having a lion on your side.

Psychic Power - Creative Channel

According to astrology, Leo is the sign of creativity and self-expression. Leo people are natural leaders and often have a strong presence that can be hard to ignore. They are also very intuitive and have powerful psychic abilities. When it comes to their creative side, Leo people are extremely creative and have no problem coming up with new ideas. They are also very passionate; this often comes through in their creative work.

There's no denying that Leo people are creative souls. They have a natural knack for self-expression and are not afraid to put their heart and soul into their art. Whether writing a novel, painting a masterpiece, or sculpting a beautiful statue, they pour every ounce of their passion and creativity into their work.

This commitment to their art is what sets Leo people apart from the rest, as they're not afraid to pour their whole hearts into their creations. As a result, their art is always beautiful, moving, and full of life. For them, creativity is a way to express themselves and connect with the world around them. So, consider trying Leo's psychic power if you're looking for a creative channel to explore. You may be surprised at what you discover.

Affirmation - "I Follow My Bliss"

When it comes to living a fulfilling life, it is vital to follow your bliss. It means finding and pursuing the things that bring you joy. It means saying yes to the things that excite and inspire you and saying no to the things that don't. It means listening to your heart and intuition and taking actions that align with your deepest desires.

When you live in this way, you are tapping into your true potential and creating a life rich with meaning and purpose. So, whatever your bliss may be, make it a priority in your life. Follow your heart's longing and see where it takes you. You may just be surprised at how wonderful life can be when you live in alignment with your highest self.

This affirmation is perfect for anyone looking to live a more authentic and fulfilling life. If you feel like you're off track or unsure what your bliss is, this affirmation can help you get back on track. Simply repeat it to yourself whenever you need a reminder to follow your heart. And before you know it, you'll be living the life of your dreams.

Sagittarius - The Hunter

People born under Sagittarius are often called "The Hunters" because they are always looking for new and exciting experiences. They are adventurous, love to travel, and are always up for a challenge. Sagittarius people are also very honest and have a strong sense of justice. They are always searching for the truth and are not afraid to speak their mind. So, if you're looking for someone who is always up for an adventure and who will always tell you the truth, then a Sagittarius is the person you want in your life.

Zodiac Symbol - The Archer

Without mentioning the Archer, the Zodiac's iconic symbol, no discussion of Sagittarius would be complete. Like the Archer, those born under this sign are always ready to aim for their goals. The Archer is also a symbol of truth and justice, two of Sagittarius's most important values. It is no surprise then that the Archer is such an important symbol for this sign. After all, it represents everything that Sagittarius people stand for.

The Archer is also a powerful symbol of protection. With their keen eyesight and a steady hand, the Archer is always ready to defend those they love. The Archer is a reminder that, no matter what life throws in your direction, you always have the power to meet it with strength and courage. It reminds you that you are never alone and always someone is watching over you.

Strengths - Optimistic, Jovial, Honest

As a Sagittarius, you are known for your optimistic outlook on life. You see the glass as half-full, and this positive attitude is infectious. People are drawn to your cheerful nature, and you can always find the silver lining in any situation. You are also known for your sense of humor. You love to laugh and make others laugh, and you are always up for a good time. Your friends know that they can always count on you for a good laugh.

Honesty is another one of your Sagittarius strengths. You always speak your truth, even if it isn't what people want to hear. You believe that honesty is the best policy, and people appreciate your forthrightness. These are just a few reasons why people love being around you. As a Sagittarius, you are truly one of a kind.

Weaknesses - Impulsive, Tactless, Restless

Sagittarius is one of the most optimistic signs of the Zodiac. They always look for the silver lining, and their glass is always half full. However, these sunny dispositions come with some drawbacks. One of the biggest Sagittarius weaknesses is that they can be impulsive. They hate being stuck in one place and are always ready for a new adventure. This can lead them to make rash decisions without thinking things through.

Additionally, Sagittarius can be tactless. They are straightforward and honest, but they sometimes lack diplomacy. They may say things without considering how they will affect others and can be insensitive. Lastly, Sagittarius is a restless sign; they get antsy when staying in one place for too long. They need constant stimulation, and they can easily get bored. If you are dating a Sagittarius, be prepared for a wild ride!

Traits of Those with This Moon Sign - Intellect, Wisdom, Truth

If you're looking for a sign known for its intellect, wisdom, and truth, look no further than Sagittarius. Those born under this sign always seek knowledge and are known for their love of learning. They are also incredibly honest and always speak their mind. This can sometimes get them into trouble, but they truly believe in the power of honesty and integrity.

If you're looking for a sign that things will work out, look no further than a Sagittarius. These optimistic folks are known for their positive outlook on life and are always ready with a joke to lighten the mood. Sagittarians can find the silver lining regardless of what life throws at them.

This positive attitude is one of the many things that make Sagittarians such great friends. They're always up for a good time, and their good-natured humor will surely put a smile on your face. So, if you're feeling down, just remember that there's a Sagittarius out there who's ready to make you laugh.

Psychic Power - Clairvoyance

Sagittarius is known for being an intuitive sign, and this psychic power is one of the ways that intuition manifests. Clairvoyance is the ability to see beyond the physical world and into the spiritual realm. For Sagittarians, this psychic power can be a valuable tool for understanding themselves and making decisions about their lives. While not all Sagittarians are clairvoyant, those who *are* find that it often enhances their ability to connect with others and understand the hidden dynamics at play in any situation.

With their natural curiosity and desire for knowledge, Sagittarians who are clairvoyant can be a valuable asset to any team or organization. Those seeking to develop their psychic power can learn more about clairvoyance by studying the lives and work of Sagittarius-born people who are known for their intuition and insight, such as writer Paulo Coelho and actress Whoopi Goldberg.

Affirmation - "I am Open to New Ideas and Beliefs"

Sagittarius is a sign that is always open to new ideas and beliefs. The affirmation "I am open to new ideas and beliefs" is a reminder that Sagittarians should never stop learning. This affirmation can also be used by those seeking to develop their psychic power of clairvoyance. By affirming that they are open to new ideas and beliefs, Sagittarians can open themselves up to the spiritual realm and develop their intuition.

If you're a Sagittarius, chances are you're the type who is always open to new experiences. You're curious and adventurous and always looking for new things to learn. That's why this affirmation is perfect for you. It reminds you that you're open to new ideas and beliefs and always learning and growing. Keep this affirmation in mind when feeling lost or unsure of yourself. Remember that you can adapt and change and that there is always more to learn. Embrace your curiosity, and let it lead you on an amazing journey.

Bold moons stimulate us to take risks, be honest, open-minded, and optimistic. They offer us a chance to let our intuition guide us. This chapter has examined the three bold moons of Aries, Leo, and Sagittarius. Each of these signs is known for its courage, honesty, and optimism.

Aries is a sign of great strength and determination. Those with this moon sign are natural leaders and are always up for a challenge. They are also incredibly brave, and their impulsivity can lead to great things. However, Aries people need to learn to channel their energy, or they will quickly become overwhelmed. They also need to be patient with others, as their short temper can sometimes make them seem impatient. But they will be unstoppable if they can find a balance between these qualities.

Leo is a sign that is often associated with strength, courage, and leadership. Those born under this sign are usually natural leaders with a strong sense of self. They are also very confident and enthusiastic and have no trouble lending their support to a cause they believe in. Leo people are also very loyal and will stick by you through thick and thin. So, if you're looking for someone to help you achieve your goals, a Leo is the person you want on your team.

Sagittarius is a sign that is known for its optimism, sense of humor, and love of learning. Those born under this sign always seek knowledge and are known for their honesty and integrity. Sagittarians are also known for their psychic power of clairvoyance. If you're looking for a sign that is always up for a good time and can see beyond the physical world, look no further than Sagittarius!

Knowing each sign's characteristics can help you better understand yourself and those around you. It can also give you some insight into how to best utilize the energy of the current moon phase. So, whatever your sign, make sure you use the energy of the bold moons to your advantage. Be brave, honest, optimistic, and most importantly, yourself. The world needs your unique talents and qualities, so don't be afraid to shine your light.

Chapter 5: Thoughtful Moons: Libra, Aquarius, and Gemini

In astrology, three zodiac signs are known for their thoughtful and reflective natures - Libra, Aquarius, and Gemini. These signs are known for their intelligence and ability to think abstractly. They're quick-witted and often have a sharp tongue, but they also deeply understand the world around them. These signs are excellent at solving problems.

This chapter will explore the thoughtful moons of Libra, Aquarius, and Gemini, discussing the strengths and weaknesses of each sign and the traits those with these moon signs portray. We'll also explore the psychic powers associated with each sign and offer an affirmation to be used to harness the power of these thoughtful moons.

Thoughtful Moons

If you're looking for someone who is always open to a deep conversation, you can't go wrong with a Libra, Aquarius, or Gemini. These three signs are often considered the thoughtful moon signs or air moons. They're known for thinking deeply about complex topics and expressing their ideas clearly.

Libra, Aquarius, and Gemini are all about introspection and intellectualism. Governed by the element air, these signs are known for their quick wit and abstract thought. They're always asking questions and seeking to understand the world around them. These signs are excellent at problem-solving and are always looking for new ways to see things.

When it comes to conversation, these signs are always ready to dive in and explore whatever is captivating their imaginations. Whether you're talking about your latest passion project or simply catching up on the news, you can always count on a Libra, Aquarius, or Gemini to keep the conversation interesting. So, if you need a stimulating discussion, be sure to seek out one of these thought-provoking signs.

Libra - The Balanced

Libra zodiac symbol.
Denis Moskowitz, CC BY-SA 4.0 <https://creativecommons.org/licenses/by-sa/4.0>, via Wikimedia Commons; https://commons.wikimedia.org/wiki/File:Libra_symbol_(Moskowitz,_variable_width).svg

People with the moon in Libra are known for their ability to see both sides of every issue. They can find the middle ground and see all sides of an argument. They're natural peacemakers, and their diplomatic skills can come in handy in any situation.

However, Libra is also an air sign, which means they can sometimes be emotionally detached. If you're looking for someone to understand your feelings, you may want to look elsewhere. But a Libran friend is a great choice if you're looking for someone who can help you see all sides of a situation.

Zodiac Symbol - The Scales

The Libra zodiac symbol is the scales, which represent balance, harmony, and justice. Libras are known for their even-keeled nature and ability to see both sides of every issue. This can make them superb mediators and diplomats, but it can also mean they have trouble making decisions. After all, how can you choose one side when both sides seem equally valid?

The scales of justice are a powerful symbol for Libras, reminding Librans there is always another perspective to consider. At their best, the Libra scales represent a deep commitment to fairness and equity. But at its worst, the scales can represent indecision, impartiality, and a lack of personal conviction. As with all things in life, balance is key. And that's something that Libras understand better than anyone else.

Strengths - Diplomatic, Cooperative, Graceful, Perfectionist

If you have a Libra moon, you are known for your diplomacy and cooperation. You are also graceful and have a strong sense of justice. Perfectionism is another one of your strengths – you strive for balance in all areas of your life. You are a gifted communicator and often use your skills to resolve conflicts. You are also an excellent listener, which makes people feel heard and understood.

People appreciate your calm demeanor in challenging situations. You have a natural ability to see both sides of every issue, which makes you a fair and impartial observer. Others can count on you to be objective and level-headed, and your ability to see the big picture is one of your greatest strengths!

Weaknesses - Indecisive, Gullible, Manipulative

While Libras are known for their gentle and diplomatic nature, they also have a few weaknesses that can sometimes hold them back. One of the most notable is indecisiveness. Libras are notorious for taking forever to make even the simplest of decisions, often agonizing over every little detail. This can often leave them feeling frazzled and stressed out.

Another weakness is gullibility. Because they are so eager to please others, they can sometimes be taken advantage of by those who are more manipulative. Finally, Libras can also be quite controlling in relationships. While they may not mean to be, their need for balance and harmony can sometimes come across as bossy or domineering. While these weaknesses can be frustrating, understanding them can help Libras to overcome them and live a more fulfilling life.

Traits of Those with This Moon Sign - Analytical, Intellectual, Social

Libras are known for their analytical minds and ability to see sides of any issue. They are highly intelligent and often use their quick wit to make others laugh. Many Libras are excellent communicators and are natural-born diplomats. They are also highly social beings who enjoy being around others.

Libras are cooperative and often work well in team environments. They are also gifted mediators who can see both sides of any conflict. However, their need for balance can sometimes make them seem indecisive. Libras are also known for their perfectionism, which can often lead to them feeling stressed and frazzled.

And, because they are always seeking balance in their lives, they are often very fair-minded. If you know Libra, you can be sure that they will always be willing to listen to your point of view and strive to find a fair compromise for everyone involved.

Psychic Power - Telepathy

Libra is the sign of balance, which also extends to their psychic abilities. Libras are excellent at using their telepathic powers to communicate with others, whether it's sending a simple message or reading someone's thoughts. They're also very good at understanding the emotions and motivations of others, which makes them excellent mediators.

Libras are also gifted at using their psychic abilities to create harmony and balance in their lives. They can often sense when something is out of balance and use their powers to correct it. This can be anything from finding a lost object to helping someone in need. While Libras are often very gentle and diplomatic, don't underestimate their ability to use their psychic powers to get what they want.

Regarding using their telepathic powers for healing, Libras are especially gifted. They can use their abilities to help others heal emotionally, mentally, and physically. A Libra is a great person to talk to if you're looking for someone to help you develop your psychic abilities. They're patient and supportive and have a wealth of knowledge to share.

Affirmation - "I Balance Myself and Others with Ease"

If your sun, moon, or rising sign is in Libra, this affirmation is for you! As a sign of balance, Libra is all about maintaining harmony within ourselves and others. We often do this by compromise and diplomacy, seeking to find the middle ground in every situation. However, remember that balance doesn't always mean "50-50." Sometimes we need to put our own needs first, even if that means upsetting the apple cart.

By affirming that we can balance ourselves and others easily, we remind ourselves that sometimes it's okay to put our needs first. We also remind ourselves that we can find harmony in every situation, no matter how difficult it may seem. When we're feeling centered and grounded, we're better able to show up for the people and causes we care about. So go ahead and repeat this affirmation to yourself whenever you need a reminder of your inner strength and power.

Aquarius - The Visionary

People with this moon sign are known for their visionary minds and their ability to see the future. Aquarians are often ahead of their time, and their unique perspectives can sometimes make them seem like they're from another planet. They are natural-born rebels who always push the envelope and challenge the status quo.

Aquarians are also humanitarian souls who care deeply about making the world a better place. And, because they are so original, they are often very creative people. If you know an Aquarius, you can be sure that they will always have something interesting to say!

Zodiac Symbol - The Water Bearer

Aquarius is the eleventh astrological sign in the Zodiac, originating from the constellation Aquarius. The symbol of the

Water Bearer represents a person who is humanitarian, independent, and intellectual. The Aquarius symbol is one of the most recognizable in the Zodiac. It depicts a person pouring water from a pitcher, and it is often associated with the element of air.

Aquarians are also known for being friends with everyone and always seeing the best in people. Although they can be shy at first, they are great conversationalists once you get to know them. Being fluid and adaptable like the water they represent, they go with the flow and are always up for anything. So, if you ever find yourself needing a friend to talk to, look for someone born under the sign of Aquarius. You're sure to find a compassionate listener who will always be there for you.

Strengths - Progressive, Original, Humanitarian, Independent

Aquarius is the eleventh sign of the Zodiac, and those born under this sign are often known for their progressive and humanitarian views. They are also independent and original thinkers who are not afraid to swim against the tide. Aquarians are often outgoing and sociable but can also be fiercely independent. This makes them excellent friends, as they are always willing to lend a listening ear but are also not afraid to speak their minds.

Regarding relationships, Aquarians need space and freedom to feel truly fulfilled. They are loyal and honest partners who will always fight for what they believe in. However, they will quickly move on if they feel restricted or trapped. Overall, Aquarius is a sign that is full of contradictions, but that is what makes them so unique and interesting.

Weaknesses - Unpredictable, Detached, Rebellious

Aquarians are known for their independent and rebellious nature. They are often seen as unpredictable and detached, but this is only because they like to march to the beat of their own drum. Aquarians value their freedom above all else, often going to great lengths to maintain their autonomy. While this can be a strength, it can also be seen as a weakness.

Aquarians can be so determined to do things their way that they often refuse to compromise or listen to reason. This can make them appear inflexible and unyielding, which can damage relationships. Additionally, Aquarians can have a hard time connecting with others on an emotional level. They tend to keep their feelings close to the vest, making them seem indifferent or uncaring. However, those who know an Aquarius well know that they are simply guarded by nature and that they have a deep well of compassion and empathy.

Traits of Those with This Moon Sign - Inventive, Imaginative, Eccentric

People born under the Aquarius sign are often described as inventors and visionaries. They are often ahead of their time, and their ideas can be seen as eccentric or even radical. Aquarians are usually very intelligent and have a sharp mind for solving problems. They are also very independent and value their freedom highly.

Aquarians are known for their independent streak, humanitarianism, and intellectual curiosity. They are often ahead of their time, and their unconventional ideas can sometimes make them seem like outcasts. But Aquarians are also compassionate and loyal friends who are always willing to stand up for what they believe in.

Ultimately, Aquarians are unique individuals who see the world in their special way. While they can sometimes be seen as aloof or detached, they are also extremely compassionate and caring. They are often very supportive friends and will go out of their way to help others. Whether you are an Aquarius yourself or you know someone who is, there is no denying that this sign has a lot to offer.

Psychic Power - Remote Viewing

Aquarius is known for its strong psychic abilities, and one of its most powerful gifts is remote viewing. Aquarians can see distant objects or events, even ones not within their sight line. Aquarians often use this ability to gain insights into difficult problems or to find lost objects.

In some cases, Aquarians have even been known to use their remote viewing abilities to predict the future. While remote viewing is a natural talent for many Aquarians, it can also be developed through practice and study. For those interested in developing their psychic abilities, learning how to remote view can be a valuable first step.

Affirmation - "I am Connected to the Collective Unconscious"

As an Aquarius, you are known for your progressive and humanitarian views. You can see the world from a broader perspective and often find yourself championing the underdog. You are also highly independent and value your freedom above all else. However, there is another side to you that is often misunderstood.

You are also deeply connected to the collective unconscious. This spiritual connection allows you to tap into a greater source of knowledge and wisdom. It is also the source of your intuition and psychic ability. When you tune into this connection, you can receive guidance and insights to help you navigate your life path. The next time you feel lost or alone, remember that you are never truly alone. You are always connected to the collective unconscious.

Gemini - The Communicator

Gemini symbol.
SeLarin CC BY-SA 3.0 < https://creativecommons.org/licenses/by-sa/3.0/deed.en> via Wikimedia Commons, https://commons.wikimedia.org/w/index.php?curid=136896

Geminis are known for their communication skills. They are quick-witted and have a sharp mind for words. Geminis are also natural-born negotiators. They can see both sides of every issue and often mediate between two opposing parties. While they are excellent communicators, Geminis can also be known for being two-faced. They can be charming and persuasive when they want to be, but they can also be manipulative and insincere. Geminis need to learn to use their communication skills for good rather than for evil.

Zodiac Symbol - The Twins

Gemini is one of the most popular zodiac signs, and it's no wonder why. The Twins are known for their charismatic personality and ability to see both sides of every story. Gemini is a natural communicator; they love meeting new people and learning new things. They're also quick-witted and adaptable, able to think on their feet and make snap decisions.

Gemini thrives on change and excitement, and they're always up for a challenge. A Gemini friend is the perfect companion if you're looking for an adventure. Whether you're exploring a new city or trying a new activity, they'll be right by your side, ready to take on anything. So, look to the Twins for guidance if you're feeling lost or just need someone to talk to. You won't be disappointed.

Strengths - Witty, Clever, Imaginative, Communicative

Gemini is an air sign, and those who belong to this astrological sign are known for their quick wit and clever words. Gemini people are often very imaginative and have no problem developing new ideas. They also have a natural gift for communication, which helps them express themselves effectively.

Regarding relationships, Gemini people are often very friendly and easy to get along with. They enjoy being around others and are often the life of the party. However, they can also be somewhat erratic and may have trouble committing to one person or thing for too long. Overall, Gemini people are intelligent, creative, and fun-loving individuals who enjoy spending time with others.

Weaknesses - Restless, Superficial, Inconsistent, Nervous

Gemini, the zodiac twins, are known for their dual nature. On the one hand, they are lively and fun-loving, always ready for a good time. On the other hand, they can be easily distracted and have short attention spans. They may also come across as superficial or even two-faced, as they can be hard to pin down.

Gemini can also be quite restless, both mentally and physically. They may have a hard time sitting still or focusing on one task for too long. And when it comes to decision-making, they can often waver back and forth, never quite sure which option is best. So, while Gemini may be a lot of fun to be around, they can also be frustratingly inconsistent and nervy.

Traits of Those with This Moon Sign - Versatile, Youthful, Intellectually Sharp

Gemini is an air sign represented by the twins, and these twin energies are reflected in a Gemini person's ability to see both sides of every issue. Gemini is a youthful sign, and its energy is perhaps best understood as the eternal student. They're also known for their versatility, flexibility, and adaptability. There's an inherent curiosity in Gemini that leads them to be constantly exploring and learning. They enjoy keeping their minds sharp by indulging in intellectually stimulating conversations and activities.

Gemini people are some of the most fun-loving, friendly, and engaging people you'll ever meet. Although they're not always the most reliable people, they do typically have good intentions. Gemini people are also quick-witted and often use humor as a way to deflect or diffuse tense situations.

Psychic Power - Psychokinesis

It is said that those born under the Gemini sun sign are endowed with special psychic powers. One of these is psychokinesis, or the ability to move objects with the mind. This may seem like a far-fetched notion, but many documented cases exist of people using psychokinesis to influence their surroundings. One famous example comes from Ingo Swann, a psychic who was able to use his abilities to obscure an image on a photograph being taken of him from a distance.

While such feats may seem impossible, they can be explained by the fact that thoughts are energy, and energy can be used to influence matter. Therefore, people with strong mental focus and concentration may be able to harness their psychic power to move objects, if even in a small way. So, if you know someone with the gift of psychokinesis, don't be too quick to write them off as a fraud - they may just have supernatural powers!

Affirmation - "I Communicate My Thoughts and Feelings Easily"

If you were born with the moon in Gemini or your "moon sign" is Gemini, this affirmation is for you! The moon represents our emotions, and Gemini is the sign of communication. When you easily communicate your thoughts and feelings, you create deeper connections with the people in your life. So, this affirmation is all about expressing yourself clearly and confidently.

You also make it easier for others to understand and support you. And when you can express yourself freely, you open up a world of possibilities. So let this affirmation be a reminder that you have the power to communicate your truth and that doing so can bring joy, understanding, and abundance into your life.

The thoughtful moons of Libra, Aquarius, and Gemini offer a unique perspective on the world. These signs are known for their intelligence and ability to think abstractly. They're quick-witted and often have a sharp tongue, but they also deeply understand the world around them. These signs are excellent at problem-solving and are always asking questions. If you need a stimulating discussion, be sure to seek out one of these thought-provoking signs.

This chapter has covered the three thoughtful moons of the Zodiac; Libra, Aquarius, and Gemini. These signs bring a unique perspective to the table, and they're all excellent at problem-solving. If you ever need a stimulating discussion, be sure to seek out one of these signs.

While Libras are often gentle and diplomatic, they also have a strong psychic power that can be used to get what they want. If you know Libra, be sure to listen to their point of view and compromise with them to find a fair balance for everyone. And, if you're looking for someone to help you develop your psychic abilities, an Aquarius is a great person to talk to. They have a wealth of knowledge to share and are always willing to help others find balance in their lives.

Gemini people are some of the most fun-loving, sociable, and engaging people you'll ever meet. If you know a Gemini, be sure to take them up on their offer to grab a coffee or go for a walk. You're sure to have an interesting conversation, and you may even learn something new.

These are just a few of the things that make the thoughtful moons of Libra, Aquarius, and Gemini so special. If you know someone with a Moon in one of these signs, appreciate them for their uniqueness. And, if you're ever feeling lost, ask one of these signs for help. They're always happy to offer their guidance.

Chapter 6: Grounded Moons: Taurus, Virgo, and Capricorn

Being grounded means being firm in your convictions and sticking to your guns even when the going is tough. You know who you are, what you want, and how to get it. You're confident, booming, and can handle anything life throws at you. In astrology, three signs, in particular, are known for being grounded. These signs are Taurus, Virgo, and Capricorn.

Ruled by the element of earth, these signs are all about practicality, hard work, and stability. They're not afraid to roll up their sleeves and get their hands dirty. They're patient, reliable, and always keep their eye on the prize. If you have a moon in one of these signs, you're probably a pretty grounded individual. This chapter will teach you everything you need to know about the grounded moons in astrology.

This chapter will cover what it means to have a grounded moon, the strengths and weaknesses of each sign, and what it's like to have a moon in one of these signs. So, if you're ready to learn all there is to know about the grounded moons in astrology, keep reading!

Grounded Moons

When it comes to astrology, having a grounded moon sign means the individual is pretty level-headed and down-to-earth. They don't let their emotions get the best of them and are not easily rattled.

They know what they want out of life and are not afraid to go after it. They are confident, successful, and always seem to have everything under control.

Individuals with a grounded moon sign are usually practical. They're not the type to take unnecessary risks or make impulsive decisions. They like to plan things out and always think before they act. This level-headedness ensures that they always make the best possible decisions.

Grounded moons are also known for being hard workers. They're not afraid to put in the hours and always hustle to achieve their goals. They're disciplined, organized, and always stay focused on what's important. Lastly, grounded moons are known for their stability. They're not the type to let their emotions get the best of them. They're always in control and never let anything shake their foundation.

Taurus - The Bright One

Taurus symbol.
Bruce The Deus, CC BY-SA 4.0 <https://creativecommons.org/licenses/by-sa/4.0>, via Wikimedia Commons: https://commons.wikimedia.org/wiki/File:Deus_Taurus.png

People with a moon in Taurus are some of the most grounded individuals you'll ever meet. They're down-to-earth, practical, and always level-headed. Those born under this sign are also famous for their love of luxury and appreciation for life's finer things. If you have a Taurus Moon sign, you are especially gifted in matters of the heart. You are a natural romantic who loves to be surrounded by beauty. You are also a loyal friend, and people know they can count on you to be there for them when they need you.

In terms of their career, these people have a great eye for detail and are very good at bringing their creative visions to life. They also have a strong work ethic and are not afraid to put in the hard work necessary to achieve their goals. Regardless of their area, they always put their all into it and strive for excellence. This dedication often leads to great success.

Zodiac Symbol - The Bull

The symbol for this sign is the Bull, which represents strength, determination, and stubbornness. Like a bull, people with this sign are often headstrong and refuse to back down from a challenge. They're also incredibly loyal, reliable, and hardworking. While they can be stubborn, they always stick to their convictions and never give up on what they believe in.

People born under this sign are often reliable and down-to-earth. They take their commitments seriously and can be counted on to follow through. Taurus signs also have a strong sense of materialism and enjoy the finer things in life. While they can be quite practical, they also deeply appreciate beauty. If you have a Taurus friend, you know that they are usually loyal and trustworthy. But beware – if you cross them, they can be fiercely stubborn, just like the Bull.

Strengths - Loyal, Stubborn, Generous

Loyalty and stubbornness are two of the most commonly cited characteristics concerning the strengths of those born under the Taurus sign. Those who know a Taurus well can attest to their steadfast nature in terms of interpersonal relationships and in their pursuit of goals. Once a Taurus has set their mind on something, they are unlikely to be swayed from their course. This focus and determination can be a great strength, helping the Taurus to achieve their aims.

In addition, Taureans are often very generous, whether it is with their time, their possessions, or their words of encouragement.

They are people who are always willing to lend a helping hand, and their efforts are often greatly appreciated. Consequently, loyalty, stubbornness, and generosity are all qualities that contribute to the strength of those born under the Taurus sign.

Weaknesses - Possessive, Jealous, Resentful

We all have our strengths and weaknesses, and when it comes to astrology, this is especially true for those with the moon in Taurus. One of the biggest weaknesses is that they can be quite possessive and jealous. If they feel like someone is taking something away from them that they feel entitled to, they can react negatively. They may also hold onto resentment and bitterness for a long time after someone has wronged them.

Another weakness of people with this sign is that they can be quite stubborn and set in their ways. Once they make up their mind about something, changing it can be challenging. However, on the positive side, people with the moon in Taurus are usually very loyal and reliable friends. They may not be the most exciting people in the world, but those who know them well appreciate their steadiness and dependability. They are also patient and slow to anger, which can be a calm presence in times of stress.

While Taurus moons have many outstanding qualities, they are not without their flaws. People with this moon sign can sometimes be stubborn, inflexible, and set in their ways. They can also be possessive, materialistic, and too comfortable with the routine. However, their loyalty, reliability, and hard work often outweigh their negative traits.

Traits of Those with This Moon Sign - Stubborn, Dependable, Patient, Persistent, Generous

If your moon sign is Taurus, you are probably familiar with some of the most common traits associated with this astrological sign. People with Taurus moon signs are often seen as being stubborn, dependable, patient, and persistent. They are also often very generous and enjoy the finer things in life. You may identify with some or all of these qualities.

However, everyone is unique, and your moon sign is just one part of your astrological profile. So even if you have some of the more negative traits associated with Taurus, plenty of other positive qualities still make you who you are. Embrace all aspects of yourself, and don't be afraid to show the world what makes you special.

Taurus is an earth sign, and those born under this sign are known for their practicality and down-to-earth nature. However, Taurus also strongly connects to the psychic and spiritual world. Those born under this sign are often gifted with psychic powers, such as psychometry. Taurus is also a sign of great determination and stability.

Those with this Moon Sign are usually loyal and reliable friends. They may have some negative traits, such as being stubborn or set in their ways, but their positive qualities often outweigh their negative ones. If your Moon Sign is Taurus, remember that you are always in control of your destiny. Embrace all aspects of yourself, and don't be afraid to show the world what makes you special.

Psychic Power - Psychometry

Taurus is an earth sign, and those born under this sign are known for their practicality and down-to-earth nature. However, Taurus also strongly connects to the spiritual world; those born under this sign are often gifted with psychic powers. One of the most common Taurus psychic powers is psychometry, which is the ability to read the energy of objects. Those with this power can often tell things about an object's history simply by holding it in their hands.

This power can be used greatly by detectives and others who work to find lost objects or solve crimes. However, it can also be a great asset in everyday life, helping to find lost keys or locate a lost wallet. If you suspect that you have psychometry, try holding an object and see if you can sense anything about its past. You may be surprised at what you discover.

Affirmation - "I am Stable and Secure"

If your Moon Sign is Taurus, you are known for your practicality, determination, and stability. These qualities make you an excellent friend and reliable ally. You are loyal and trustworthy. People know they can rely on you to keep your word. You are also a natural leader with a talent for inspiring others to achieve their best. You have a strong sense of security and are comfortable with the routine.

Change can be difficult for you, but you are always willing to adapt if necessary. You are confident and sure of yourself and know what you want in life. Keep this affirmation in mind when you need a reminder of your strength and stability. "I am stable and secure." Remember that you are always in control of your own destiny.

Virgo - The Pure One

The Virgin Maiden traditionally represents Virgo, and the moon in Virgo suggests purity, innocence, and a need for orderliness. Those with a Virgo Moon tend to be analytical and systematic in their approach to life. They like to have things just so, and they can be extremely critical if things don't meet their high standards.

Virgos are usually quiet and reserved but can also be fiercely independent. They often have a sharp wit and are not afraid to use it. Virgos are loyal friends and reliable partners. They aren't the most spontaneous people but always follow through on their commitments. A Virgo moon is a good choice if you're looking for someone practical and down-to-earth.

Zodiac Symbol - The Virgin

The Virgin Maiden is a popular image that has been associated with the astrological sign of Virgo for centuries. According to legend, Virgo is the only human sign of the zodiac, and she represents all that is pure and innocent in the world. Often depicted holding a bunch of wheat or a flower, the Virgin Maiden is a symbol of fertility and abundance.

In recent years, however, some people have questioned whether this image represents Virgo. After all, Virgo is a sign that is often associated with hard work and practicality. Nevertheless, the Virgin Maiden remains a popular symbol of Virgo, and she continues to be revered by many as a symbol of innocence and purity.

Strengths - Analytical, Practical, Hardworking

One of the best things about having a Virgo Moon sign is that you are usually very analytical and practical. These strengths can help you in all sorts of situations, whether you are trying to figure out a problem or you are working on a project. You tend to be a hard worker, which can mean that you are successful in many areas of your life.

If you need to have someone look at something objectively, chances are good that a Virgo Moon sign will be able to do just that. Additionally, if you need someone to help get things done, a Virgo Moon sign can often be counted on to lend a hand. All in all, these strengths can make Virgo Moon signs precious people to have around.

Weaknesses - Perfectionist, Overcritical, Worrier

Virgo is an earth sign, and those with Virgo as their Moon sign are known for their practicality and level-headedness. However, Virgos can also be highly perfectionistic, always striving to meet sky-high standards. This can sometimes lead to them being overcritical, both themselves and others.

Virgos are also notorious worriers, and they can often be found fretting over minor details. While these qualities can be seen as weaknesses, they also help to make Virgos hardworking and reliable. Ultimately, it's up to each Virgo to learn to balance their perfectionism with flexibility and their worrying with trust. Doing so can make the most of their innate strengths and live a happier, more fulfilling life.

Traits of Those with This Moon Sign - Precise, Perfectionist, Analytical, Helpful, Hardworking

If you have a Virgo Moon sign, you will likely be precise, perfectionist, analytical, helpful, and hardworking. You are loyal and supportive of those you care about but can also be judgmental and critical of them. You like to be in control and often take on too much responsibility. You may find fault with others and yourself and can be your own worst critic. You are loyal and supportive of those you care about but can also be judgmental and critical of them.

You have a strong sense of duty and responsibility and are often the one who is called upon to help others. You tend to worry a lot and can be pretty indecisive. But you are also intelligent, resourceful, and have great common sense. Virgo Moons make great friends, employees, and bosses. They are always willing to lend a helping hand and are usually the go-to person when someone needs advice or assistance.

If you have a Virgo Moon sign, you will likely be precise, perfectionist, analytical, helpful, and hardworking. You like to be in control and often take on too much responsibility. You may find fault with others and yourself and can be your own worst critic. You are loyal and supportive of those you care about but can also be judgmental and critical of them.

Psychic Power - Clairvoyance

According to astrology, each zodiac sign has unique traits and abilities. For those born under the sign of Virgo, one of their psychic powers is clairvoyance. This power allows them to see beyond the veil of physical reality and into the spiritual realm. Many Virgos find that they can use this power to help others. For example, they may be able to see into someone's future and offer guidance that can help them avoid making bad choices.

Additionally, Virgos often have a strong sense of intuition, leading them to make decisions based on their gut feelings rather than logic. As a result, Virgos can often navigate difficult situations with relative ease. Overall, clairvoyance is just one of the many psychic abilities that those born under the sign of Virgo possess.

Affirmation - "I am Healthy and Whole"

As a Virgo, you are naturally health-conscious and detail-oriented. You take pride in taking care of yourself and those around you and always look for ways to improve your well-being. This full moon is perfect for reaffirming your commitment to your health and well-being. Repeat this affirmation to yourself: "I am healthy and whole."

Allow yourself to feel the truth of these words in every cell of your body. Fill yourself with the light of this full moon, and let it infuse you with strength, vitality, and clarity. Remember that you are worthy of care and attention and that you are capable of creating a life that is healthy and whole.

Capricorn - The Accomplished One

Capricorn zodiac symbol.
Google, Apache License 2.0 <http://www.apache.org/licenses/LICENSE-2.0>, via Wikimedia Commons: https://commons.wikimedia.org/wiki/File:Green_Capricorn_emoji.svg

If your lunar sign is Capricorn, you are known as "The Accomplished One." Capricorns are disciplined and hardworking, always striving for success. They are natural leaders, and their ambitious nature ensures that they are always moving forward in life. Capricorns are practical and realistic, preferring to stick to tried-and-true methods rather than taking risks. However, this does not mean they are unwilling to take on new challenges - they simply approach them with a level head and a clear plan.

Capricorns are ambitious and hardworking, always striving to reach the top. They are practical and down-to-earth, preferring to stick to proven methods rather than taking risks. Capricorns are loyal and dependable friends, but they can also be quite unforgiving if they feel betrayed.

Capricorns are also patient and level-headed, able to stay calm in the face of adversity. However, they can also be stubborn and inflexible, unwilling to change course even when it is clear that something isn't working. But overall, Capricorns are reliable people who make loyal friends and partners. If you're looking for someone who will always be there for you, a Capricorn is a perfect sign.

Zodiac Symbol - The Goat

The Capricorn zodiac symbol is the Goat. The Goat is an enduring and determined creature that is always moving forward.

Capricorns are known for their ambition and determination. Like the goats, they are constantly striving to reach the top. They are hard workers who are not afraid to put in the extra effort to achieve their goals.

Capricorns are also practical and down-to-earth. They are patient and level-headed, preferring to make slow and steady progress rather than taking risks. This cautious approach means that Capricorns often achieve great things in life. They may not be the zodiac's most exciting or impulsive sign, but their disciplined nature ensures they are always moving forward.

Strengths - Responsible, Disciplined, Self-control

Those born under the Capricorn moon sign are often considered responsible and disciplined. They are often able to maintain self-control, even in difficult situations. This can be a great strength, as it allows them to stay calm and focused when things get tough. Capricorns are often natural leaders because they can stay calm under pressure and make clear-headed decisions. This can be an asset in both their personal and professional lives.

When it comes to relationships, Capricorns are often loyal and reliable partners. They value stability and security and will do whatever it takes to maintain a healthy relationship. While some may see them as boring or predictable, those close to them know that they are simply dependable people.

Weaknesses - Know-it-all, Stubborn, Unforgiving

Capricorns are known for their strong work ethic, determination, and discipline. However, these qualities can also be seen as weaknesses. Capricorns can come across as know-it-alls who are always right. They can also be quite stubborn, sticking to their opinions even when they are wrong.

Additionally, Capricorns can have difficulty forgiving people who have wronged them. They hold onto grudges and may even seek revenge. While these qualities can be seen as negative, they make very loyal friends and reliable employees. If you can handle their sometimes-tricky personality, a Capricorn is a friend for life.

Traits of Those with This Moon Sign - Ambitious, Serious, Disciplined, Self-control, Organized

If you know someone with a Capricorn Moon sign, they are likely to be ambitious, serious, disciplined, and self-controlled. They are often very organized and may even have a structured daily routine that they stick to. This can sometimes make them seem inflexible, but it also means they are reliable and consistent. They are usually good at saving money and may even be a bit stingy with their finances.

Capricorns are often attracted to power and status and may aspire to reach a high level in their careers. They can be excellent leaders but may also be overly critical and demanding of those around them. Over time, their ambition and discipline will usually lead them to achieve their goals. So, if you know a Capricorn, be prepared for them to be driven and determined - but also fair and just.

Psychic Power - Channeling

If your Moon Sign is Capricorn, you may be interested in exploring your psychic abilities. One of Capricorns' gifts is the ability to channel information from higher realms. This means you can connect with beings on a higher frequency and receive guidance and wisdom from them. Learning how to quieten your mind and connect with your intuition is essential to developing your channeling ability.

Meditation can be a helpful tool for this. Once you have learned how to still your mind, you can begin to focus on your breath and open yourself up to receiving guidance. You may find that you receive advice through thoughts, images, or even words. Trust whatever comes through for you, and don't be afraid to experiment with different ways of channeling. With practice, you will develop stronger connections with the highest realms and receive powerful guidance that can help you on your path.

Affirmation - "I am Successful and Respected"

As a Capricorn, you are known for your hard work and dedication. You are ambitious and driven and always looking for ways to improve yourself. That's why it's important to remind yourself that you are already successful and respected. Just because you haven't reached your goals yet doesn't mean you aren't deserving of success and respect. Believe in yourself, and don't let anyone else tell you otherwise. Keep working hard, and eventually, you will achieve the success you deserve.

Grounded Moons are known for their hard work, determination, and discipline. The three signs of the Grounded Moon are Taurus, Virgo, and Capricorn. People with these Moon signs are often ambitious, serious, reliable, and consistent. They may be attracted to power and status and have strong psychic abilities. If you know someone with a Grounded Moon, they are likely to be a loyal friend and a driven worker. Keep these things in mind when interacting with someone with this Moon sign.

Chapter 7: Emotional Moons: Pisces, Scorpio, and Cancer

In astrology, water signs have a well-deserved reputation for being emotional. Those with their moon in Pisces, Scorpio, or Cancer feel things deeply, and their emotions tend to be more intense than other signs. While water sign people can be a lot to handle, they are also some of the most loving, caring, and compassionate people you will ever meet.

This chapter will explore what it means to have an emotional moon sign. We will look at the Pisces, Scorpio, and Cancer moon signs and see what makes them so emotional. We will also explore the strengths and weaknesses of each sign, the psychic powers associated with them, and an affirmation for each sign that you can use to harness the power of your emotional moon.

Emotional Moon

Each of the water signs has its way of expressing emotions. For Pisces, it is through creativity and imagination. Scorpio's emotions are intense and passionate, while Cancer's feelings are nurturing and compassionate. Having an emotional moon means that your emotions are strong, and you feel things deeply. You may find yourself being more sensitive than others, and you may need to be careful not to get too caught up in your emotions. However, you can also use your feelings to your advantage.

Your emotions can be a source of power and can be used to create positive change in your life. If you can harness them, you can be a powerful force for good. Remember that your emotions are just a part of who you are. They do not define you, and they should not control you. You can use them to your advantage.

Pisces - The Sign of Emotions

Pisces is the final sign of the zodiac, and this water sign is often seen as being deeply emotional and sensitive. Those born under this sign are often compassionate and caring, seeing the best in others even when they might not see it in themselves. Pisces moon signs can also be highly creative, using their imagination to see beyond the here and now. This empathy and creativity can make them terrific friends, but their emotions can also lead to some challenges.

Pisces moon signs can sometimes be overwhelmed by their feelings, leading them to withdraw from others. They may also have difficulty saying no, leading to them taking on more than they can handle. However, when Pisces can stay connected to their emotions, they can be a source of great strength and healing for those around them.

Zodiac Symbol - The Fish

The Pisces zodiac symbol is the fish. It represents the dual nature of Pisces, as well as their emotions. The two fish swimming in opposite directions represents Pisces' opposing forces, such as their creativity and emotions. The fish also represent Pisces' connection to the water element. Water is a powerful force, and Pisces' emotions are just as powerful.

Pisces is a highly intuitive sign, and their emotions often give them insight into the hidden meanings of things. They are also often in tune with the emotions of those around them, making them very compassionate people. The symbol also represents Pisces' connection with the spiritual world.

Strengths - Compassionate, Artistic, Intuitive, Gentle, Wise

Known for their compassion and artistry, they also have a deep well of intuition and wisdom. When the Pisces Moon is strong in your chart, you are likely to be a kind and gentle soul who is in touch with your feelings and the feelings of others. You may be drawn to creative pursuits and have a strong spiritual practice. You are likely to be a good listener and to have a knack for seeing both sides of every issue. You may also find yourself being called upon to provide sage advice to friends and loved ones.

You are likely to be a calm and easygoing person, but when the Pisces moon is especially strong, you may feel more emotional than usual. This is not necessarily a bad thing - it just means that you are in touch with your feelings and the feelings of those around you. Emotions can be powerful but can also be handled with compassion and understanding. You will likely be a natural healer and counselor when the Pisces moon is strong in your chart.

Weaknesses - Overly-Sensitive, Moody, Pessimistic, Lacks Boundaries

As anyone who has ever been in a relationship with Pisces knows, they can be sensitive souls. They feel things deeply and can easily get their feelings hurt. They can also be quite moody, going from happy to sad to angry in an hour. And because they are so sensitive, they tend to see the world through a pessimistic lens.

People with a Pisces moon assume that others are out to hurt them and that bad things will always happen to them. This can make them lack boundaries. They have trouble saying "no" and often get taken advantage of as a result. Pisces moons need to learn how to build up their emotional resilience and set healthy boundaries if they want to avoid being taken advantage of by others.

Traits of Those with This Moon Sign - Creative, Romantic, Imaginative, Sympathetic

Those with a Pisces moon are known for being creative, romantic, imaginative, and sympathetic. If you have a Pisces moon, you probably enjoy spending time alone, daydreaming, or just being lost in your thoughts. You may find yourself drawn to creative pursuits such as writing, painting, or music. You may also be attracted to more spiritual or mystical subjects.

Pisces moon people are often very compassionate people. If you have a Pisces moon, you likely have a strong intuition and can be very sympathetic toward others. You may find yourself drawn to helping professions such as teaching, social work, or counseling. Whatever career path you choose, you will likely approach it with imagination and creativity.

Psychic Power - Clairsentience

Pisces people are blessed with psychic power. One of their gifts is clairsentience, which is the ability to feel the energy of other people and places. Pisces are very compassionate and can often sense the emotions of others. They are also very intuitive and strongly connected to the spiritual realm. When they use their clairsentience, they can pick up on other people's vibes and places. This allows them to learn things that they wouldn't otherwise know.

Pisces people are natural healers and can often instinctively help others. They are also great at advising because they can see both sides of every issue. If you know someone with a Pisces moon, consider yourself lucky. You have found a true friend who will always be there for you.

Affirmation - "I am Open to the Guidance of My Higher Power"

If you have a Pisces moon, your affirmation should be "I am open to the guidance of my higher power." This will help you connect with your intuition and the spiritual realm. It will also help you to trust the guidance that you receive. Remember, your intuition is always there to help you. All you need to do is listen.

By affirming that we are open to this guidance, we can create a channel for it to flow through. We can trust that we will be given the answers we need and that we will be supported on our journey. Take some time to quiet your mind and listen for the voice of your higher power. It may come in the form of a thought, a feeling, or an image. Trust what you receive, and allow it to guide you forward.

Scorpio - The Sign of Power

Scorpio symbol.
Google, Apache License 2.0 <http://www.apache.org/licenses/LICENSE-2.0>, via Wikimedia Commons: https://commons.wikimedia.org/wiki/File:Green_Scorpio_emoji.svg

People with a Scorpio moon are known for being passionate, intense, and powerful. If you have a Scorpio moon, you likely approach life with great intensity. You are likely to be drawn to intensity in all its forms. You approach everything with great passion, whether it's your work, relationships, or hobbies.

You can use it for good when you are in touch with your power. You can be a force for positive change in the world. You can also be a great leader and motivator. When you are out of touch with your power, you may find yourself feeling lost and directionless. You may also struggle with self-destructive behaviors.

Scorpio is one of the most misunderstood signs of the zodiac. Because of its association with death and rebirth, it is often seen as dark and foreboding. But the truth is that Scorpio is a sign of great power. Scorpios are passionate, intense, and fiercely loyal. They are also natural leaders, always ready to take charge when necessary.

Regarding relationships, Scorpios are in it for the long haul. Once they have committed to someone, they will do whatever it takes to make the relationship work. So, if you're looking for a strong, passionate, and reliable partner, look no further than a Scorpio.

Zodiac Symbol - The Scorpion

The Scorpio zodiac symbol is the scorpion, which is a powerful and dangerous creature. They are also very passionate and intense. When you see a scorpion, it reminds you that you have great power. Use your power wisely and for good. Scorpio is a sign of transformation, so use your power to make positive changes in your life and the world.

This symbol also reminds us that we all have a dark side. Scorpions can be dangerous and destructive. We all have these qualities within us, but we must learn to control them. If we can harness our power and use it for good, we can achieve great things.

Strengths - Resourceful, Brave, Passionate, Stubborn, True Friend

Scorpio is known for being one of the zodiac's most intense and passionate signs. People born under this sign are often resourceful, brave, and stubborn. They are also some of the most loyal and true friends you will ever have. If you have a Scorpio friend, you'll have a fiercely good protector and friend. They are also usually very intuitive and can read people very well. However, their intensity can sometimes be overwhelming, and they can hold grudges for a long time. But if you can handle their intensity, Scorpio is a great friend to have.

Weaknesses - Jealous, Obsessive, Suspicious, Anxious

Scorpios are known for their passion and intensity, which can also lead to negative traits. Scorpios are often very jealous and possessive, especially in relationships. They can be obsessive about the people and things they care about and very suspicious of others. This can make Scorpios seem anxious and paranoid. However, these weaknesses can also be turned into strengths.

Scorpios who learn to control their jealousy are very loyal and protective partners, and those who learn to channel their obsessions can succeed in their chosen field. Scorpios who learn to trust themselves can also be calm and confident in any situation. So, while they may have some darkness in their hearts, they also have the potential for great strength.

Traits of Those with This Moon Sign - Intense, Resilient, Passionate, Mysterious

If you were born under a Scorpio Moon, congratulations - you've got one of the zodiac's most intense and resilient energies! Scorpio moons are known for their passion and mystery and are often incredibly successful in whatever they put their minds to. If you're looking to capitalize on your natural Scorpio moon traits, here are a few things to keep in mind.

First, Scorpio is all about intensity. Whether it's your emotions or goals, you tend to go all-in, which can be both good and bad. On the plus side, it means that you're usually very successful at whatever you set your mind to. But on the downside, it can also mean that you burn out quickly or that you're always on the go without taking time to rest and recharge.

Secondly, Scorpio moons are incredibly resilient. You have an amazing ability to pick yourself up after setbacks and keep going, which is an invaluable quality in life. Finally, Scorpio moons are often very passionate. You have a deep well of emotion within you, and when you care about something - or someone - you care. This can be both a strength and a weakness.

Psychic Power - Clairvoyance

Clairvoyance is the ability to see clearly beyond the five physical senses. Scorpios have an innate understanding of this sixth sense and often use it to their advantage. While some people might shy away from their psychic abilities, Scorpios embrace them. They are unafraid to explore the unknown and often use intuition to guide them through life.

Thanks to their keen insights, Scorpios can often see things others cannot. This allows them to make better decisions and navigate through life with ease. When it comes to matters of the heart, Scorpios are especially gifted. Their ability to see the future gives them a leg up regarding relationships. They know who is right for them and who isn't, which helps them avoid heartache down the road.

If you're lucky enough to have a Scorpio in your life, consider yourself fortunate. These individuals are true treasures. Thanks to their unique abilities, they can help you see things in a different light and teach you how to trust your intuition.

Affirmation - "I Trust My Intuition"

Trusting your intuition can be difficult, especially if you're used to second-guessing yourself. But if you have a Scorpio moon, your instinct is likely one of your strongest assets. Scorpios are known for their psychic ability and are often very in tune with their emotions. As a result, they are often very good at reading people and understanding their motives.

When making decisions, trusting your gut can be the best course of action. After all, your Scorpio moon knows things you may not be consciously aware of. So, if you find yourself second-guessing your choices, take a step back and listen to what your intuition is telling you. Chances are, it will lead you in the right direction.

Cancer - The Sign of Nurturing

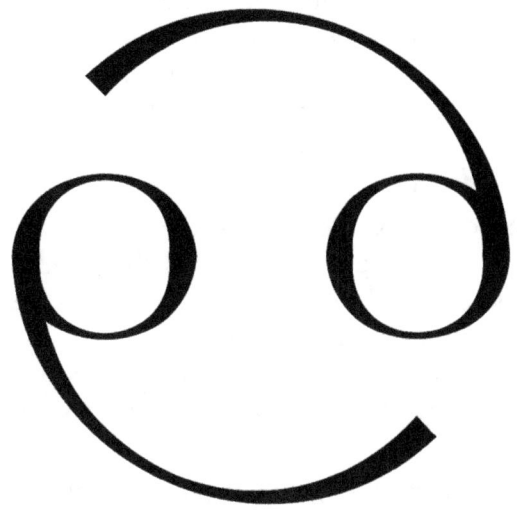

Cancer zodiac symbol.
Denis Moskowitz, CC BY-SA 4.0 <https://creativecommons.org/licenses/by-sa/4.0>, via Wikimedia Commons:
https://commons.wikimedia.org/wiki/File:Cancer_symbol_(Moskowitz,_variable_width).svg

Cancer is a sign of nurturing. Those born with the Cancer moon sign are often extremely caring and compassionate, always looking out for the needs of others. Cancerians are particularly family-oriented and create close-knit bonds with those they love. These caring qualities make Cancerians natural caregivers and are often drawn to professions such as teaching or nursing.

Cancer is also a very emotional sign. Those born under this sign feel things deeply and are often very sensitive. This can sometimes make them seem moody or clingy, but it also gives them a great deal of compassion and empathy. Cancerians are often very intuitive, and they have a strong connection to their emotions.

The Cancer moon is a time when these qualities are amplified. Cancerians may feel more emotionally volatile than usual. However, this can also be a time when they can connect with their emotions more intensely. This can be a powerful time for a Cancerian to connect with their inner self and to nurture their own needs as well as the needs of others.

Zodiac Symbol - The Crab

The Cancer zodiac symbol is the crab. This symbol represents the qualities of nurturing, family, and emotion. People born under this sign are often very protective of their loved ones and are emotionally in tune with those around them. They can be quick to anger if they feel someone they care about is being threatened, but they are also some of the most loving and supportive people you could ever hope to meet.

Cancers are often excellent at creating a warm and welcoming home, and they usually put the needs of their family before their own. If you know a Cancer, be sure to thank them for their amazing ability to nurture and care for those they love. If you are a Cancer moon sign, take some time for yourself. Though it is essential to care for others, it is also critical to nurture your own needs.

Strengths - Tenacious, Highly Imaginative, Loyal, Emotional, Persistent

Cancerians are known for their tenacity, loyalty, and emotional strength. They are often highly imaginative and can see things differently than others. They are often highly imaginative and can see things in a different way. All of these strengths make Cancerians ideal friends and partners.

If you're looking for someone who will stand by you and help you through thick and thin, a Cancerian is a perfect friend for you. They will always be there for you, no matter what your circumstances. And their imagination means they can often devise creative solutions to problems.

Weaknesses - Sensitive, Moody, Pessimistic, Lacks Boundaries

While the Cancer moon sign has many strengths, it also comes with some challenges. Those born under this sign tend to be highly sensitive and easily moody. They may also be quite pessimistic and lack boundaries. This can make them susceptible to manipulation by others. However, with awareness and a commitment to personal growth,

Cancerians can maximize their strengths and minimize their weaknesses by working on their self-awareness and setting healthy boundaries. Those around them will benefit from their innate caring nature, loyalty, and ability to create a warm and inviting home.

Traits of Those with This Moon Sign - Nurturing, Protective, Compassionate, Sensitive

People with the Cancer moon sign are some of the most nurturing and compassionate people you will ever meet. They are very protective of their loved ones and tend to be highly sensitive to the emotions of those around them. They are often quick to anger if they feel someone they care about is being threatened, but they are also some of the most loving and supportive people you could ever hope to meet.

Those with Cancer moon are often very sensitive to the needs of others and quick to offer a helping hand. They are naturally able to make others feel comfortable and safe, and they are usually loyal and generous friends. However, Cancers can also be quite moody, and their emotions can fluctuate rapidly. They may withdraw into their shells when feeling overwhelmed or hurt, emerging only when they feel ready to face the world again.

If you have a Cancer moon, you may find the different phases of the moon strongly influence your moods. During the full moon, you may feel especially energized and creative, while during a new moon, you may crave solitary time to reflect and rejuvenate. Regardless of your moon sign, we all have a little bit of Cancer in our charts. So next time you're feeling nurturing or protective, remember to thank your Cancer moon!

Psychic Power - Clairsentience

If you've ever had a gut feeling about something, you may have experienced clairsentience. This psychic power is all about sensing energy and associated emotions and can manifest in several ways. For example, you may suddenly get a strong feeling that something bad is going to happen. Or you may meet someone for the first time and instantly get a "bad vibe" from them.

Cancer people are often very intuitive and are drawn to careers in which they can help others, such as counseling or social work. If you think you may be clairsentient, you can do a few things to develop your abilities. Meditation is a great way to clear your mind and focus your energy. You can also try keeping a journal to document your experiences. You can learn to harness the power of clairsentience by tuning into your intuition.

Affirmation - "I am in Tune with the Universe"

Cancer is a water sign, and they may also be quite sensitive to the energies around them, picking up on the emotions of others easily. For cancer people, it can be helpful to connect with a higher power or cosmic force that can offer guidance and support. This doesn't have to be a traditional god or goddess - it could simply be the universe's energy.

The essential thing is to feel that you are connected to something larger than yourself, something that can offer guidance when you need it most. By affirming that "I am open to the guidance of my higher power," cancer people can strengthen their connection to this powerful source of support.

Water signs are often associated with emotions, and this is especially true for Cancer, Pisces, and Scorpio. Those with a Cancer moon tend to be highly nurturing and compassionate, while those with a Pisces moon may be more sensitive and introspective. Scorpios may be the most intense of all the water signs, and their emotions can run deep.

Regardless of what your moon sign is, we all have a little bit of each of these signs in our charts. So next time you're feeling emotional, remember to thank your watery moon!

Chapter 8: Getting to Know Your Psychic Powers

Psychic powers are special abilities that allow individuals to sense, feel, and see beyond the five physical senses. Though anyone can develop psychic abilities, some people are born with a natural inclination towards them. Psychic abilities often first during childhood or adolescence but can lie dormant until later in life. There are many different psychic abilities, each with its specialties and functions. Understanding your psychic powers can help you to live a more balanced and fulfilling life.

This chapter will explore the different types of psychic abilities and what they can do. Furthermore, it will provide a table of which psychic abilities are associated with each moon sign. Finally, it will explore how understanding your psychic abilities can improve different areas of your life.

The Different Types of Psychic Powers

1. The Four Clairs

The four Clairs are the psychic abilities of Clairvoyance, Clairaudience, Clairsentience, and Claircognizance. Though some people are more gifted than others, we all have at least some psychic ability. Clairvoyance, or clear seeing, is the ability to see beyond the physical world. This might manifest as sensing a presence in the room, seeing ghosts or angels, or having vivid dreams or precognitive visions.

Clairaudience, or clear hearing, is the ability to hear beyond the physical world. This might manifest as human and non-human voices or sounds that no one else can hear. Clairsentience, or clear feeling, is the ability to feel beyond the physical world. Or it could be gut feelings or hunches about people or situations, empathy for others, or knowing things without knowing how you know them.

Lastly, Claircognizance, or clear knowing, is the ability to know beyond the physical world. This might manifest as sudden realizations, "a-ha!" moments, déjà vu experiences, or an innate understanding of complex concepts. So next time you have a hunch about something, trust your gut. You just might be tapping into your psychic abilities.

2. Precognition

Precognition is the ability to see into the future. This could show up as dreams or visions of future events, a sense of knowing what is going to happen before it does, or a "gut feelings" about something. Precognition is a powerful ability that can be used to help make decisions, avoid danger, or simply know what will happen.

Precognition, also called prescience or future sight, is the ability to see events that have not yet transpired. Although it is often associated with paranormal activity, precognition is a fairly common experience. For example, many people report having dreams that later come true or feeling a sense of déjà vu when encountering a new situation.

Some research suggests that precognition may be more likely to occur when people are tired or stressed because their ability to focus is reduced. They can filter out irrelevant information. Precognition is still not fully understood by science, but it remains an intriguing subject for further study. The ability to see into the future can be a valuable asset in many different areas of life.

3. Retrocognition

Have you ever had a dream where you relive a moment from your childhood? Or maybe you've been in a new place, and it suddenly feels very familiar? These are both examples of retrocognition - the experience of knowing something without any previous knowledge. Retrocognition can also happen when we see things in our dreams that we have never seen before – yet they feel familiar.

There are many possible explanations for retrocognition. Some believe it is a kind of intuition or sixth sense that lets us tap into hidden knowledge. Others think it may be a form of déjà vu, where our brain momentarily confuses past and present experiences. It is also possible that retrocognition is a way for our minds to make sense of new information by connecting it to things we already know. Whatever the cause, retrocognition is a fascinating phenomenon that can give us a glimpse into our hidden memories and abilities.

4. Psychokinesis

Psychokinesis, also known as telekinesis, is the ability to move objects using only the power of your mind. This may sound like something out of a science fiction movie, but there have been many documented cases of people using psychokinesis to move objects. In most cases, the objects that are moved are small and lightweight, such as paper or coins.

However, there have also been reports of people using psychokinesis to move larger objects, such as furniture. While the jury is still out on whether or not psychokinesis is a real phenomenon, there is no denying that it would be a handy ability to have! Imagine being able to clean your house or cook dinner without lifting a finger. Psychokinesis may not be a reality for everyone, but it is certainly an intriguing possibility.

5. Mediumship

Mediumship is the ability to communicate with the spirits of the dead. This ability is said to be latent in all of us, but it is only developed in some people. Mediums use their gifts to comfort the bereaved and offer messages of hope and guidance from the other side.

There are different types of mediumship, including mental mediumship and physical mediumship. Mental mediumship involves receiving messages from the dead without any physical manifestation. This can happen through clairaudience (hearing voices) or clairsentience (sensing spirits).

On the other hand, physical mediumship involves materializing the spirits of the dead, so they can be seen and heard. This is done through scrying (seeing visions), table-turning (moving objects), and direct-voice communication (hearing voices).

If you think you have mediumistic abilities, develop them with the help of a qualified teacher. This will ensure that you use your gift positively and not become overwhelmed by negative energies. With practice, you can learn to channel your psychic ability and use it to help others.

6. Empathy

Empathy is the ability to sense and understand the emotions of others. It's a psychic ability that allows you to feel what others feel as if their emotions were your own. This can be a powerful tool for understanding and connecting with others, but it can also be overwhelming if you're not used to it.

If you're an empath, you may find yourself picking up on the emotions of those around you even when they're not explicitly expressed. You might also be highly sensitive to your environment and feel drained after being in crowded or chaotic places. Some empaths are also claircognizant, which means they receive information about people and events through psychic means.

Empathy is a gift that can be used to help others, but it's important to set boundaries so you don't absorb other people's emotions to the point of causing yourself harm. It's also important to develop coping mechanisms for dealing with the sometimes-overwhelming onslaught of information that can come with this ability. With practice, empathy can be a valuable tool for building deeper relationships and creating positive change in the world.

7. Channeling

Channeling is a psychic ability where a person can receive and transmit communication from other entities, both human and non-human. The entity may be a spirit guide, an angel, a demon, or even an extraterrestrial being. Channeling can be conscious or unconscious, often happening when the person is in a trance. Channelers use their abilities to receive guidance, healing, or information from the other side.

Although channeling is often associated with New Age practices, it is a very ancient ability practiced by cultures worldwide. It's not always accurate, and using your common sense when working with a channeler is necessary. For those who are open to the experience, channeling can be a powerful way to connect with the unseen realms.

8. Automatic Writing

Automatic writing is a psychic ability where a person channels information from their subconscious mind onto paper. This can also be a conscious or unconscious action; the messages received can provide insights into the future or offer guidance on specific problems.

Although anyone can learn to do automatic writing, it is often considered a natural gift developed over time. With practice, it is possible to sharpen this skill and use it to obtain more accurate and detailed information. In addition to being an interesting party trick, automatic writing can be a valuable tool for personal growth and self-discovery.

9. Psychometry

Psychometry is a psychic ability where people read the energy of objects and learn about their history. This information can be revealed through physical sensations, emotions, or mental images. To read an object, a psychometrist will typically hold it in their hands or place it against their forehead. Psychometry can be used to learn about an object's past owners, origins, or any significant events it has been involved in.

While some people are born with this ability, it can also be developed through practice and meditation. People interested in developing their psychometric abilities may want to try working with different types of objects, such as jewelry, tools, or even photographs. With time and practice, anyone can learn to harness the power of psychometry.

10. Tarot Reading

Tarot readings can be used to explore the past, present, or future.
https://www.pexels.com/photo/assorted-tarot-cards-on-table-3088369/

People have been using tarot cards for divination for centuries. The practice likely originated in the 14th century, and the first known tarot deck was created in Italy in the 15th century. Tarot reading is a form of fortune-telling that uses a deck of 78 cards. The deck is divided into two sections, the Major Arcana and the Minor Arcana. The Major Arcana consists of 21 cards representing major life events, while the Minor Arcana consists of 56 cards representing more everyday concerns.

Tarot readings can be used to explore a person's past, present, and future. To get a reading, the seeker shuffles the deck and pulls out a certain number of cards, which the reader interprets. While tarot readings are not considered to be 100% accurate, they can be useful for gaining insights into a person's life.

Table: Psychic Powers of Moon Signs

Moon Signs	Psychic Abilities
Aries	Claircognizance
Taurus	Psychometry

Gemini	Psychokinesis
Cancer	Emotional Empath
Leo	Creative Channel
Virgo	Physical Empath
Libra	Telepathy
Scorpio	Mediumship
Sagittarius	Clairvoyance
Capricorn	Channeling
Aquarius	Remote Viewing
Pisces	Clairsentience

How Understanding Psychic Powers Can Improve Life

Psychic powers have been shrouded in mystery for centuries. Still, recent advances in psychology and neuroscience are beginning to shed light on these abilities. While some people may be skeptics, there is now a growing body of scientific evidence that suggests that psychic powers are real. And more importantly, understanding these abilities can improve your life. Here's how:

1. General Life Improvement

Psychic abilities can be used to improve your life in several ways. For example, using your clairvoyance to make better decisions can lead to improved relationships, increased success at work, and more money in the bank. Studies have shown that people who can see into the future tend to make better decisions about their careers and personal relationships.

People who can read other people's minds tend to be more successful in negotiations and social interactions. Finally, people with a strong connection to the spiritual world tend to be more resilient in facing adversity. So, if you're interested in learning more about psychic powers, don't be afraid to do some research. Understanding these abilities could lead to a better life for you and those around you.

2. Love Life

Everyone wants to be loved and to love in return. But sometimes, things don't go according to plan. That's where understanding psychic powers can come in handy. After all, love is just another form of energy, and psychic abilities allow you to tap into and manipulate different forms of energy. By understanding how psychic powers work, you can use them to improve your love life in several ways.

For example, if you're having trouble finding Mr. or Mrs. Right, you can use psychometry to learn more about potential partners. Or, if you're already in a relationship, but things are starting to fizzle, you can use telepathy to communicate better with your partner. So, if you're looking for a little extra help in the love department, why not try understanding psychic powers? It just might be the boost your love life needs.

3. Career

Many people are interested in psychic powers and what they can do. However, few people realize that understanding psychic powers can also positively impact their careers. For example, those who can read minds or see the future can use these abilities to their advantage in a business setting. Understanding what others are thinking can better anticipate their needs and wants. Those who can see the future can use this knowledge to make better decisions about investments, strategic planning, and more.

In short, those who understand psychic powers can use them to give them a leg up in their career. So, if you're interested in using your psychic abilities to improve your career, start by researching and learning all you can about these powers. With a little understanding, you can start using your psychic abilities to catapult yourself to success.

4. Finances

Psychic abilities can manifest in many ways, from being able to read people's thoughts to predicting the future. Understanding and harnessing your psychic powers can help improve your finances. For example, let's say you have the ability to read people's thoughts. You can use this to your advantage by reading people's cues and knowing when they're about to make a financial mistake. By warning them ahead of time, you can help them avoid making poor decisions that could cost them money.

Or let's say you have the ability to see into the future. You can use this knowledge to make wise investments that will pay off down the road. You can also use it to steer clear of financial pitfalls that others may not see coming. So, if you've ever wondered whether or not you have psychic powers, now is the time to start exploring them. Who knows? You may just find that they hold the key to improving your financial situation.

5. Health

A recent study found that people who reported having psychic experiences were more likely to have good mental health. Moreover, they were more likely to report higher well-being and life satisfaction levels. This suggests that understanding and experiencing psychic powers can positively impact health.

While more research is needed to confirm these findings, they provide an intriguing glimpse into the potential benefits of psychic powers. If further studies confirm the link between psychic powers and health, it could revolutionize our understanding of both mental and physical health.

6. Friendship

By understanding more about psychic abilities, we can learn how to better use them to improve our friendships. For example, studies have shown that telepathic people are better able to understand the thoughts and feelings of others. This ability can be used to build closer relationships with friends through empathy and understanding.

Moreover, those who are psychically gifted often have a strong intuition. This intuition can be used to help friends in times of need or trouble. Finally, people with psychic abilities often deeply connect to the spiritual world. This connection can be used to provide comfort and guidance to friends who are experiencing difficult times.

7. Family

Many people are interested in psychic powers and what they can do. While some people may be interested in using them for personal gain, others may want to use them to improve family relationships. Psychic powers can be used to communicate with loved ones who have passed away, to get messages from the other side, or simply connect on a deeper level. By understanding how psychic powers work, you can use them to your advantage and improve your family life.

Psychic abilities are based on energy; you can learn how to channel it for positive purposes by understanding how energy works. When you use your psychic abilities to benefit your family, you can create strong bonds, heal old wounds, and even resolve conflict if you are interested in improving your family life.

Psychic powers have long been a source of fascination, and recent years have seen a surge in popular interest in the topic. For some people, understanding psychic powers is a way to connect with the spiritual world. Others see it as a way to gain insight into their own lives and relationships. Regardless of your reasons for looking into psychic powers, there are some key things to keep in mind.

First, it's important to remember that everyone has psychic abilities. We all can sense things beyond the physical realm. However, some people are more attuned to their psychic abilities than others. If you're interested in exploring your psychic powers, there are a few ways to do so. You can try meditating or practicing visualization exercises. You can also consult with a professional psychic for guidance.

When it comes to spirituality, there is no one right path. Everyone has a unique relationship with the spiritual world. However, understanding psychic powers can help you deepen your spirituality and connect with the divine in new ways. If you're open to exploring your psychic abilities, you may be surprised at what you discover about yourself and the spiritual realm.

Chapter 9: Tapping into the Four Clairs

In the previous chapters, we discussed the four Clairs: Clairvoyance (clear seeing), Clairsentience (clear feeling), Claircognizance (clear knowing), and Clairaudience (clear hearing). Now let's focus on how to tap into these abilities. Each person has all four Clairs, but one is usually stronger than the others. You can develop the weaker Clairs with practice. For example, if you want to improve your ability to see clearly, you can try visualization exercises. If you want to become more attuned to your feelings, you can journal about your emotions each day.

You can develop stronger psychic abilities by working on your weaker Clairs. This chapter will focus on accessing each of the four Clairs. We will discuss which moon signs are most likely to have strong abilities in each area and the best methods for tapping into your abilities.

Clairaudience - Clear Hearing

Clairaudience can hear things that are not within the range of normal human hearing. This may include hearing voices or sounds from other dimensions. Clairaudience is often associated with clairvoyance or clear seeing. However, it is possible to have one without the other.

Many people who develop their abilities find that the first one is clairaudience. This is because it is easier to receive auditory information than visual information. For example, you may hear a voice telling you to turn left while driving, even though there is no one else in the car. Or you may suddenly hear a song playing in your head that you haven't thought of in years.

If you suspect you have clairaudience, pay attention to the thoughts and messages that come into your mind. You may be surprised at how accurate they are!

Moon Signs Most Likely to Have Clairaudience - Gemini

Gemini is one of the most intuitive signs of the zodiac, and they are known for their sharp minds and quick wit. Gemini is also a highly adaptable sign, which makes them well-suited to developing clairaudience. This ability allows Gemini to receive guidance from their higher selves or spirit guides, and they can use this guide to navigate through life's challenges. If you're a Gemini, you may find that you can hear messages from your guides when you quiet your mind and focus your attention inward.

Whether you're a Gemini or not, know that anyone has the potential to develop clairaudience. If you're interested in exploring this ability, start by meditating and practicing self-reflection. Over time, you may find that you can hear voices or sounds that offer guidance and insight.

How to Access Your Clairaudience - Reading, Meditating

If you're looking to develop your clairaudience, you can do a few things to get started. One is to start paying attention to the sounds around you - both external and internal. External sounds can include things like running water, birds singing, or children laughing. Internal sounds can include the sound of your breath or heartbeat. As you become more attuned to the sounds around you, you may notice patterns or messages you wouldn't have noticed before.

Another way to do it is through meditation. Meditation helps to quiet the mental chatter that can prevent you from hearing intuitive guidance. While there are many different ways to meditate, one simple method is to focus on your breath and count each inhale and exhale.

As you become more relaxed, you will start to notice thoughts, images, or words coming into your mind. These may be messages from your higher self or spirit guides. Trust whatever comes up, and don't be afraid to write it down or share it with someone else. With a little practice, you'll be surprised at how easy it is to access your clairaudience!

The Best Method to Tap into Your Clairaudience - Reading about Intuition

Many people don't realize this, but one of the best ways is actually by reading about intuition. Why? Because by reading about something, you are effectively tapping into your intuition and subconscious mind, which is where your clairaudience ability lies.

When you read about how to develop your intuition or how to interpret the signs and symbols that your intuition gives you, you are effectively training your mind to become more aware of these things. And the more aware you are of your intuition, the easier it will be for you to interpret the signs and messages that it gives you. So, if you want to develop your clairaudience ability, make sure to spend some time reading about intuition and developing your understanding of it.

Claircognizance - Clear Knowing

Claircognizance is the ability to know something without understanding how you know it. It's often described as a "gut feeling" or a hunch. Claircognizance differs from intuition, which is when you get a sense or feeling about something. With Claircognizance, you just know something without any explanation. For example, you may meet someone for the first time and suddenly know that they will be important in your life, even though you don't know why.

Some people experience Claircognizance as a physical sensation, like a tingling in their body or a headache. Others just have a clear understanding of something without any physical sensations. Claircognizance is one of the many ways that we receive information from the Universe. If you're attuned to it, you can use Claircognizance to guide your decisions and choices in life.

Moon Signs Most Likely to Have Claircognizance - Aries

Aries is the first sign of the zodiac, and those born under this sign are often seen as natural leaders. Aries are known for their fiery temperament and competitive nature. They are always up for a challenge, and they are never afraid to speak their mind. When it comes to Claircognizance or clear knowing, Aries is one of the most likely signs of possessing this ability.

For Aries, Claircognizance might feel like a gut feeling or a hunch about something. If you were born under this sign, you might find that you have a natural knack for reading people and situations. You may also find that you have an inner understanding of the Universe and your place in it. Psychic abilities are often thought to be more common in children than adults, but Aries disproves this theory. If you have Claircognizance, trust your instincts, and don't be afraid to follow your heart.

How to Access Your Claircognizance - Questioning, Asking for Guidance

If you're wondering how to access your Claircognizance, the first step is to start questioning everything. Ask yourself why you believe what you believe and whether there might be another way of looking at things. Trust your intuition, and don't be afraid to question authority figures or so-called experts. Remember that nobody knows everything and that even the wisest person still has room to grow.

Asking for guidance from your Higher Self or the universe is another great way to develop your Claircognizance. When you're unsure of what to do or where to go next in life, simply ask for guidance and then listen for the answer. It may come in the form of a gut feeling, a sudden urge to take action, or a clear knowing that this is the right path for you.

The Best Method to Tap into Your Claircognizance - Work on Your Intuition

Intuition is our built-in guidance system, and it's always trying to communicate with us, but we often ignore it or second-guess it. Trusting your intuition takes time and practice, but it's worth the effort. Here are some tips:

- Pay attention to your gut feelings. If something feels off, it probably is.
- Learn to meditate. This will help you still your mind and better hear the quiet voice of your intuition.
- Listen to your dreams. Your subconscious mind often communicates with you through symbols and metaphors in your dreams.
- Keep a journal. Writing down your thoughts and feelings will help you become more attuned to

Clairsentience - Clear Feeling

Clairsentience is the psychic ability to feel or sense information. A clairsentient person picks up on the emotions and energy of others and the environment around them. They might get a "gut feeling" about something or just have a sense that something is off. Clairsentience can also manifest as empathy, which is the ability to feel what others are feeling.

Clairsentience is one of the most common psychic abilities and is also one of the easiest to nurture. If you're interested in exploring your clairsentience, there are a few simple exercises you can try. Spend time in nature, and pay attention to how you feel. Meditate regularly, and focus on your breathing. And finally, practice being "in the moment" by being present and aware of your surroundings. With a little practice, you'll soon be able to sense almost anything.

Moon Signs Most Likely to Have Clairsentience - Cancer, Pisces, Scorpio

The three moon signs most likely to have clairsentience are Cancer, Pisces, and Scorpio. Cancer is a water sign; as such, they are very intuitive and in tune with their emotions. This gives them a strong ability to sense the emotions of others, even when those emotions are not explicitly expressed. Pisces is another water sign, and like Cancer, they are extremely attuned to the emotional energy around them.

Pisces also has a strong connection to the spiritual realm, enhancing their ability to sense things beyond the physical world. Scorpio is the final sign on our list, and like Cancer and Pisces, they too have a strong connection to emotions and energy. Scorpio is also a very intuitive sign, and they are known for their keen instincts and sharp intellect. All of these factors contribute to their strong

How to Access Your Clairsentience - Listening to Your Emotions

To access your clairsentience, start by paying attention to your emotions throughout the day. Again, question everything. Ask yourself what you're feeling and why. Be curious about what your emotions are trying to tell you. You may also want to try keeping a dream journal or try automatic writing, as these can also help develop this ability. With a little practice, you can learn to listen to your emotions and use them as a guide on your journey toward greater psychic awareness.

The Best Method to Tap into Your Clairsentience - Journaling

A little-known fact is that journaling is one of the best methods to develop your clairsentience. This doesn't have to be anything complicated. Simply write down your thoughts and feelings about different situations throughout the day, as in a stream of consciousness. Pay attention to any gut feelings you have about people or situations, and trust your intuition.

Over time, you'll find that you can more accurately read people and situations and have a stronger sense of intuition overall. So, if you're looking to develop your psychic abilities, start by keeping a journal and tapping into your clairsentience.

Clairvoyance - Clear Seeing

Clairvoyance is the ability to see clearly. It's a form of extrasensory perception (ESP) that allows you to perceive things that are not apparent to your physical senses. Clairvoyance is sometimes referred to as "the sixth sense." Clairvoyants see visions, symbols, or colors when they receive psychic information. Others may just "know" things without knowing how they know them.

Some people are born with this gift, while others develop it through meditation and prayer. Clairvoyance is not just about seeing the future; it's also about gaining insights into relationships, careers, and other areas of your life. If you feel you have this ability, many books and websites are available to help you develop your gift.

Moon Signs Most Likely to Have Clairvoyance - Scorpio

Clairvoyance is the ability to tap into a sixth sense, or what some refer to as the "third eye." This extrasensory perception allows one to see Auras, energy fields, and past lives. Clairvoyance is mostly associated with the positive aspects of spirituality, but it can also be used for evil deeds. A person's Moon Sign plays a big role in their psychic abilities.

Scorpio is one of the most psychic signs of the Zodiac, and they are known for their ability to see into the future. Their intense emotions and penetrating eyes give them an extrasensory perception that other Signs lack. If you know a Scorpio, chances are they have had a Clairvoyant experience at some point in their life.

How to Access Your Clairvoyance - Visualization, Imagination

One of the most common ways to access this ability is through visualization. You can often receive clear psychic impressions about what is happening by quieting your mind and picturing a scene in your imagination. This is because your imagination is a powerful tool for tapping into the collective unconscious or the universal storehouse of knowledge.

When you focus on a particular image, you can often access information that would otherwise be hidden from you. In addition, you can often manifest your desires into reality by using your imagination to visualize the desired outcome. So, whether you're trying to gain insights about the future or manifest your deepest desires, accessing your clairvoyance through visualization can be a powerful tool.

The Best Method to Tap into Your Clairvoyance - Scrying

Many people want to know how to develop their clairvoyance or psychic ability. Out of all the methods available, scrying is undoubtedly the best way to begin tapping into this power. Scrying is a divination form involving gazing into a reflective surface to promote trance-like states and visions. Water is the most commonly used scrying medium, but other surfaces such as mirrors, crystals, and even fire can be used.

The key to successful scrying is to relax the mind and body and allow yourself to become open to whatever visions may come. With practice, you can interpret the symbols and images you see in new and exciting ways. Who knows what insights you may gain about yourself and the world around you? Scrying is an incredible tool for self-discovery and personal growth, so why not try it?

The four Clairs, or forms of extrasensory perception, are Clairvoyance, Clairaudience, Clairsentience, and Claircognizance. Each of us can tap into these abilities, but some are more gifted than others. If you feel you have a strong connection to one or more of these abilities, there are many ways to develop your gifts.

This chapter has only scratched the surface of what is possible with psychic abilities. Go ahead and explore these abilities further and see what hidden talents you may possess. The world is waiting for you to discover your true potential!

Chapter 10: Turning Your Psychic Powers On and Off

We all have psychic abilities, but not all of us know how to use them. Some people are born with natural psychic ability, while others have to work a little harder to develop their skills. But whether you're a natural or not, it's crucial to know how to turn your psychic abilities on and off. This chapter will teach you why it's essential to have an ON/OFF button for your psychic abilities, how to create one, and how to access it. We'll also review when and how often you should turn your power on and off.

The ON/OFF Button

Everyone has some degree of psychic ability, but most people don't know how to harness it or don't bother to try. If you're someone who wants to develop their abilities, it's essential to have an ON/OFF button. Knowing when to turn them on or off is key to keeping your abilities sharp and avoiding information overload.

The ON/OFF button is necessary to protect yourself because it gives you control. When your powers are turned on, you're more susceptible to picking up on other people's thoughts and emotions. You're also more likely to be influenced by outside forces, such as entities or spirits.

If you're not careful, you can easily become overwhelmed by all the information coming at you. That's why it's important to be able to turn your abilities on and off. You can use your ON/OFF button to control when you want to work with your psychic abilities and when you need a break from them.

The Importance of Turning Your Psychic Powers On and Off

There are many reasons to be able to turn your abilities on and off. For one thing, it can help to prevent burnout. It can be overwhelming and exhausting if you're constantly bombarded with information from the spirit world. Learning to control your psychic abilities can help you focus and use your energy more efficiently. It can also help you protect yourself from negative energies.

When your psychic powers are turned off, you're less vulnerable to outside influences and can better control your energy field. In addition, turning your psychic powers on and off can help you develop a stronger connection with the spirit world. By opening yourself up to messages from the other side, you can gain insight and guidance that you might not otherwise receive. With practice, you'll learn how to control your psychic abilities and use them to improve your life.

Creating Your Own ON/OFF Button

Now that you know why it's important to have an ON/OFF button for your psychic abilities, it's time to learn how to create one. The first step is to identify what works for you. Some people find it helpful to visualize a physical switch that they can flip on and off. Others prefer to imagine a barrier that they can put up around themselves.

The vital thing is to be clear and specific about what you want, whichever method you choose. The more specific you are, the easier it will be to create your ON/OFF button. Here are some ways to get started:

1. **Visualization**

One of the simplest and most effective ways to create an ON/OFF button is to visualize it. For this method, you can either imagine a physical switch that you can flip on and off or a barrier that you can put up around yourself. Alternatively, you can visualize yourself closing and opening a door or drawing a curtain around yourself.

Picture a switch in your mind's eye to create a physical switch. It can be any kind of switch, such as a light switch or a power switch. Now, visualize flipping the switch to the OFF position. As you do, feel your psychic abilities shutting down. To create a barrier, imagine a wall or force field around you. Start to visualize it going up around you, starting from your feet and moving up to your head. Once the barrier is in place, you will feel your psychic abilities shutting down.

2. Affirmations

Another way to create an ON/OFF button for your psychic abilities is to use affirmations. For this method, you'll need to come up with a short, simple phrase that you can say to yourself to turn your abilities on or off. Some examples of affirmations include:

- "I am turning on my psychic abilities."
- "I am now open to receiving guidance from the other side."
- "I am now closing myself off to outside influences."

Once you've chosen your affirmation, repeat it to yourself several times. As you do, picture your psychic abilities turning on or off. The key is to believe what you're saying. The more conviction you have, the more effective your affirmation will be.

3. Crystals

Crystals can also be used to create an ON/OFF button for your psychic abilities. For this method, you'll need to choose a crystal that resonates with the protection energy. Some good choices include black tourmaline, obsidian, and hematite. Once you've chosen your crystal, hold it in your hand and visualize your psychic abilities turning on or off. As you do, feel the crystal's energy working to protect you.

4. Meditation

Meditation is another effective way to create an ON/OFF button for your psychic abilities. For this method, find a quiet place to sit or lie down. Close your eyes and take a few deep breaths. As you breathe in and out, visualize your psychic abilities turning on or off. Feel the energy of your abilities shifting as you change your visualization.

5. Rituals

You can also use rituals. For this method, you'll need to choose a simple action that you can do to symbolize turning your abilities on or off. Some examples of rituals include lighting a candle, saying a prayer, or burning incense. Choose whichever action feels right for you. The essential thing is that you do it with intention.

As you act, visualize your psychic abilities turning on or off. This is a powerful way to change your energy and focus on your intention. Feel the energy of your abilities shifting as you complete the ritual. The more you do this, the more effective it will be.

Accessing Your ON/OFF Button

Now that you know how to create an ON/OFF button for your psychic abilities, it's time to put it into practice. The next time you find yourself in a situation where you need to turn your abilities on or off, take a moment to visualize your ON/OFF button. See it in your mind's eye, and then take action to flip the switch or activate the barrier. You may also want to carry around a physical representation of your buttons, such as a piece of jewelry or a crystal. This can help you to remember to use it when you need to.

Here are some additional tips to help you get the most out of your ON/OFF button:

1. Check-In with Your Body

Before you turn your psychic abilities on or off, it's crucial to check in with your body. Pay attention to how you're feeling physically and emotionally. If you're feeling any resistance or discomfort, it may be best to leave your abilities turned off for the time being. Being in a state of resistance will only block your ability to receive guidance. Instead, focus on opening yourself up to receiving advice when you're in a state of receptivity.

2. Set an Intention

Set an intention when you use your button. This will help you focus your energy and align with your desires. For example, if you're trying to turn your abilities off, your intention might be to protect yourself from outside influences. If you're trying to turn your abilities on, your intention might be to receive guidance from your intuition. Choose whichever intention feels right for you at the moment.

3. Be Patient

Don't expect results immediately. Getting used to using your ON/OFF button can take some time. And even when you do get the hang of it, there will still be times when your abilities won't work the way you want them to. This is normal and to be expected. The important thing is to keep practicing and to have faith that your abilities will develop in time.

4. Be Aware Of Your Energy Levels

Your energy levels can also affect your psychic abilities. If you're tired or run down, your abilities will likely weaken. On the other hand, if you're feeling energetic and enthusiastic, your abilities will be stronger. Pay attention to how you're feeling and use that information to decide whether it's a good time to turn your abilities on or off.

5. Practice Regularly

The more you practice using your button, the easier it will become. So, make sure to use it often, even when you're not trying to do any reading or work with your psychic abilities. The more familiar you are with the sensation of turning your abilities on and off, the easier it will be to do it when you need to.

6. Practice Mindfulness

Mindfulness is an essential part of using your psychic abilities. When you're trying to control your abilities, be aware of your thoughts and emotions. If you get caught up in your thoughts, take a few deep breaths and focus on the present moment. This will help you to clear your mind and focus on your intention.

7. Take Breaks

Like anything else, too much of a good thing can be detrimental. If you find yourself getting overwhelmed or stressed out, take a break and give yourself some time to recover. This will help you to avoid burnout and keep your abilities strong.

Learning how to turn your psychic abilities on and off is a valuable skill. It will help to protect you from outside influences and to focus your energy. To get the most out of your ON/OFF button, practice regularly and set an intention when you use it.

With time and practice, you'll develop a strong understanding of how to use your abilities and when it's best to turn them on or off.

Conclusion

The moon's position at your time of birth is what determines your moon sign. Moon signs are essential to astrology and can give you insight into your psychic powers. Moon signs represent the emotional side of our personalities and can play a role in everything from love and relationships to our creative output.

When it comes to psychic abilities, moon signs can provide some clues as to what we may be gifted at. For example, water signs such as Cancer and Pisces are often known for their strong intuition, while air signs like Gemini and Aquarius are often associated with psychic powers of the mind.

This informative guide covered the basics of moon signs, the four psychic powers, and how your moon sign affects your psychic abilities. You should now have a good understanding of what your psychic powers are and how to tap into them. Remember, everyone has psychic abilities, and with a little practice, you can develop yours too.

Moon signs represent the emotional side of our personalities and can play a role in everything from love and relationships to our creative output. While moon signs don't necessarily dictate our lives, they can give us insight into our own emotions and how we relate to others. The information in this guide can help you better understand your emotions and how they might affect your psychic abilities.

This guide has covered everything you need to know about moon signs and psychic abilities in three parts. Part One presented the basics, including moon signs and their relation to psychic powers. Part Two explored the different psychic abilities associated with each moon sign, and Part Three provided tips and advice on how to develop your psychic abilities.

Chapter 1 looked at what moon signs are and how they're determined. Chapter 2 explored the four psychic powers and how they're related to our moon signs. From Clairvoyance and Clairsentience to Clairaudience and Claircognizance, we explored the four main psychic powers. Chapter 3 delved into how your specific moon sign affects your psychic abilities.

Part Two of this guide explored the different moon signs in more depth. Chapter 4 examined Aries, Leo, and Sagittarius and how their bold personalities impact their psychic abilities. Chapter 5 examined Libra, Aquarius, and Gemini and how their thoughtful nature can help or hinder their psychic abilities.

In Chapter 6, we looked at Taurus, Virgo, and Capricorn and how their grounded approach to life can affect their psychic abilities. Finally, Chapter 7 looked at Pisces, Scorpio, and Cancer and how their emotional nature can impact their psychic abilities. Each of these chapters provided information on the positive and negative aspects and how those traits can impact psychic abilities.

In Part Three, we explored how to unlock your psychic powers. Chapter 8 looked at getting to know your psychic powers and how to use them for your benefit. In Chapter 9, we looked at the four Clairs and how they can help you to develop your psychic abilities. Finally, in Chapter 10, we looked at how to turn your psychic powers on and off.

By now, you should understand your psychic abilities and how to develop them further. Remember, everyone has psychic abilities, and with a little practice, you can develop yours too.

Part 2: Sun Signs

Secrets of Star Sign Astrology, Sun-Moon Astrology Combinations, Your Personality Type, and More

Introduction

The stars can tell you who you are and who you are destined to be. The secrets behind this lie in your Sun sign. The Sun shines in the center of your natal chart, the map of celestial bodies at the time of your birth, influencing the energies of all other objects around it. Sun signs are studied by a specific branch of astrology that reveals your innermost desires, goals, instincts, beliefs, and what the universe may have in store for you in the future. It can help you understand why you think, feel, and behave in general or even in specific situations and why other people's personalities may differ when compared to yours.

You may be familiar with some basic astrological terms if you check your horoscope. However, by introducing you to a more specific astrological language, this book will help you discover your Sun sign more confidently. You will learn what the terms Sun signs and Moon signs refer to and how they are related to the zodiac. You will see how the Sun determines the standards you use to measure yourself and which you show to the outside world. You will also understand how the moon defines the marks you would like to leave behind, even if you are not aware of them yet.

Both the Sun and the Moon influence the main events of your life, and they guide you on your path to becoming the type of person their combination indicates you will be. You will also learn that your Sun sign is only the core of your personality. The other aspects of your natal chart, such as your zodiac sign, house placement, the phase of the moon, or the quality of the element ruling the season of your birth, outline your personality in finer detail.

Sun sign astrology can be a valuable tool to uncover the hidden strength you can use to persevere in life. You can think of your Sun sign as a vessel for all the different potential you can unearth. The opportunities you can reveal from a detailed study of your birth chart can be surprising. So, if you are ready to delve into the hidden depths of your personality, the only thing you have to do is keep reading this book. Although the Sun sign is just a piece of the larger whole, knowing what it holds for you can enormously impact your spiritual growth and happiness.

Chapter 1: Introducing Astrology

If you have spent even a tiny bit of time on social media lately, you have probably encountered astrology. Memes about star signs and their effect on a person's personality are more popular than ever, and terms like Mercury retrograde and Mars retrograde have become part of daily conversation. In short, astrology is no longer the realm of older people and those who are out of touch. It has gone mainstream.

That said, if social media is your first real introduction to astrology, it can be enormously confusing to try and understand how it works. While most of us know our star signs, that information is almost everything we know on the topic. We may read our horoscopes, but we are unaware of how they were crafted and how other parts of our natal chart may affect our lives.

Before exploring astrology in detail, you first need to understand what astrology is. With a strong base knowledge of the subject, you will better understand the importance of your star sign and how the slightest changes in the skies can affect your life.

Understanding Astrology

According to Merriam-Webster, astrology is *"the divination of the supposed influences of the stars and planets on human affairs and terrestrial events by the positions and aspects."*

Pretty clear, right?

You are probably even more confused after reading that definition.

In essence, astrology studies celestial objects, like the stars and planets. Based on observations about their positions, astrology can make predictions about a person's life or how events in our lives and on earth will unfold.

It is essential to remember that astrology is not an exact science. Perfecting astrological analysis can take a lifetime, and even veteran, experienced astrologers learn more and refine their processes daily.

History of Astrology

This practice has a long history. Astrology can trace its origins to the 3rd millennium BC, and scholars today believe it developed along with calendar systems that were used to predict the changes in seasons. People would interpret the movement of celestial objects as communication from the gods and, for a period of time, astrology and astronomy were indistinguishable from one another.

Astrology spread far and wide from its origins in Mesopotamia, India, and China. Astrological systems in these countries are very different from the ones we know today in the West, and exploring Indian and Chinese astrology would need entire books dedicated to them.

However, in terms of astrology, as we know it today, you can trace back its roots to Egypt and Greece. One of the peoples who learned astrology from the Mesopotamians were the Persians, and, following their conquest of Egypt in 525 BC, they introduced the subject to their own lands. Following Alexander the Great's occupation of Egypt in 332 BC, the Egyptians, in turn, introduced the Greeks to astrology.

For a time, astrology took two different directions and developed differently in Ptolemaic Egypt and Greece. In Ptolemaic Egypt, three different forms of astrology, Mesopotamian, Babylonian, and native Egyptian, combined to produce the first type of horoscopic astrology. The horoscopes used by the Ptolemaic Egyptians were very different from horoscopes as we understand them today, but they formed the basis without which today's Western astrology would be completely different.

The Egyptian astrology.
See page for author, CC BY 4.0 <https://creativecommons.org/licenses/by/4.0>, via Wikimedia Commons: https://commons.wikimedia.org/wiki/File:Astrology;_the_Egyptian_zodiac._Coloured_engraving_by_J._Cha_Wellcome_V0024917.jpg

The Greeks continuously explored new astrological concepts, including the newly developed horoscopic astrology. However, one of the most popular types of astrology was theurgic astrology, which was focused on helping a person's soul ascend to the stars and reach the gods.

Greek influence also helped spread astrology in Rome, especially following the Roman conquest of Greece. For a portion of time following the Roman conquest, astrology was relegated to a study with minor importance and only concerned the lower classes of society. Astrology was also significantly associated with Babylon. Babylonia was known as Chaldea in Rome, and the link between the Babylonians and astrology was so deep that they used the term "Chaldean wisdom" to refer to any form of divination involving the planet and the stars.

Over time, astrology rose to prominence once more in Rome. The first references to astrology in Roman texts were from the writings of Cato and Juvenal in the 2nd century BC, both of whom caution against the divinatory powers of the "Chaldeans" and their astrologers. However, by the time of Augustus (who ruled from 27 BC to14 AD), astrology was used as a way to legitimize the emperor's right to rule. Augustus' stepson and heir, Tiberius, was the first emperor to have a court astrologer. The astrologer, Thrasyllus of Mendes, was also a personal friend of the emperor.

Most astrological texts from the Roman Empire were written in Greek, emphasizing the importance of the Greeks in the development of astrology. However, this also meant that following the downfall of the Western Roman Empire and the decline of the Greek language in Western Europe, astrology also declined in popularity once again.

While astrology was rising and falling in popularity under the Romans, it was also enormously popular in the Islamic world. This was the first time astrology and astronomy were differentiated, and Arabic astrology texts would become extremely popular in Europe.

These Arabic texts led to a resurgence of interest in the subject in Europe during the 10th century, and Greek and Roman theories were revived in the 12th and 13th centuries. By the 13th century, doctors had combined medicine with astrology, and by the 1500s, they were legally required to calculate the position of the moon before performing complex medical procedures like surgeries in some parts of Europe.

However, the differentiation of astrology and astronomy also meant a loss of interest in the subject from the scientific community. There was little scientific focus on it by the end of the 18th century.

Among the public, however, astrology has always ebbed and flowed. Popularity in the subject declined at the end of the Renaissance and has been up and down ever since. It would regain a strong following by the 1960s, a following that has continued to this day.

How Astrology Works

Astrologers study the connections between celestial activity and events on earth. These earthly events can affect one single person or society at large.

The events affected by the movement of celestial objects can be anything from your interpersonal relationships and career to your health or any aspect of your life. Astrologers who work with individuals will also create a birth (or natal) chart for those requiring one.

A birth chart is essentially a snapshot of what the sky looked like at the exact moment and location of your birth. The sky is divided into 12 sections or signs, and your birth chart not only allows astrologers to understand what positions the planets, Sun, and Moon were in when you were born but also a host of other information that allows them to make predictions.

Other astrologers only look at the signs under which you were born. These signs (the 12 zodiac signs) are based on the date of your birth, and astrologers look at the movement of planets and other bodies in and out of the section of the sky that "belongs" to your sign to make predictions and write horoscopes.

Astrologers also use your natal chart for other purposes, such as determining who you should marry, your compatibility with your current partner (based on both your natal charts), and much more. They can also use it to help you better understand your personality and path in life, as well as what your life focus should be.

Other parts of your birth chart include:

- **Houses:** There are 12 houses in each birth chart, each representing a different part of your life, such as relationships, career, etc. Your birth chart allows an astrologer to understand in which house each celestial body was placed at your birth.
- **Degrees:** This is the precise location of a planet. Its general location tells you which sign it is in, while the degree essentially serves as the planet's home address. Degrees are important when predicting transits and can help astrologers determine how a particular day, week, or

month may affect your chart.
- **Aspects:** A way to determine how planets and other celestial bodies interact with each other.

Other Aspects of Your Natal Chart

Natal charts, and astrology in general, are not strictly predictive. A natal chart reading, for example, can give you a better understanding of existing behavioral patterns, both the good and the bad.

This light into your life may feel uncomfortable, but after a few sessions with an astrologer, you will feel better and more connected with yourself. Additionally, it could also help spark healthy changes in your life, allowing you to develop a new personality without first having to go through the process of recognizing negative behavioral patterns.

Armed with your natal chart, an effective astrologer can tell you what goals your soul wants to achieve in its current lifetime, both in your career and otherwise. They can then help you interpret those goals. This is especially effective for people who are unsure of what path they want to take

You can also find other information, such as any trauma your soul has from a past life. Birth charts can also provide an insight into your family life, including your relationships with close family members such as parents and siblings (if you have any). It can give you a better understanding of any familial trauma you may be carrying and help you get started on resolving these issues.

Reading Birth Charts

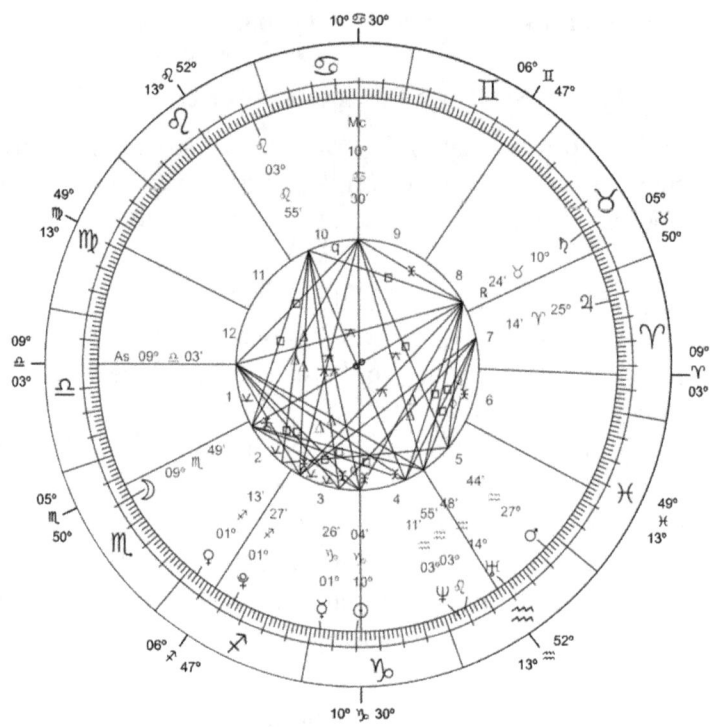

Sample birth chart.
Fred the Oyster, CC BY-SA 4.0 <https://creativecommons.org/licenses/by-sa/4.0>, via Wikimedia Commons: https://commons.wikimedia.org/wiki/File:Astrological_Chart_-_New_Millennium.svg

Originally, a person would have to be a trained astrologer to be able to effectively read your birth chart. Creating these natal charts requires a lot of math. This meant that you would have to confirm that your astrologer knew and understood math sufficiently before getting a natal chart reading.

However, modern-day readings could not be more different. As long as you know the exact time, date, and location of your birth, you can plug in this information to one of many similar websites online and receive a basic natal chart within seconds. While these charts do not give you near the level of detail professional charts do, they can often be a good starting point for people interested in the practice.

Additionally, these services often do not interpret or analyze your results. Instead, they either offer you a complete chart for you to interpret or a summary of the key points, including your ascendant and the location of the planets in your chart. While some services also provide interpretations, these are generally computer-generated and more generic interpretations than you would receive from a skilled astrologist.

If you plan to read your own chart, here are some key tips to help you with your analysis:

- **The Sun Sign:** Your Sun sign represents who you are at all times, regardless of what you are doing, who you are with, or how your life changes
- **The Moon Sign:** Your Moon sign represents the side of you that is more "hidden," a side that very few people are privy to, and the part of you that guides you when you feel lost. It plays an important part in your decision-making process.
- **The Ascendant Sign:** Your ascendant sign depends on which constellation was on your horizon at the exact moment of your birth. The ascendant sign changes far more frequently than the Sun or Moon signs – every hour or two, which is why astrologers place so much emphasis on knowing the exact hour of your birth. This sign (also known as your rising sign) represents how others see you, and it is usually the first part of yourself you show to new people.
- **Inner Planets:** The inner planets are Mercury, Venus, Mars, the Sun, and the Moon. Each of these planets carries a different meaning, but in general, these planets help you understand your core personality traits and your basic needs and desires. Mercury controls your communication style and your mind, Venus rules your romantic relationships, and Mars has sway over your actions and overall energy. Your core personality traits change depending on which signs these planets are in.

- **Outer Planets:** Jupiter, Saturn, Uranus, Neptune, and Pluto are the outer planets. They rule over more abstract aspects of your life. Jupiter rules over your luck and progress, Saturn over your self-discipline and your fears, Uranus over change in general, Neptune rules over your dreams and your healing ability, and Pluto over your power in general and transformative abilities.

- **Your Ruling Planet:** Your ruling planet is the planet associated with your ascendant sign. The planet's qualities give you insight into who you are, what things and attributes you value, and what motivation and principles rule your behavior. You are also more affected by the movements of your ruling planet than those of other planets. For example, if your ruling planet is Mercury, you will be more affected by Mercury retrograde than people with a different ruling planet.

- **The Midheaven Sign:** Some astrologers also focus on your midheaven sign. This sign is the highest point at the top of your chart and represents the southernmost high point above the horizon at the exact moment of your birth. Your midheaven sign allows you to better understand your career and life path. It helps you understand where you should aim to be in your life, what path you should follow, and what mark you are destined to leave through your achievements. It is, essentially, a representation of all your achievements as seen through other people's eyes, including the eyes of society, and can help you further explore your life goal.

Analyzing the intricate details of a natal chart can be challenging, especially if you have no previous experience. If you misinterpret a single movement, you could misinterpret your entire chart.

So, while getting overarching themes from a computer-generated natal chart is possible, it is always best to see a professional if you want a proper reading. They will better help you understand the intricate movement of the stars and how they affect your life on earth.

So, Why Astrology?

Now that you have a better understanding of astrology, the next question many people ask is, "Why should I care?" While astrology is popular, belief in it is certainly not universal, and many people do not understand how a natal chart or the daily horoscope can help them.

For people who believe in astrology, its value lies in the predictions it can offer about a person's life. While you may not be able to change everything that an astrologer predicts, knowing it is coming will allow you to better prepare and anticipate the effects.

However, even if you are on the fence about your belief in astrology, exploring it further on your own or with a trained astrologist can benefit you.

Studies have shown that astrology can encourage self-reflection in individuals, helping them to better understand themselves and the world around them. Additionally, astrology offers people a chance to make sense of the world's chaos, giving them a sense of control they may have otherwise lacked. It can help them deal with negative life events and uncertainty.

People are particularly drawn to astrology during tumultuous times in their personal lives and the world around them. For example, astrology found greater popularity in the United States during the Great Depression and in Germany in the years between the two world wars. The insight astrology provides you with deals with the realities of life better, which is why people turn to it in challenging periods during their lives.

Additionally, many people find it hard to cope with a sense of ambiguity and uncertainty, especially when making plans for the future. Astrological predictions help give you the knowledge and information you need to make informed decisions for yourself and the people around you.

As we have discussed in this chapter, one of the most important parts of astrology is your Sun sign. While you probably already know your Sun sign, you have also likely realized that there is more to it than simply your daily or weekly horoscope. Now that you understand the importance of astrology and how Sun signs play into astrology, this book will help you explore the impact your sign can have on your life.

In the next chapter, you will learn more about the effect of the planets on your life and their function as a source of energy. It will help you to understand how astrologers use the placement of the planets to make predictions about you, the world, and other people.

We will then explore the zodiac signs in further detail, including their elements, qualities, personality, and positive and negative traits. Following this, we will explore the 12 houses, what zodiac signs they are ruled by, and what aspects of your life they represent and rule.

Next, we will move on to helping you discover your Sun and Moon signs. The Sun-Moon combination of your signs can help you to better understand your personality than those individual signs. We will also look at the Sun-Moon combinations according to their respective elements. We'll cover all four elements: earth, air, water, and fire.

By the time you finish reading this book, you will have a good understanding of your Sun and Moon signs and how they affect your life. This will help you better understand any horoscopes you consult in the future and give you the knowledge needed to help you shape your life going forward.

So, what are you waiting for? All that is left now is to turn the page to the next chapter and continue reading!

Chapter 2: Planets: The Source of Energy

As you have learned from the previous chapter, planets have played an enormous role in astrological predictions since the practice began. Each heavenly body is a key to birth charts in astrology because their energy is associated with intrinsic human characteristics and values. While each astrological planet has its own energy source, they are also influenced by other entities in the solar system. Depending on their interaction, their combined force affects people's behavior differently. This chapter discusses how astrology uses planet placements, movements, and qualities to provide predictions and insights into the world and the human psyche. By learning the characteristic energies and glyphs linked to each planet, you can learn how they affect your natal chart and how you can determine their influence.

Astrological Planets and Birth Charts

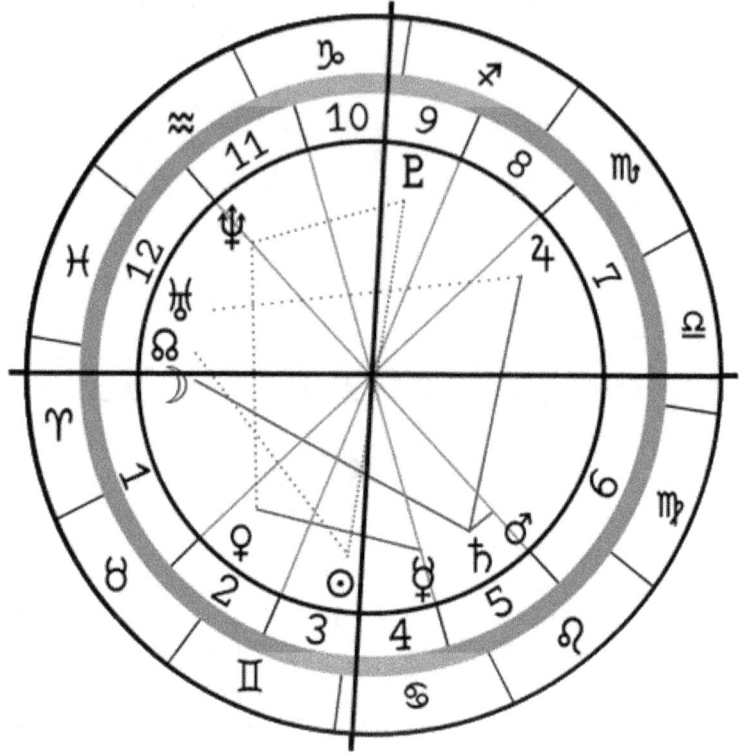

Sample birth chart with signs and planet glyphs.
Rursus, CC BY-SA 3.0 <https://creativecommons.org/licenses/by-sa/3.0>, via Wikimedia Commons: https://commons.wikimedia.org/wiki/File:Birth_chart.svg

The astrological planets rule over zodiac signs and are located in one of the 12 zodiac houses. Your birth chart is a complex trove of information that reveals the precise location of each heavenly body and zodiac sign when you entered this world. From that time on, they will have influenced you. Depending on their location at the time you were born, each planet has a different impact on your life. In ancient astrology, the planets themselves were seen as representations of characteristics people may display throughout the course of their lives. Today, we know that not only do planets determine human traits, but they also affect different areas of our lives, determining how they will play out. By drawing from this symbolism, you can peek into any aspect of your life, from health to relationships to professional development.

It is important to note that the astrological planets are not represented similarly on all birth charts. Some will show the planets displayed in the same constellation while, in others, they are located at greater distances from another. For a more precise reading, it is recommended to go with a natal chart that displays the exact distance between the planets, as this can be crucial to their astrological function.

Astrological Planets and Their Energies

Before you can learn how to make or read a birth chart, you must understand the basic meaning of each astrological planet. This will allow you to interpret their positioning in your chart and what their movements can bring you in the future.

The Sun and the Moon, the two astrological bodies visible to the naked eye most of the time, were the most studied heavenly bodies for centuries. And to this day, we know that their energies affect our lives the most. However, as soon as astronomers and astrologers began observing the other planets in the solar system, it soon became evident that these objects can also influence our characteristics and behavior. At first, people were only aware of the effects of Mercury, Venus, Mars, Jupiter, and Saturn, as the rest of the planets were considered to be too far from the Sun. Nowadays, we know that Uranus, Neptune, and even Pluto can influence our lives depending on their position and movement.

Here is an overview of all the heavenly bodies, including their placements and energies in life and within yourself.

Sun

Keywords: Primal personality, ego, stamina, consciousness, vitality

Glyph as Seen on One's Birth Chart: ☉ - Shield with a circle inside it

Placement in the Solar System: Center, providing energy to all the planets and celestial bodies

Time to Transit between Signs: 1 month

What It Represents within You: Your ego, vital energy, and the core of your personality.

What It Represents in Life: Collective focus, community energy, and strength

While it is considered to be a star – not a planet – in astrology and birth charts, the Sun is the most important object in them. Why? Because this luminary object determines the positions of all other planets and zodiac signs at any given time, determining the birth signs of every individual person. Its impact is so broad that it can influence entire communities and nations, independently of the characteristics of individual members.

When it comes to your own personality, the Sun is what determines what comes after the phrase "I am." It brings out your *core personality*, which is determined by the location of the Sun in the sky at the time you came into this world. This planet will also influence how you express your creativity and how you use your vital life force. Since the Sun transits into another sign each month, you can get more precise information about your personality.

Moon

Keywords: Emotions, mood, unconsciousness, desires, instincts, and habits

Glyph as Seen on One's Birth Chart: ☽/☾ - A crescent from either side

Placement in the Solar System: Between Venus and Mars, close to the earth

Time to Transit between Signs: 2-3 days

What It Represents within You: Your soul and inner desires

What It Represents in Life: Collective inner power of all humans beings

Like the Sun, the moon is not a planet in astronomy, and it has far less impact on the movement of other planets. However, according to astrology, the moon has just as much influence as other celestial bodies on your birth and life cycle. Its close proximity to earth provides us with a unique source of emotional power, lending entire communities confidence to rise and overcome difficulties.

Interestingly enough, the position of the moon at the time you were born can bring forward characteristics that are vastly different from the ones provided by the location of the Sun at the same time. Since it focuses more on your feelings and intrinsic senses, this planet is more likely to show you who you *want to be* rather than *who you think you are*. It can also reveal how to best nurture your emotions to get what you desire. To learn all of this, you must uncover the exact location of the moon on your natal chart, as the transit time of 2-3 days can make a vast difference in your fate.

Mercury

Keywords: Communication, rational thinking, intellect, language skills, and natural intelligence

Glyph as Seen on One's Birth Chart: ☿ The head and the winged cap of Mercury

Placement in the Solar System: Closest planet to the Sun, absorbing the most energy of all planets

Time to Transit between Signs: 3-4 weeks

What It Represents within You: Your rational mind and natural communication style

What It Represents in Life: Mental power of a community and the effects of the media and global economy

Mercury is the planet responsible for communication - or the lack of it. On the one hand, the strong influence of this planet comes from its energy, which is the closest planet to the Sun. The other reason Mercury affects human lives is that it is the second closest planet to earth. Its quick transit period means that it can cause quick mood shifts in entire communities, bringing the members closer to each other or pushing them apart.

The energy of Mercury can determine how you receive, process, analyze and transmit information about your environment. Mercury can affect everything from daily routines to communication in complicated long-term relationships. It can also counteract the emotional influence of the moon, allowing you to process everything through rational thinking. While often encouraging you to explore complex ideas, Mercury will also prompt you to think them through entirely. Since the planet transits every 3-4 weeks, knowing its precise location is needed if you want to uncover how it affects you.

Venus

Keywords: Love, emotional attachment, relationships, beauty, art, and harmony

Time to Transit between Signs: 4-5 weeks

Glyph as Seen on One's Birth Chart: ♀ - The female symbol

Placement in the Solar System: The second closest to the Sun, located between Mercury and Earth

What It Represents within You: Your language and romantic and aesthetic preferences

What It Represents in Life: The emotional energy of a community and the sense of connection between all members

Even though it is often viewed only as the planet of love, Venus has much more influence in people's lives than just facilitating romantic relationships. Its energy is known to resolve conflicts by prompting people to display empathy, compassion, and social grace instead of disdain or fear, even toward those they do not know. Venus encourages the masses to seek out different types of relationships, which is how communities are formed. It brings harmony whenever and wherever it is needed.

Venus also affects our ability to manage our finances, although this varies depending on individual values. Depending on its location at the time of your birth, Venus will provide you with different core values. And everything you do in your finances and relationships must align with these values. Venus is often used in love-match comparisons as it can tell you how a person wants to be loved. A match can also come out in art and sense of style, especially in friendships and other types of non-romantic relationships.

Mars

Keywords: Need for action, aggression, sex, desire, passion, competition, and courage

Time to Transit between Signs: 6-7 weeks

Glyph as Seen on One's Birth Chart: ♂ - The male symbol

Placement in the Solar System: Fourth planet from the Sun, located between Earth and Jupiter

What It Represents within You: Your passion, determination, and sex drive

What It Represents in Life: Collective focus and levels of high passion and aggression

Being the closest planet to the Earth, Mars has an incredibly powerful hold on our physical energy. Often called masculine energy, the physical drive of Mars provides different levels of endurance and encourages people to act, even when they feel unable to do so. However, this may often come out as aggression and willingness to cause conflicts, leading to community distress. This planet also rules passion and sexuality, acting as a complementary tool to the emotional connections developed with the help of Venus.

Depending on its position on your birth chart, Mars can offer some insight into what physical activity will work best for your body. For some people, this planet only provides low levels of physical energy, so they are only able to engage in passive exercise. Others are blessed with the ability to take up intense activities or even choose the intensity they want to engage in. While typically a great motivator, when in retrograde, Mars can cause even people willing to take action to step back and wait.

Jupiter

Keywords: Luck, optimism, growth, abundance, expansion, and understanding

Time to Transit between Signs: 12-13 Months

Glyph as Seen on One's Birth Chart: ♃ - A hieroglyph of an eagle

Placement in the Solar System: The fifth planet from the Sun, located between Mars and Saturn

What It Represents within You: Where you will find your true luck

What It Represents in Life: Collective sense of hope, empowerment, and growth

Since it is the largest planet in our solar system, Jupiter was the first one discovered after the Sun and the Moon. This probably explains why it has so many influential roles, including the ones in religious beliefs and faiths, philosophy, and even luck. Jupiter has excited people about their fate and helped them accept it for centuries. Depending on its location on one's birth chart, people believed, and still believe, that it can bring luck.

Jupiter's energy can make you want to seek out and explore new adventures with joy, passion, and enthusiasm. Even though this planet may push you out of your comfort zone, it will only be to show your new horizons. It shows you that you can experience all this in many forms as long as they keep you happy and help you grow. Remember that the luck and abundance it promises on your natal chart may come in a different form than you would expect it to arrive.

Saturn

Keywords: Law, structure, discipline, restriction, responsibility, ambition, and obligation

Time to Transit between Signs: 2-3 Years

Glyph as Seen on One's Birth Chart: ♄ - An ancient representation of a sickle or scythe

Placement in the Solar System: The sixth planet from the Sun, located between Jupiter and Uranus

What It Represents within You: The place where your responsibility lies and the life lessons you learn

What It Represents in Life: Global structures, inducing community, governments, and collective karma

Saturn also has a long-term effect on people's lives, often showing up in stages to show the path one is meant to take. It often guides younger community members, particularly when they become young adults ready to contribute to society. If Saturn returns at this time, it will guide the youngsters through a series of tasks they must complete to find their identity and purpose in life.

As an individual, Saturn will help you through all the milestones of your life, ensuring that you learn the responsibilities that come with your life's purpose. It will encourage you to keep up the hard work and work towards your goals. Depending on which house the planet was in when you were born, you may thrive on structure. This will also allow you to view each challenging task as an opportunity to grow instead of an obstacle.

Uranus

Keywords: Unpredictable changes, reformation, eccentricity, rebellion, newness

Time to Transit between Signs: 7 Years

Glyph as Seen on One's Birth Chart: ♂ - Combined signs symbolizing the Sun and the spear of Mars

Placement in the Solar System: The seventh planet from the Sun, located between Saturn and Neptune

What It Represents within You: Your eccentric side and how you express it

What It Represents in Life: Science, progressive and future-oriented communal growth, technology, digital communication

Uranus is often called the modern planet, not just because its impact on human societies has been discovered long after the first six planets. Nothing can provide people with more inspiring energy than Uranus. In fact, its effects on human evolution and advancements have been so great that it even surprised astrologers. The planet prompts generation after generation to develop numerous innovations in science and technology. Although this often means breaking the rules, as history has shown, this can sometimes be more beneficial for the common good than anyone has thought.

Regarding individual characteristics, Uranus is responsible for eccentricities, unexplained need for change and liberation, and even rebellion. Depending on which zodiac house the planet was in when you were born, Uranus will either lend you the energy to fight against injustice or move past it in a totally unexpected, innovative way. The energy of this planet will encourage you to express your individuality in various degrees and forms, including in the form of art, technology, and science.

Neptune

Keywords: Intuition, dreams, mysticism, visions, delusion, imagination,

Time to Transit between Signs: 10-12 Years

Glyph as Seen on One's Birth Chart: ♆ - The trident of Neptune

Placement in the Solar System: The eighth planet from the Sun, located between Uranus and Pluto

What It Represents within You: Your dreams, imagination, and your creative and mystical side

What It Represents in Life: Global artistic interests, community outrage, spirituality, religion, and illusions

As the second to last astrological planet in our solar system, Neptune is linked to slow and mystical influences. It inspires different generations with different dreams, visions, and illusions. Neptune can also determine people's values and ideals, equipping them with different degrees of the ability to see the truth. This is particularly true if the planet shifts into retrograde, which sometimes undoes the effects of the previous illusion.

Depending on its location at the time of your birth, it may encourage you to only accept the truth from yourself and from those around you. That being said, the most beneficial effects of this planet come from the sense of oneness with the universe it can provide. Remember, Neptune can be tricky; just as it can lend you its energy for psychic influences, it can also hide the truth from you.

Pluto

Keywords: Power, evolution, transformation, death, and rebirth

Time to Transit between Signs: 12-15 Years

Glyph as Seen on One's Birth Chart: ♇, - A monogram made from the letters P and L or a bident with an orb

Placement in the Solar System: Located after Neptune, the farthest planet from the Sun

What It Represents within You: Your ability to transform your life and your soul's rebirth

What It Represents in Life: Global sources of power, including financial institutions, and governments

Even though Pluto lost its status as a planet in astronomy, in astrology, its place as one of the most influential celestial bodies remains the same. Due to its slow transit time and location in the solar system, Pluto's effects are much subtler. Yet, they can be equally profound, especially as they are mostly known for their transformative qualities. Its energy allows communities to thrive and empower themselves through different institutions, which may or may not be for the common good.

While the effects of the moon can come with darker psychological aspects for the masses, this is rarely the case for individuals. Pluto can lend you varying amounts of regenerative powers depending on its location at the time of your birth. So, if you notice that your life is not heading in the direction you wanted it to, you can transform into a better version of yourself by letting go of the past and looking toward the future.

Chapter 3: Zodiac Signs: The Type of Energy

Zodiac Symbols.
https://commons.wikimedia.org/wiki/File:Zodiac_(PSF).png

While astrological planets are known to be a powerful source of energy, the zodiac signs represent a different type of power. And the reason you need to consider this when examining your natal chart is twofold. For one, zodiac energy is subtler than that of your ruling planet. While planets can determine your core personality, the rest of your traits come from the energy of the zodiac signs and houses. Second, the planets move through the zodiac signs, mixing their energies with the signs and creating combinations that give unique qualities to each individual person. In addition, each sign has a ruling planet which influences its overall energy output. This energy, albeit not as strong as the planets, can vary greatly depending on whether the sign is under the influence of its ruling planet or another one near it at any given moment. This chapter will teach you about the associations of each zodiac sign and how their energy influences people's lives.

Zodiac Sign Associations and Qualities

Before delving into the specific energies of each zodiac sign, you need to learn a little more about their association with the four cardinal elements. Apart from being ruled over planets and the power of their houses, each zodiac sign is influenced by one of the four elements of nature, Air, Earth, Fire, and Water. These elements give each zodiac sign different qualities, determining the undertone of personality traits. However, not only do the four elements represent a distinctive quality, but within each of them, there are also unique nuances called quadruplicities. They are three unique qualities within each element:

- **Mutable:** The most *adaptable* quality, allowing the signs that possess it to persevere in any situation. However, it can also make them indecisive even in situations when time is of the essence or if their future depends on making a definite decision.
- **Cardinal:** The signs with a cardinal trait are open-minded and always ready to think about the bigger picture. Unfortunately, they will not always follow through with all the magnificent ideas they come up with when they brainstorm about a crucial aspect of life.
- **Fixed:** The most dependable and strong-willed signs; these are not afraid to face any challenge. Their stubbornness to overcome will occasionally place them in uncharted territories they are not equipped to explore.

Each of these qualities can be found in each element, and their combination will create distinct personality traits in the different zodiac signs. Below, you will see which sign is associated with which elements and which quality of the said element.

Aries

Nickname: The "I am" sign
Zodiac Symbol: ♈- The ram
Birth Month: March 21 - April 19
Element: Fire
Quality: Cardinal

As a cardinal fire sign, Aries is known for being dynamic, competitive, impulsive, and fearless, all of which come from the sign's active and masculine archetype. They have an insatiable appetite for conquering new goals, whether winning a prize or acquiring a new skill. And the higher the stakes for this new goal, the better for the Aries. They also focus on communicating their beliefs to the outside world, which makes them great leaders. Aries knows how to adapt and innovate. They also have a way of getting others to follow their lead by enticing fierce competition.

Positive Traits: Aries is always ready to take action, even if this means overcoming a limiting belief or fear. People born under this sign do not hold grudges and will always let you know where you stand with them. Aries can be great athletes as they always focus on their performance.

Negative Traits: Since Aries prefers to act according to their own beliefs, they are not keen to listen to advice and will even avoid conversations for this reason. When they communicate, they tend to be direct, which is often conceived as cruel and insensitive.

Taurus

Nickname: The "I have" sign
Zodiac Symbol: ♉ - The bull
Birth Month: April 20 - May 20
Element: Earth
Quality: Fixed

The fixed quality of this earth sign makes it the most resolute and grounded of all the zodiac signs. Not only is Taurus keen on standing their ground, but they will do it so stubbornly that most people find it easier to just go along with them. And they will definitely take their time with everything. Despite this, the archetype of the Taurus personality is peaceful and indulgent. As long as no one bothers them when they are working on their own goal, they will be happy to share the fruits of their hard labor. They will enjoy it themselves too, along with any luxury they can get their hands on!

Positive Traits: Patience is a virtue that Taurus holds in high esteem. When faced with difficulties, they are resourceful and receptive. Taurus are skilled at arts and crafts and have the know-how to appreciate other creators' work too.

Negative Traits: Their peaceful nature often makes Taurus seem too complacent, even in situations that clearly are not working in their favor. They can be so fixated on their own creations that they will not even notice when they are being taken advantage of.

Gemini

Nickname: The "I think" sign

Zodiac Symbol: ♊ - The twins

Birth Month: May 21 - June 20

Element: Air

Quality: Mutable

As a mutable air sign, Gemini is the living embodiment of the famous "mercurial" quality. They use their witty and lighthearted nature to charm everyone around them. This is great because they can choose with whom to share a good talk and who will be the perfect company for a quiet moment, both of which they enjoy from time to time. Gemini is always keen to explore new ideas, which allows them to adapt to any circumstances and make the necessary changes to better their lives and the lives of those around them.

Positive Traits: The primary strength of Gemini lies in their intelligent and curious nature. Gemini will make the best of whatever situation they find themselves in. Their playful disposition allows them to easily establish communication with everyone they meet.

Negative Traits: Gemini's ability to jump from one interest to another can make people think that they will never know which "twin" they will be dealing with on any given day. This may earn them the reputation of being untrustworthy and emotionally distant.

Cancer

Nickname: The "I feel" sign

Zodiac Symbol: ♋ The crab

Birth Month: June 21 - July 22

Element: Water

Quality: Cardinal

Cancer is a cardinal water sign, which means they have a nurturing, compassionate and sentimental nature. The moon also influences their personality, which helps them dream about how to create the perfect home for their family. They may also represent a strong, supportive presence for their community. That said, Cancer typically prioritizes their relationships with their loved ones instead of creating new ones. They will give them everything that is in their power, and sometimes even more. If this happens, they will retreat for a bit of self-care so they can be up and ready to help others as soon as possible.

Positive Traits: Cancer has a kind and giving nature and is always ready to show emphasis and care for others. While they want to share what they can, they will not overwhelm you with unwanted advice or even their presence but will wait for you to become comfortable with them.

Negative Traits: Cancer can become so emotionally involved with their environment that it is hard for them to let go and make changes when needed. They may also project their willingness to help others, which can result in unhealthy, co-dependent relationships.

Leo

Nickname: The "I will" sign
Zodiac Symbol: ♌ - The lion
Birth Month: July 23 - August 22
Element: Fire
Quality: Fixed

Leo is typically confident, optimistic, generous, and cheerful as a fixed fire sign. Their charismatic nature makes it easy for them to connect with those around them, and this is only one of the things that they can accomplish, whatever their aim in life is. The other reason is that they will always prefer to take action instead of waiting for a solution. Even though they believe in luck, they have more confidence in achieving their goals. Their radiant energy is contagious, often inspiring their followers to change their own lives.

Positive Traits: Leo is a natural-born leader whose primary strength lies in their confidence. They are also always optimistic and will always find things they can be happy about. Not only do they lead with courage, but they are also very generous to those who rely on them.

Negative Traits: Being fixated on their own opinions often gets Leo in trouble, as they often have issues admitting they are wrong. Their tendency to steal the limelight may also make them seem ruthless and power-hungry. That can even lead them to forget those who helped them along their path to success.

Virgo

Virgo symbol.
Google, Apache License 2.0 <http://www.apache.org/licenses/LICENSE-2.0>, via Wikimedia Commons: https://commons.wikimedia.org/wiki/File:Green_Virgo_emoji.svg

Nickname: The "I analyze" sign
Zodiac Symbol: ♍ - The virgin
Birth Month: August 23 - September 22
Element: Earth
Quality: Mutable

Despite being an earth sign, the mutable quality of Virgo pushes their mind to work on several different frequencies at all times. Virgo loves to research whatever project they might be interested in and work hard for their goals. This goal is often helping others, like securing finances or meeting health needs. Virgo thrives on serving their nearest and dearest and will always make sure they know who to turn to with their problems. They are also detail-orientated and will keep all the information they gather neatly organized.

Positive Traits: Virgo is gifted with an incredible skill of adaptability, which, combined with their meticulous nature, makes them quick learners. They can decide what is useful and what is not at a moment's notice. However, instead of taking full advantage of it for themselves, they pride themselves on using this skill to help others.

Negative Traits: The highly functional mind of a Virgo can easily become overwrought with worries, which may or may not only exist only in their minds. They also tend to over-identify when their help is needed and can become overprotective of their loved ones.

Libra

Nickname: The "I relate" sign
Zodiac Symbol: ♎ - The scales
Birth Month: September 23 - October 22
Element: Air
Quality: Cardinal

As the cardinal air sign, Libras were born to bring justice, peace, and happiness into the lives of others. They appreciate beautiful art and being surrounded by like-minded people. While they prioritize bonds with particular individuals, this is never to their own benefit. Whether it is a working relationship, romantic relationship, or friendship, they will do everything to keep the other person happy. They will also stand up for what they believe in, especially if it benefits their loved ones. Libras tend to have romantic dreams, which they are not afraid to follow.

Positive Traits: Libras are great communicators and listeners and always try to see things from everyone else's perspective. They can put others first and care for others' well-being before they think of their own. Libras rarely get angry and give plenty of opportunities to those who wronged them to redeem themselves.

Negative Traits: Libras often cannot focus on their own goals because they are distracted by everyone else's problems. To keep the peace, they can compromise their values but will resent this later.

Scorpio

Nickname: The "I transform" sign

Zodiac Symbol: ♏ - The scorpion

Birth Month: October 23 - November 21

Element: Water

Quality: Fixed

This mysterious water sign is known for valuing their privacy above anything else in life. They seek power and are willing to work hard for it but rarely reveal their true motives to others. Scorpions demand attention not because they speak loudly but because they listen and take their time to get to know you. People are often drawn to their magnetic presence. They often seek solitude for spiritual purposes, as it gives them time and space to ponder. They may even turn from people they have a close emotional bond with if pressed too hard on personal matters.

Positive Traits: Whether they are committed to art, studies, or anything else, Scorpions are hard workers. They are also receptive and patient and are keen to learn the dynamics of any relationship by simply letting others speak or act first.

Negative Traits: Those born under this sign are slow to trust and have trouble revealing their weaknesses or asking for help. Despite this, they expect others to show the same intense emotions they feel but hide or show very little of them.

Sagittarius

Nickname: The "I see" sign

Zodiac Symbol: ♐ - The archer

Birth Month: November 22 - December 21

Element: Fire

Quality: Mutable

The free-spirited Sagittarius is always ready to seek a new adventure, although they rarely do this when in the company of other people. However, they like to socialize if they stay in one place long enough. In these times, they will be the life of the party, entertaining everyone with unfiltered tales about their latest adventure or philosophical discoveries. They are passionate about their beliefs and want to share them with everyone else before they change. Because as a mutable sign, Sagittarius is born to change constantly and will unconsciously seek this change.

Positive Traits: They are bold and optimistic and will let you see the brighter side of life in any situation. Their belief that everything will work out eventually gets rewarded with their adventure taking them to a place they are happy to explore. They are also fiercely independent and not afraid to tell you if they have a problem with someone invading their privacy.

Negative Traits: Due to their adventurous spirit, they are known to be non-committal. If they feel like it, they will not hesitate to make last-minute changes in their plans, even if this means breaking commitments with others.

Capricorn

Nickname: The "I use" sign

Zodiac Symbol: ♑ - The sea goat

Birth Month: December 22 - January 19

Element: Earth

Quality: Cardinal

As a cardinal earth sign, Capricorn is always motivated to achieve its goals. Despite being down-to-earth and traditional in many ways, Capricorns pride themselves on setting as many tasks for themselves as possible. If needed, they will employ industrious methods to persevere and will never stop their diligent work until they do. Although they tend to avoid large gatherings when accompanied by people they trust and enjoy being with, Capricorns exhibit a dry and often dark sense of humor. They can also show you the benefits of taking a pragmatic but proactive approach to any challenge.

Positive Traits: Capricorns are good judges of characters and will render a fair verdict if asked to rule in a dispute. They are also remarkably cool-headed and will always survey all the possibilities before deciding the proper way to pursue a goal.

Negative Traits: Capricorns tend to hold everyone around them to the same work ethic they possess, often leading to conflicts. They can even cease contact with people who fail to live up to these standards or are unwilling to put up with their grueling pace.

Aquarius

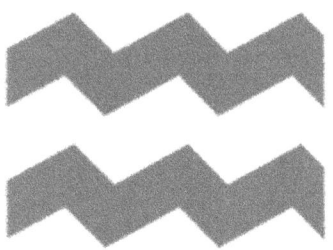

Aquarius symbol.
Google, Apache License 2.0 <http://www.apache.org/licenses/LICENSE-2.0>, via Wikimedia Commons: https://commons.wikimedia.org/wiki/File:Green_Aquarius_emoji.svg

Nickname: The "I know" sign

Zodiac Symbol: ♒ - The water-bearer

Birth Month: January 20 - February 18

Element: Air

Quality: Fixed

The ever-cool Aquarius stays true to its name and its fixed air quality. While they seem eccentric, people born under this sign are only in pursuit of their own individualistic ideals and beliefs. They believe in progress and are willing to help others, but their social life is somewhat superficial. They cultivate many relationships but will avoid deep and intimate connections. It is not uncommon for Aquarius to gravitate towards non-traditional arrangements, whether in work or private life. They find conventions boring and one-dimensional, so they will avoid them at all costs.

Positive Traits: The primary strengths of Aquarius lies in their intelligence and ability to find a fresh perspective. After examining a problem, they will always be able to come up with innovative solutions, which allows them to adapt to any circumstances.

Negative Traits: Their love for the complex forces them to view life as nothing more than a puzzle to be solved. Their abstract ideas can be hard to relate to. They use humor to deflect feelings or make others feel inferior when they feel attacked.

Pisces

Nickname: The "I believe" sign

Zodiac Symbol: ♓ - Two fishes

Birth Month: February 19 - March 20

Element: Air

Quality: Mutable

As a mutable air sign, Pisces is not only tuned in to their own emotions but is also empathetic to the feelings of others. They have the ability to heal emotional wounds and can speak up when someone needs counseling. Despite their high level of inner awareness, they find it easier to express their emotions through art than through regular speech. They often have a dreamy and romantic quality to them which comes from their keen sense of imagination and tendency to seek out spiritual explorations. They enjoy contemplating life and finding out how to adapt to new circumstances.

Positive Traits: Pisces is sympathetic and receptive to other people's feelings and ideas. They are always ready to offer helpful spiritual advice and as much of themselves in any relationship as possible. They can retain an air of innocence, no matter how many challenges they may face in life.

Negative Traits: Pisces take comments to heart and are easily emotionally wounded, especially regarding their art. Their selfless nature makes them needy and vulnerable to co-dependent relationships and toxic energies emanating from their environment.

Chapter 4: The Houses: Where the Energy Manifests

Anyone interested in learning a bit more about astrology will immediately come across the concept of the houses, and it can be quite difficult to understand in the beginning. However, if you have made a habit of checking your daily horoscope, then that is the start of delving deeper into astrology and all of the incredible details the practice entails. Astrology combines the study of many different disciplines, from astronomy to history, and getting to know the houses allows for a deeper appreciation for this much-maligned yet sophisticated art form. In addition to the planets and the signs themselves, the houses are an integral part of the moving elements behind the creation of birth charts. So, what are houses? This chapter will clear up some common misconceptions and will introduce you to the heart of not only astrology but where most metaphysical energies in this world manifest.

What Is a House?

Let us start from the very beginning and explain precisely what the concept of a house means in astrology. Basically, there are twelve ecliptic planes in astrology that divide up time and place as soon as someone is born. From there, their unique energies manifest, informing every other element that makes up the personality and destiny of an individual. If you look at a birth chart, you will find that each house is numbered counter-clockwise from the point of the first house. Also, they tend to be laid out in a very particular way in one's birth chart, with each house presiding over various aspects of one's life, including things like major relationship milestones, financial quandaries, and so on. Therefore, they are crucial to help us to better understand what may come later in our lives. Think of it this way. The houses form a vital part of your birth chart, which should be treated as a map of your life that can offer guidance if you choose to use it.

Houses and Symbols

The planets were aligned in different houses and signs when you were born. When you take the time to outline a birth chart yourself or go to an astrologer, they will take the time to interpret its meaning. That involves deciphering each planet's role and the house within that sign and mapping any obstacles or moments of good fortune that will happen to you. On every rotation, the planets will visit any of the twelve houses, lighting up different parts of your birth chart, which in turn energizes particular characteristics of the house. Astrologers tend to use twelve houses to predict several areas in your life that will come into focus, which could allow you to take the best possible action.

The birth chart is, of course, circular in nature. If you were to draw a circle and move clockwise, the first house could be found at what is noted as nine o'clock. This first house is often referred to as the cusp of the "beginning border," and as you move throughout the zodiac wheel, you will do so in a counter-clockwise direction. This movement is meant to represent the soul's evolution from the personal, the first house, to the greater society, the twelfth house.

Personal Houses

So, now you know that the houses on a birth chart are meant to track one's evolution as an individual to their rightful place in a collective. We can now break this down further and study the first six houses, which are referred to as *personal houses*.

Personal houses dominate our private and immediate lives. They cover our personal journeys, our environments, and our relationships with siblings, peers, and parents. In essence, they define our own particular expressions of who we are. An interpretation of someone whose chart possesses several planets in the first six houses is that they may have trouble leaving the nest, for example. Or, they may be inordinately attached to their childhood friendships, unable to make new connections as adults since nostalgia rules their thoughts. This is just one way in which seeing the houses in your charts may be able to tell you more about yourself, which is a dynamic that will be explored further in this chapter.

- **The First House**

The First House is often referred to as the House of the Self. Its cusp is the home of the Ascendant, the sign that resides on the eastern horizon at the exact moment of your birth. It lays the foundations for how you can define yourself as a person and who you will become. It also speaks to the individual's realization of their ultimate potential. The First House is ruled by the star sign Aries and the planet Mars.

This particular house rules early childhood. Everything from your first attempts at walking to your emergent worldview, regardless of how childlike and unformed, is considered to reside here. It answers key questions on how your personality will develop and the different elements that will inevitably shape your life. To sum up, the first house speaks to the parts of your personhood that are currently in existence and will solidify later.

- **The Second House**

The Second House is referred to as the House of Possessions. Of course, it alludes to what we actually own, although it is not limited to material possessions. It also refers to less tangible things we own, such as our feelings, our unique capabilities, and needs and wants. So, when someone tells you to "own up to it," in terms of astrology, you are presenting ownership over the Second House and all that it entails, which means that you are in full possession of your being. This house corresponds with Taurus.

As a quick note, of course, specific possessions are also found in the Second House, and these can run the gamut from earned income, the wealth you were born into, any debts you may have accrued, and so on. This house refers to all you own, both in the tangible and intangible sense.

- **The Third House**

This house is often referred to as the House of Communication, which means any and all communication that occurs between the self and anyone that person holds dear, such as brothers and sisters, schoolmates, or even neighbors. Communication here is meant in both the written and verbal sense, so intentionality is a big part of it. In general, it is meant to highlight the role of intelligence in one's life by underscoring the importance of any mental connections one makes with others. The Third House is ruled by Gemini together with the planet Mercury.

The House of Communication effectively underscores the importance of early education in how we can think and communicate with others, and even traveling to different environments falls within this rubric since external forces also shape this particular capacity. Basically, our ability to listen, think, process, and share falls under the Third House.

- **The Fourth House**

The Fourth House is more literal than the House of the Home. This alludes to any place where we can put down our roots. As we lay our foundation and plant ourselves firmly onto the ground, there is a circular nature to our journey. The Fourth House addresses our beginning, as well as old age, and our final resting place. This house is ruled by Cancer and the Moon.

So, this idea of the Fourth House refers to something concrete but also more conceptual since it relates more clearly to a period when and where we feel grounded. A sense of peace follows, and that is definitely the kind of energy that this particular house manifests. When you can create or find a home, it means you can find a meeting place, a sanctuary of sorts for yourself and others.

- **The Fifth House**

The Fifth House is also referred to as the House of Pleasure. Here, *pleasure* means both bodily and intellectually spurred pleasure. Whenever you have a burst of creativity and can perform the simple act of creating anything, this is a form of pleasure. So, while this house does, in fact, refer more concretely to the acts of procreation and children, it also addresses the creation of arts and culture. This is the house that spurs questions of self-satisfaction and how that could be derived in your everyday life. The Fifth House is ruled by the star sign Leo and the Sun.

So, romantic affairs definitely fall under this house, but emotional satisfaction can be derived in various ways. It can refer to acts that some people might call vices, such as gambling and the willingness to take risks. It also refers to more bucolic activities, like games and hobbies, or anything you may find engaging.

- **The Sixth House**

The last of the personal houses, the Sixth House, is also called the House of Health. Of course, it refers to your physical integrity, but it also encompasses one's ability to maintain good health in the face of adversity. Whether there is a moment of personal crisis, a health scare, or a severe reversal of fortune, these changes are all tracked by the Sixth House. Our ability to prioritize our health inevitably defines the kind of person we become, so this is an especially important house within the realm of astrology. The Sixth House is ruled by the star sign Virgo and the planet Mercury.

Interpersonal Houses

Houses seven through twelve are called the interpersonal houses, which tend to govern our relationships, travels, professional journeys, relationship with society, and spirituality over the course of our life. If a person has a lot of planets in these houses, they may be career-focused, meaning they have effectively left the past behind and focus solely on their present.

- **The Seventh House**

This is typically referred to as the House of Partnership. This is the house in which we begin to move away from the self and toward how we interact with another, namely, a partner. It also points to one's desire to accomplish something, whether it is for the sake of their relationship or society. When we can contribute to a cause or help someone else, we feel that we have a concrete purpose in life. This is the kind of work that the Seventh House tends to dominate. It is ruled by the star sign Libra and the planet Venus.

This is not to say that the Seventh House focuses solely on these lighter elements. It also encompasses the darker aspects of our relationships with others. Toxic romantic partners, divorces, and even lawsuits fall under this house.

- **The Eighth House**

This house is sometimes called the House of Sex. Here, the relationships previously alluded to are put under a microscope, and the house rules over these interactions and how they can allow us to either grow or falter. It is important to note that it does not only allude to bodily pleasure, but the Eighth House also focuses on any aspect of our life that means we are entwined with someone else. So, even things like inheritance, alimony, taxes, or any kind of financial support can fall under this house. It is ruled by Scorpio and the planets Mars and Pluto.

Unlike the House of Pleasure, creative pursuits aren't underscored here. Rather, this house focuses on how our relationships with these tangible assets, be they monetary or bodily, relate to our personal journey.

- **The Ninth House**

This is also called the House of Philosophy. As you have probably guessed, this house indicates our search for meaning and how that influences our life trajectory. By trying to understand the things we see and feel around us, we are also probing deeper into the meaning of life, even if it may not seem that way at first. This house is ruled by the star sign Sagittarius and the planet Jupiter.

While we may learn everything, for example, at school, coming face to face with our ideals and the compromises we sometimes have to make is a big part of this sign. The Ninth House also governs our quest for spirituality and, ultimately, how we understand the world will be governed by this house.

- **The Tenth House**

The Tenth House is also called the House of Social Status. It governs where we are regarding our career path and our general place in society. It also rules how we interact with our communities at large or any fame or renown that may have become part of who we are. So, achievement is deeply tied to this house which, in turn, informs us of how we see ourselves and how the community sees us. It is ruled by the star sign Capricorn and the planet Saturn.

Basically, our relationship with the individual or the group is highlighted by the Tenth House. For those interested in making an impact, paying special attention to this part of the birth chart is important. Social status here does not mean the capitalist sense of the word, but rather how we can lead fruitful lives in the service of others.

- **The Eleventh House**

This house, also referred to as the House of Friends, understands the power of the collective, and is thus informed by the idea that there is strength in numbers. It can refer to things like clubs, organizations, social groups, and even professional associations. The underlying concept of the Eleventh House is that the group can define what individuals are capable of doing. It is ruled by Aquarius and the planets Saturn and Uranus.

The Eleventh House argues that our desire to work toward the greater good with our network of friends is our humanity manifesting that particular energy. While the individual's work is important, it holds that the total sum of everyone's efforts will have the greatest impact on the world.

- **The Twelfth House**

The last of the houses is called the House of the Unconscious. This means the realm of sorrow or anything unseen by the naked eye. This state can help us succeed or make do with our failures. Basically, the two polar opposites of success and failure tend to fall within the realms of this house. When we think about our strengths or weaknesses, we are essentially thinking about The Twelfth House. It is ruled by Pisces as well as the planets Jupiter and Neptune.

Working in Tandem

The twelve houses inform and underscore different elements of our personalities and how we can develop in the future. Each one on its own is simply one piece of the puzzle, and you need to look at them collectively in a birth chart to understand the different meanings they embody.

Some people's birth charts will heavily gravitate toward other houses, which is completely normal. If one house in your birth chart currently has no planets, then that is okay. This is important information to hold onto because it shows how you currently relate to that part of your life, and you will be allowed to consider how to change it.

Each of these houses is responsible for emanating specific energy from our being that best informs who we are and how we live our lives. Some people feel that the information presented by houses is fairly concrete; therefore, our entire life is already accounted for, without any room for improvisation. Of course, this is a big mistake. Astrology is a means to understand and guide how we wish to behave or present ourselves in the future. Few things are set in stone, and life is full of surprises. Astrology allows you to explore what you would like to do next.

A birth chart is basically a zodiac wheel that follows the earth's yearly trip around the Sun, which is why it is divided into twelve ellipses, each corresponding to a particular house. Through the unique prism of these wheels, you can see different ways of looking at your personality. The zodiac sign is, ultimately, just one part of the equation. The rest of the information comes from the houses and the planets that reside within each, as sketched throughout the chart.

Therefore, the twelve houses collectively represent all aspects of human life and, when viewed in tandem, can provide you with invaluable information moving forward. The planets will reveal themselves rather emphatically in different areas of your life, as represented by the houses and where they fall on your natal chart. An important note about houses and energies is that they do not really emanate energies in that way, adding color or flow into your life. Rather, the energies tend to manifest within each of these houses. So, each house not only represents different areas of your life but your own experience of it. As you look throughout the chart, whether on your own or with the astrologer, you can figure out how the different pieces fit together and decide how you would like to move forward.

Chapter 5: Discovering Your Sun Sign

Sun signs are vital in astrology as they represent a person's true identity. Although there are various types of zodiac signs, Sun signs are known to be the most common and popular ones. They are usually the first thing that comes to mind when someone asks you, "What is your zodiac sign?" Just like the sun shines every morning in the sky, your Sun sign is the part of you that shines out to the world. It is your essence and the driving force that allows you to express yourself and showcase your qualities and who you really are. Your Sun sign is the answer to "who are you truly?" Each person has their own unique personality traits that set them apart and showcase their individuality. Your Sun sign represents the qualities that define your truest self. It can show you your potential and who you can be. It opens up a world of possibilities and shows you the impact you can leave on the world.

In this chapter, we will discuss the 12 Sun signs so you can learn more about your sign and your various interesting qualities.

Aries (March 21 – April 19)

Nickname: The fierce fire sign
Zodiac Symbol: The Ram
Glyph: ♈

Identity: Aries are known to be competitive and must always be number one in everything. So, it is quite fitting that it is the first sun sign in the zodiac. Their boldness, ambitions, stubbornness, and occasional ruthlessness are the qualities that drive them to climb to the top and be the best. They are true individuals who are never afraid to be themselves. An Aries is known for their courage and fearlessness. They jump head first and are never afraid to take a risk. Being natural-born leaders, Aries will often take charge because they believe they can do anything they want. Ruled by Mars, the planet named after the god of war, Aries are known for their explosive temper and are always ready for battle.

Aries Role in Society

This competitive sign is only after one goal, to be the best. For this reason, you will often find Aries in leadership positions. They are energetic, dynamic, confident, and spontaneous, which makes them an inspiration to everyone around them.

Famous Aries

- Reese Witherspoon
- Elton John
- Sarah Jessica Parker
- Keira Knightley
- Mariah Carey
- Lady Gaga
- Pharrell
- Kristen Stewart
- Emma Watson
- Fergie

Professions

- Soldier
- Politician
- Entrepreneur
- Race car driver
- Personal trainer

Struggles: Aries struggle with finishing projects because they are extremely impatient and easily get bored. They crave novelty which is often why they leave projects unfinished to start new ones. Because they often juggle many things at once, Aries can forget to relax and burn themselves out.

Positive Traits
- Courageous
- Energetic
- Natural Leaders
- Confident
- Optimistic
- Passionate
- Independent
- Generous
- Honest
- Organized

Negative Traits
- Reckless
- Impulsive
- Impatient
- Angry
- Aggressive
- Selfish
- Competitive
- Attention-seeker

Taurus (April 20–May 20)

Nickname: The sensual sign
Symbol: Bull
Glyph: ♉

Identity: Taureans thrive in routine, stability, and familiar environments. Just like Aries, they are stubborn and will succeed in anything they set their mind to. However, they do not have Aries' fiery attitude. In fact, Taureans move at a slower pace. They usually enjoy relaxation and being in quiet and soothing environments. Ruled by Venus, Taureans are known to be the most sensual sign in the zodiac. They love luxury, comfort, and beauty.

Taurus Role in Society

Taureans are dependable individuals because of how stable they are. People often rely on them; they are always the "rock" others can lean on in times of need. People always depend on the Taureans in the group when it comes to group projects, whether at work or school. Thanks to their determination and productivity, they can serve as a strong foundation in any group project.

Famous Taureans

- Queen Elizabeth II
- Robert Pattinson
- The Rock
- Channing Tatum
- Adele
- George Clooney
- Jon Cena
- Barbra Streisand
- Janet Jackson
- Sam Smith

Professions

- Lawyer
- Chef
- Designer
- Teacher
- Engineer

Struggles: Taureans struggle with a few things. Jealousy is one of their biggest struggles, whether in romantic relationships or when someone has something they want. They can also be very stubborn, which sometimes costs them. Additionally, Taureans move slowly and may require encouragement and motivation to keep going.

Positive Traits
- Sensual
- Reliable
- Patient
- Kind
- Intelligent
- Organized
- Hard-working
- Honest

Negative Traits
- Stubborn
- Lazy
- Jealous
- Perfectionist
- Possessive

Gemini (May 21–June 21)

Nickname: The curious

Symbol: Twins

Glyph: ♊

Identity: Geminis are known for their communication skills. They are social butterflies who love meeting new people. Geminis' whole identity revolves around their chatty and charming attitude. They are quick-witted and can talk about different topics and strike up conversations with anyone they meet. This is probably the result of their curious, knowledgeable, and intellectual nature.

Gemini's Role in Society

Geminis love to throw parties and do anything that can bring everyone together. They make friends with every stranger they meet. Well-spoken, social, and outgoing, they are the life of the party, and they bring excitement and fun conversations wherever they go.

Famous Geminis
- Johnny Depp
- Marilyn Monroe
- John F. Kennedy
- Angelina Jolie
- Prince
- Morgan Freeman
- Tom Holland
- Helena Bonham Carter
- Paul McCartney
- Chris Evans

Professions
- Teacher
- Social worker
- Architect
- Technical support
- Stockbroker

Struggles: Geminis struggle to keep things to themselves. They love gossiping and chatting but do not understand that other people's secrets are not theirs to share. They do not know where to draw the line between what to share and what to keep to themselves.

Positive Traits
- Curious
- Sociable
- Creative
- Sense of humor
- Intellectual
- Charismatic

- Savvy

Negative Traits
- Gossip
- Immature
- Mood swings
- Impulsive
- Superficial

Cancer (June 22–July 22)

Nickname: The heartfelt

Symbol: Crab

Glyph: ♋

Identity: If you see a sensitive person, they are most likely Cancer. Cancers are always aware of their environment and can pick up on other people's emotions. They are so intuitive that you may mistake them for psychics. Home means a lot to Cancer; it is their haven where they can rest and self-reflect. They create strong bonds thanks to their loyalty and emotional depth.

Cancer's Role in Society

Cancers are always there for the people they care about. You can depend on them for anything. They aim to spread love to everyone they meet. They love the idea of a family and often play the role of the caregiver.

Famous Cancers
- Meryl Streep
- Margot Robbie
- Chris Pratt
- Selena Gomez
- Ariana Grande
- Lana Del Ray
- Tom Hanks
- Tom Cruise

- Will Ferrell
- Gisele Bündchen

Professions
- Teacher
- Lawyer
- Gardner
- Social worker
- Childcare
- Human resources

Struggles: Due to their extra sensitive nature, Cancers are easily offended. They struggle to handle criticism or good-natured teasing.

Positive Traits
- Caring
- Loyal
- Protective
- Faithful
- Charming
- Sentimental
- Intuitive

Negative Traits
- Mood swings
- Insecure
- Vengeful
- Overly-sensitive
- Manipulative
- Pessimistic\

Leo (July 23–August 22)

Nickname: Spot-light loving
Symbol: Lion

Glyph: ♌

Identity: The celebrities of the zodiac signs, Leos, love to be the center of attention and under the spotlight. Just like their animal symbol, Leos are dominant and natural-born leaders. In their heads, Leos are celebrities and believe they should be treated like superstars. They are extremely confident and proud, but their pride and ego can get the best of them on occasion.

Leo's Role in Society

These superstars have a mesmerizing charisma that people often gravitate towards. Similar to the lion, Leos are extremely courageous, and they inspire everyone around them with their courage. They are true individuals who stand out and make an impact in society through their creative power.

Famous Leos

- Jennifer Lopez
- Daniel Radcliffe
- Mick Jagger
- Helen Mirren
- Sandra Bullock
- Terry Crews
- Jason Momoa
- Barack Obama
- Charlize Theron
- Chris Hemsworth

Professions

- Real estate agent
- Performer
- Fashion designer
- CEO
- Salesperson
- Tour guide

Struggles: Leos tend to spend all their time in the spotlight. They forget to take some time off to relax and eventually burn themselves out.

Positive Traits
- Natural-born leaders
- Strong
- Generous
- Protective
- Passionate
- Determined
- Ambitious
- Creative
- Honest
- Friendly

Negative Traits
- Arrogant
- Attention-seekers
- Stubborn
- Lazy
- Inflexible
- Competitive
- Jealous
- Proud

Virgo (August 23–September 22)

Nickname: Detail-oriented

Symbol: The virgin

Glyph: ♍

Identity: Virgos are known for being practical, logical, and dedicated. They are also detail-oriented and never leave anything to chance. Grounded and realistic, this practical sign never loses its head in the clouds. Honest and straightforward, Virgos stick to the truth even if it hurts. They are kind and supportive and use their problem-solving abilities to help their friends.

Virgo's Role in Society

Virgo's goal is to spread peace to everyone around them. They work hard on any skill they learn until they achieve perfection. As a result, at work, they usually play a vital role and ensure everything runs smoothly.

Famous Virgos
- Beyonce
- Blake Lively
- John Mulaney
- Cameron Diaz
- Zendaya
- Keanu Reeves
- Salma Hayek
- Idris Elba
- Colin Firth
- Pink

Professions
- Journalist
- Writer
- Critic
- Editor
- Detective
- Technician
- Teacher
- Translator

Struggles: Perfection does not exist, but Virgos refuse to see this fact. Their need to pay attention to every detail can be exhausting. They are afraid to make mistakes and can take themselves too seriously and forget to have fun.

Positive Traits
- Hard-working
- Kind

- Patient
- Creative
- Reliable
- Helpful
- Responsible
- Modest
- Intelligent
- Calm

Negative Traits
- Stubborn
- Picky
- People-pleasers
- Perfectionist
- Judgmental
- Anxious

Libra (September 23–October 23)

Nickname: The social butterfly

Symbol: The scales

Glyph: ♎

Identity: Just like their symbol, the scale, Libras are fair and always want to achieve justice. They try to find balance in various areas of their life. Libras are often accused of being indecisive because they take time to decide. However, they simply like to do that to weigh all their options. Ruled by Venus, Libra loves romance, harmony, luxury, and beauty. Libras are also known to be very social and love to surround themselves with people who like to have fun and avoid conflict.

Libra's Role in Society

Libras are fair idealists and are interested in achieving justice. They work toward fighting injustice because they believe they can make the world a better place. Libras are considered great teammates and will stand up to those in power when they feel someone is treated unfairly.

Famous Libras
- Serena Williams
- Will Smith
- Gwyneth Paltrow
- Hilary Duff
- Halsey
- Eminem
- Hugh Jackman
- John Krasinski
- Zac Efron
- Tyler Posey

Professions
- Dancer
- Negotiator
- Salesperson
- Host
- Diplomat
- Travel agent
- Supervisor

Struggles: Libras struggle to make decisions, whether big or small, because they have to consider all the pros and cons. This can be very exhausting as they are always afraid of making a decision they will regret. They need to understand that it is okay to make the wrong decisions every now and then. How else will they learn?

Positive Traits
- Fair
- Perfectionist
- Intelligent
- Social

- Charming
- Great listener
- Sense of humor
- Romantic
- Intuitive

Negative Traits
- Vain
- Indecisive
- Lazy
- Self-pity
- Superficial

Scorpio (October 24–November 21)

Nickname: The magnetic

Symbol: Scorpion

Glyph: ♏

Identity: Scorpios are the most determined and focused of all the signs. They will work hard, plot, and research to find something or get what they want. Extremely calculating, Scorpios treat life like a chess game and often try to be a few steps ahead of their opponent. Mysterious and enigmatic, Scorpios can be very secretive, which makes them attractive and appealing to others.

Scorpio's Role in Society

Whenever a Scorpio is passionate about a cause, they will fight for it. They do not care about the consequences. Fearless and unstoppable, they are relentless warriors who will never give up until their side wins. They believe that they can make a difference in the world through passion.

Famous Scorpios

- Leonardo DiCaprio
- Ryan Reynolds
- Katy Perry
- Drake

- Julia Roberts
- Winona Ryder
- Penn Badgley
- Emma Stone
- Ryan Gosling
- Anne Hathaway

Professions
- Surgeon
- Lawyer
- Scientist
- Detective
- Educator

Struggles: Scorpios are extremely focused, which can lead them to become a little obsessive. They never take a step back and look at the big picture.

Positive Traits
- Loyal
- Ambitious
- Determined
- Honest
- Curious
- Passionate
- Courageous
- Independent
- Persistent

Negative Traits
- Jealous
- Stubborn
- Possessive
- Controlling

- Intimidating
- Resentful

Sagittarius (November 22–December 21)

Nickname: The adventurous

Symbol: The archer

Glyph: ♐

Identity: Sagittarius is the most unique zodiac sign because of its blend of characteristics. Some of Sagittarius's unique qualities that make them stand out are adaptability, curiosity, passion, and intensity. Their adventurous spirit often leads them to explore places no one else would dare approach. This can be the result of their curious and energetic nature which loves traveling and venturing to new places.

Sagittarius Role in Society

Optimistic with childlike curiosity, they want to make people curious like them. They are always looking to inspire others and ignite their spirits. Witty and reliable, they bring peace whenever there is conflict or tension.

Famous Sagittarius

- Scarlett Johansson
- Miley Cyrus
- Don Cheadle
- Ben Stiller
- Lucy Liu
- Britney Spears
- Amanda Seyfried
- Taylor Swift
- Jamie Foxx
- Brad Pitt

Professions

- Editor
- Public relations

- Animal trainer
- Minister

Struggles: Sagittarius is adventurous and always on the lookout for something more interesting to do. However, this can make them flaky and constantly struggle to meet their plans.

Positive Traits

- Curious
- Active
- Adventurous
- Ambitious
- Friendly
- Deep thinkers
- Adaptable
- Visionary
- Bold

Negative Traits

- Restless
- Rude
- Short-tempered
- Arrogant
- Inconsistent
- Reckless
- Stubborn
- Blunt

Capricorns (December 22–January 19)

Nickname: The motivated

Symbol: The goat

Glyph: ♑

Identity: If you have ever spent time with a Capricorn, you have probably noticed that there is something special about them. It can be their fearlessness, ambition, resilience, wild side, or the fact that they never give up despite their adversity. At first glance, Capricorns may seem reserved and conservative. But they have a rebellious spirit and love to let loose every time. Traditional, responsible, and independent, Capricorns are great leaders. They are often realistic with their plans and learn from their mistakes.

Capricorn's Role in Society

Capricorns are extremely nurturing and supportive to their loved ones. The people in their lives know they can depend on them for anything. They work hard, often occupy positions of authority, and are highly respected by others.

Famous Capricorns

- Kate Middleton
- Finn Wolfhard
- Kit Harington
- Jared Leto
- Diane Keaton
- Zayn Malik
- Regina King
- Kate Moss
- Jim Carrey
- Betty White

Professions

- IT
- Editor
- Manager
- Banker
- Administrator

Struggles: Capricorns work hard but forget that playing hard is essential too. They tend to neglect themselves and other aspects of their lives because they can be workaholics. They should pay more attention to themselves and their relationships.

Positive Traits
- Realist
- Ambitious
- Persistent
- Loyal
- Discipline
- Responsible
- Team player
- Reliable
- Intelligent

Negative Traits
- Stubborn
- Pessimistic
- Serious
- Sensitive
- Picky
- Unforgiving

Aquarius (January 20–February 18)

Nickname: The quirky

Symbol: Water-bearer

Glyph: ♒

Identity: Eccentric and quirky, Aquarians definitely stand out. They are the rebels who fight for freedom. However, they can often be quiet and shy as well. Intellectual, idealistic, and deep thinkers who will never stop fighting for what they believe in. They are spontaneous, live life to the fullest, and are determined to never waste their time. Free-spirited, Aquarians believe they can change the world. They do not live by anyone's rules but their own.

Aquarius Role in Society

Aquarians love being a part of a community where they can make an impact and positive changes. They are compassionate and care about humanitarian causes. They are often the ones volunteering for social causes, and they believe they can make a difference in the world.

Famous Aquarians
- Harry Styles
- Oprah Winfrey
- Shakira
- Alicia Keys
- Michael B. Jordan
- Jennifer Aniston
- The Weekend
- Chris Rock
- Elizabeth Olsen
- Tom Hiddleston

Professions
- Inventor
- Musician
- Aviator
- Scientist
- Designer

Struggles: Unlike Leos, who thrive under attention, Aquarians struggle with being in the spotlight. They also usually guard themselves and struggle with warming up to people.

Positive Traits
- Creative
- Open-minded
- Intelligent
- Free-spirited
- Ambitious
- Original
- Friendly

- Easygoing

Negative Traits
- Inconsistent
- Unpredictable
- Impulsive
- Stubborn
- Idealistic
- Detached
- Insensitive
- Unpredictable

Pisces (February 19–March 20)

Nickname: The dreamy

Symbol: Fish

Glyph: ♓

Identity: Pisces is dreamy, and their heads are often between reality and fantasy. Compassionate, sensitive, and extremely empathetic, they can be overwhelmed by emotions. They often live in a world they have built in their imagination and are ruled by dreams and creativity. They are so optimistic that some people see them as delusional. Pisces are selfless and helpful and surround themselves with people from all walks of life.

Pisces' Role in Society

Pisces can inspire and connect with people through art, poetry, or any form of artistic creativity. Well-intentioned and compassionate, Pisces will do anything for others, even if it inconveniences them.

Famous Pisces
- Justin Bieber
- Rihanna
- Emily Blunt
- Drew Barrymore
- Millie Bobby Brown

- Eva Langoria
- Camila Cabello
- Adam Levine
- Carrie Underwood
- Bad Bunny

Professions
- Psychologist
- Nurse
- Vet
- Artist
- Philanthropist
- Physical therapist

Struggles: Pisces are generous and sweet-natured but can also be gullible. They struggle with setting boundaries and saying "no," which leads others to take advantage of them.

Positive Traits
- Generous
- Sensitive
- Empathetic
- Creative
- Compassionate
- Intuitive
- Devoted
- Forgiving
- Romantic
- Strong
- Natural leaders

Negative Traits
- Gullible
- Closed off

- Too emotional
- Moody
- Lazy
- Idealistic

Your Sun sign can teach you so much about your personality and potential. It can serve as a guide to help you work on your weaknesses and find a career where you can thrive. Learning about these signs can also help you to better understand the people in your life and what you can do for them when they are struggling. Embrace who you are and work on what you can be.

Chapter 6: Identifying Your Moon Sign

Similar to the Moon, a part of us is always hidden. This part is kept from the rest of the world and only surfaces when you are alone. To better understand who you are and unveil your deepest self, the part of you that no one can see, you need to discover your Moon sign. Most people are familiar with the Sun sign as it is the one that reflects their personality traits and who they are to the world. Although Moon signs are not as popular as Sun signs, they impact one's character and influence our lives more than them. There are two sides to each person's personality. One is governed by the Sun, while the Moon governs the other.

The Moon's presence in the zodiac at your moment of birth is what determines your Moon sign. It represents the soul's identity, a part of you located deep down that sometimes you may not even be aware of, but it greatly impacts your emotions.

While the Sun sign is responsible for your identity and basic self, the Moon sign is responsible for your emotional responses and inner and hidden self. It reflects who you are when no one is around, while the Sun sign is who you are around other people. Only those closest to you can see your Moon sign personality. Your Moon sign reflects who you are truly in your comfort zone, while your Sun sign reflects your path, mission, and true purpose in life. Your Sun sign represents your will, ego, and fundamental personality. It mainly represents who you think you are. Your Moon sign is your subconscious self and how you react to the world around you.

To learn about your Moon sign, check your birth chart or go online and enter your birth details to find out the Moon's exact location at the time of your birth. In this chapter, we will discuss the Moon's signs so you can learn about the soul of your true identity.

Aries Moon

Nickname: Desire

Zodiac Symbol: The Ram

Glyph: ♈

Identity: Similar to its Sun sign, Moon Aries is also known to be fiery and impulsive. They usually go after what their heart desires and lead exciting and spontaneous lives. Aries Moon usually represents your impatient inner child who must always get everything they want. It is all about instant gratification for this sign. Aries Moon is usually a quick thinker but does not concern themselves with small details. Trouble seems to follow them wherever they go, or maybe they are the ones who invite it? With Aries Moon, what you see is always what you get.

Aries Moon's Role in Society

Aries Moon individuals are very giving when it comes to their loved ones. They enjoy being themselves at all times and will resent anyone who tries to restrict them or interfere with their freedom. Although it is very easy to hurt Aries Moon's feelings, they can forgive you if they see you remorseful.

Famous Aries Moon

- Angelina Jolie
- Tom Hiddleston
- Rihanna
- Salma Hayek
- Pink
- Joaquin Phoenix

- Eva Langoria
- Jared Leto
- Daniel Craig
- Chris Rock

Professions
- Manager
- Executive
- Business owner
- Mechanic
- Engineer

Struggles: Aries Moon people do not accept failure, and their desire to succeed can lead them to lose their temper or be hysterical.

Positive Traits
- Optimistic
- Self-sufficient
- Enthusiastic
- Sociable
- Energetic
- Lively
- Outspoken
- Sincere

Negative Traits
- Restless
- Inconsistent
- Emotionally exhausting
- Mean
- Impatient

Taurus Moon

Nickname: Determination

Symbol: Bull

Glyph: ♉

Identity: Taurus Moon individuals are very calm and rarely get angry. They usually enjoy a luxurious lifestyle and cozy environments. These individuals are down to Earth and thrive in routine and stability. They are also extremely stubborn, and once they set their mind on something, they never waver.

Taurus Moon's Role in Society

People born under this sign are loyal and devoted to their loved ones. They thrive on developing emotional connections and nurturing relationships with others. Emotionally strong, kind, and loyal, they form bonds that can last a lifetime.

Famous Taurus Moon

- Robert Downey Jr
- Adam Driver
- Colin Firth
- Meryl Streep
- Demi Moore
- Zendaya
- Jamie Foxx
- Cameron Diaz
- Brendan Fraser
- David Boreanaz

Professions

- Artist
- Designer
- Jeweler
- Real estate agent
- Business

Struggles: Taurus Moon individuals struggle to express their emotions. They do not know how to openly talk about their problems, even to their loved ones.

Positive Traits
- Stable
- Balanced
- Focused
- Patient
- Strong
- Confident
- Loyal
- Gentle
- Reliable

Negative Traits
- Shy
- Stubborn
- Materialistic
- Lazy

Gemini Moon

Nickname: Communication

Symbol: Twins

Glyph: ♊

Identity: Free-spirited; these individuals often express themselves in a non-restricted and light manner. They thrive on intellectual and witty conversations. When communicating, they usually use information and facts. They love the spotlight and often enjoy having people fight for their attention. They can be shallow, so they usually choose partners based on what they find interesting rather than people with whom they can form deep connections.

Lunar Gemini's Role in Society

People often feel at ease around Gemini Moon individuals because of their ability to relate to others' opinions and experiences. They enjoy a good debate and may sometimes try to influence other people's opinions. Since Gemini's symbol is twins, Gemini Moon individuals are always looking for their "twin" or their other half.

Famous Lunar Geminis
- Barack Obama
- Rachel McAdams
- Jeremy Renner
- Olivia Wilde
- Hugh Jackman
- Jake Gyllenhaal
- Kylie Minogue
- Jennifer Garner
- Jonathan Groff
- Brooke Shields

Professions
- Dancer
- Librarian
- Investor
- Accountant
- Research worker
- Journalist

Struggles: Instead of confronting their feelings, people born under this sign usually dance around the subject. They struggle to understand their true feelings.

Positive Traits
- Happy
- Confident
- Realistic
- Practical
- Sociable

Negative Traits
- Deceptive
- Shallow
- Moody
- Mysterious

Cancer Moon

Nickname: Solicitude
Symbol: Crab
Glyph: ♋

Identity: People born under this sign are extremely empathetic. They can sense the energy in the room and are sensitive to other people's feelings. Trust is essential for them, and they often gravitate toward relationships where they feel supported and safe. Cancer Moon individuals are giving, nurturing, and maternal. The Moon rules the Sun sign Cancer, so if you were born under a Cancer or Cancer Moon, you would be affected by the different moon phases.

Cancer Moon's Role in Society

Cancer Moon individuals are extremely dependable and create deep relationships. They are often there for the people in their life to help them solve their problems and to provide helpful advice.

Famous Lunar Cancers
- Taylor Swift
- Dua Lipa
- Keanu Reeves
- Shakira
- Jack White
- Michael B Jordan
- Melissa McCarthy
- Kerry Washington
- Colin Farrell
- Elizabeth Olsen

Professions
- Poets
- Artists
- Musicians
- Photographer
- Psychologist
- Nurses

Struggles: They often struggle to move on and can dwell for a long time over past pain. Opening up does not come easily to Cancer Moon because they do not like to appear vulnerable.

Positive Traits
- Compassionate
- Kind
- Sympathetic
- Peaceful
- Great memory
- Romantic
- Gentle
- Affectionate
- Giving
- Tenacious
- Intuitive
- Sense of humor

Negative Traits
- Manipulative
- Victim mentality
- Irrational
- Moody

Leo Moon

Nickname: Freedom

Symbol: Lion

Glyph: ♌

Identity: Caring and giving, Leo Moon individuals enjoy expressing their love through lavish gifts. Like their Sun counterpart, they enjoy being the center of attention and usually have huge egos. They do not tolerate it when someone insults their ego and may even walk away for good. However, they do not make a strong impression as easily as Leo Sun, and they have to work harder to make an impact on others.

Leo Moon's Role in Society

Leo Moon individuals are considered great entertainers, and others enjoy their company. They also can make people completely rely on them.

Famous Leo Moon

- Paul McCartney
- Julia Roberts
- Tom Cruise
- Jamie Dornan
- Megan Fox
- Chris Martin
- Maisie Williams
- Liam Hemsworth
- Hugh Laurie
- Cobie Smulders

Professions

- Comedians
- Schools principles
- Athletes
- Boxers

- Midwives
- Astrologers
- Theater workers

Struggles: They may struggle with having huge egos that make them only focus on themselves and ignore everyone else around them.

Positive Traits
- Warm
- Creative
- Assertive
- Strong
- Decisive
- Generous
- Optimistic
- Stylish
- Determined
- Fair
- Proud

Negative Traits
- Controlling
- Bossy
- Lazy
- Dramatic

Virgo Moon

Nickname: Criticism

Symbol: The virgin

Glyph: ♍

Identity: Virgo Moon individuals thrive in an organized and structured environment. They enjoy everyday activities others find tedious, like paying the bills or running errands. Many Virgo Moon individuals are pretty content to lead a simple life and stay away from any attention.

Virgo Moon's Role in Society

They can create dynamic and comprehensive systems to help others. In fact, Virgo Moon people are always there to lend a hand, and they only feel fulfilled when they are helpful.

Famous Lunar Virgo

- Dolly Parton
- Michael Fassbender
- Madonna
- Chris Hemsworth
- Betty White
- Serena Williams
- Rami Malek
- John Travolta
- Zac Efron
- Jim Sturgess

Professions

- Banker
- Bookkeeper
- Inventor
- Literary critic
- Liberian
- Real estate agent

Struggles: Virgo Moon people can be overwhelmed with stress and worry and may struggle to handle pressure.

Positive Traits

- Fair-minded
- Compassionate
- Patient
- Logical
- Organized

- Helpful
- Social

Negative Traits
- Picky
- Critical
- Extra sensitive
- Prejudiced
- Over-thinker
- Low self-esteem

Libra Moon

Nickname: Charm

Symbol: The scales

Glyph: ♎

Identity: Libra Moon people only feel secure and complete when they have someone to share their lives with. They are usually classy and gentle, which is why many people are often attracted to them. Social interactions with loved ones are vital for Libra Moon as this is where they find emotional fulfillment. They are not the most committed individuals in relationships and usually jump from one relationship to the other.

Libra Moon's Role in Society

They are great debaters and have a knack for justice, so they will often defend their loved ones and will not give up until they win. Just as they love to have the best of everything, they enjoy spoiling the people in their lives with luxurious gifts and meals.

Famous Lunar Librax
- Leonardo DiCaprio
- Kate Winslet
- Sylvia Plath
- Walt Disney
- Nicolas Cage
- Alec Baldwin

- Bruce Springsteen
- Gena Davis
- Louis Armstrong
- Sylvester Stallone

Professions
- Banker
- Any job in finance

Struggles: Libra Moon people are idealists and are constantly chasing perfection. This can be exhausting and can prevent them from enjoying their lives.

Positive Traits
- Sympathetic
- Witty
- Social
- Charming
- Attractive
- Rational
- Diplomatic
- Creative

Negative Traits
- Critical
- Emotionless
- Passive-aggressive
- Anxious
- Dependent
- Self-indulgent
- People pleasers

Scorpio Moon

Nickname: Ulterior motivation

Symbol: Scorpion

Glyph: ♏

Identity: Scorpio Moon individuals are only comfortable when their emotions are intense. In fact, they are always seeking intense experiences and emotional excitement. They are not ones to be fooled by someone's appearance, and they can read people and understand them on a deeper level. They thrive in meaningful relationships and often have an all-or-nothing attitude.

Lunar Scorpio Role in Society

People are either attracted to or intimidated by a Scorpio Moon because of their ability to see through people's facades. Thanks to their strong intuition, many people often rely on them and trust their insight.

Famous Lunar Scorpio

- Lady Gaga
- Beyonce
- Katy Perry
- James Dean
- Jason Momoa
- Bob Marley
- Mila Kunis
- Miley Cyrus
- Selma Blair
- Elizabeth Taylor

Professions

- Surgeon
- Teacher
- Counselor
- Soldier

- Psychologist
- Engineer

Struggles: They struggle to trust others and only let people they fully trust into their lives. Scorpio Moon's secretive nature can sometimes prevent them from connecting with their loved ones.

Positive Traits
- Intuitive
- Strong
- Intelligent
- Deep
- Powerful

Negative Traits
- Secretive
- Deceitful
- Resentful
- Moody
- Vengeful
- Needy

Sagittarius Moon

Nickname: Enthusiasm

Symbol: A mythical centaur or Archer

Glyph: ♐

Identity: Sagittarius Moon is at their best when they feel free. If anything or anyone jeopardizes their sense of freedom, they can become very unhappy. They enjoy leading an active life, so you will often find them traveling to see the world or going out to meet new people. With their infectious optimism, these individuals believe in happy endings and that everything eventually works out. Straightforward and often blunt, they express themselves directly without playing mind games or dancing around the subject.

Sagittarius Moon's Role in Society

Sagittarius Moon people are very helpful and often act as teachers to their loved ones by guiding or helping them learn new things. Fair and just, they will help and fight for anyone experiencing injustice.

Famous Sagittarius Moon

- Oprah Winfrey
- Jennifer Aniston
- Nicole Kidman
- John Mulaney
- Kevin Costner
- Ellie Goulding
- Zoe Saldana
- Anthony Hopkins
- Adele
- Neil Patrick Harris

Professions

- Teacher
- Counselor
- Social worker
- Journalist
- Entertainer
- Travel agent
- Tour guide

Struggles: Sometimes, they dominate the conversation and can be condescending to those around them. They usually act as if they are the smartest people in the room. In most cases, they get away with this attitude because of their fun and cheerful personality.

Positive Traits

- Easy going
- Cheerful
- Intelligent

- Optimistic
- Upbeat
- Free-spirited
- Adaptable
- Daring
- Independent

Negative Traits
- Irresponsible
- Forgetful
- Impulsive
- Blunt
- Explosive temper
- Impatient

Capricorn Moon

Nickname: Management

Symbol: The goat

Glyph: ♑

Identity: Capricorn Moon is often in control of their emotions. Even when they are going through something or experiencing various feelings, they will often display a cool and collected demeanor. Realistic individuals, Capricorn Moon people often set attainable goals. They would rather play it safe than take risks. Security is essential to them, which is why they always plan ahead for their future, like saving money for retirement. Their self-worth usually depends on the respect they get from others which is why they work so hard to become successful.

Capricorn Moon's Role in Society

They are extremely responsible individuals, and they are the ones that you can usually count on in group projects. Lunar Capricorns are hard-working and dedicated, so they always manage to advance in their careers.

Famous Capricorn Moon
- Brad Pitt
- Reese Witherspoon
- Dwayne Johnson
- Johnny Depp
- Kate Hudson
- Matt Damon
- Rosamund Pike
- Gerard Butler
- Bryan Cranston
- Maya Hawke

Professions
- CEO
- Administrator
- Banker
- Designer
- Accountant
- Real estate agent

Struggles: Capricorn Moon individuals want nothing more than to achieve their goals and become successful. As a result, they may forget to relax and have fun now and then. They also build a wall around themselves and struggle to open up to others or express their emotions.

Positive Traits
- Competent
- Cool
- Collected
- Calm
- Organized
- Serious
- Ambitious

Negative Traits
- Mood swings
- Cold
- Selfish
- Calculating
- Controlling

Aquarius Moon

Nickname: Disinterest

Symbol: Water-bearer

Glyph: ♒

Identity: Aquarius Moon individuals are extremely analytical and usually observe and analyze other people's behavior. As children, these individuals always felt they were different from everyone else. On the outside, they may seem like social individuals, but, in reality, they are quite the loners. This is mainly because they never felt like they fit in with anyone. For this reason, they will do anything to stand out from the crowd and showcase their unique individuality. Aquarius Moon people believe they are better than others and often deny experiencing any negative emotions like jealousy or fear because they are above these "petty" feelings.

Aquarius Moon's Role in Society

You will often find Aquarius Moon volunteering for humanitarian causes. However, this is done for more philosophical reasons than to help others. They are extremely independent and detached and expect others to be the same. Since they often feel like they do not fit in, Aquarius Moon individuals always make sure to help others feel included. They wholeheartedly believe in equality and will fight tooth and nail for it.

Famous Aquarius Moon
- Billie Eilish
- John Lennon
- Britney Spears

- Marilyn Monroe
- Shawn Mendes
- Henry Cavill
- Princess Diana
- Gigi Hadid
- Morgan Freeman
- Tobey Maguire

Professions
- Astrologist
- Politician
- Humanitarian
- Explorer
- Teacher

Struggles: They usually struggle with being detached and distant from other people because of their huge egos and belief that they are better and above normal human emotions.

Positive Traits
- Observant
- Independent
- Loyal
- Trustworthy
- Charming
- Quirky
- Honest

Negative Traits
- Huge ego
- Proud
- Aloof
- Stubborn
- Distant

- Unreliable

Pisces Moon

Nickname: Anxiety

Symbol: Fish

Glyph: ♓

Identity: Pisces Moon individuals are probably the least practical people you will ever meet. However, they are extremely intuitive and easily see things from other people's perspectives. Although they are very funny, their sense of humor may seem odd to others. Daydreamers, these individuals require time to be alone with their imagination every day. During this time, they may come up with ideas to solve various problems, even though many of their solutions may seem unconventional. They are extremely empathetic and able to feel other people's emotions and experiences. Although they may seem gullible, many Pisces Moon individuals can sense when someone is manipulating them.

Pisces Moon's Role in Society

Pisces Moon individuals care so much about their close relationships and often make them a priority. Thanks to their empathetic nature, these individuals often want to help others and make the world a better place.

Famous Lunar Pisceans

- Edgar Allan Poe
- Leonardo Da Vinci
- Sarah Michelle Gellar
- Frank Sinatra
- Robert De Niro
- Elvis Presley
- Kathy Bates
- Audrey Hepburn
- Paul Newman
- Prince

Professions
- Actors/Actresses
- Artists
- Writers
- Musicians
- Poets
- Detectives
- Promoters

Struggles: They live in their heads more than in the real world. Often, they struggle to ground themselves and develop an escapist attitude.

Positive Traits
- Intuitive
- Compassionate
- Kind-hearted
- Sweet
- Sentimental
- Creative
- Empathic
- Loyal
- Sensitive

Negative Traits
- Secretive
- Indecisive
- Negative
- Submissive
- Sensitive

Your connection to the Moon is vital to help you better understand yourself more deeply. Naturally, you will find many similarities between your Sun and Moon signs. Although the Moon's presence impacts each sign, you will still find the Sun's sign's influence in each Lunar sign. Sun and Moon signs can help take you on a self-discovery journey to learn about your truest self and discover things you may not even be aware of.

Chapter 7: Sun-Moon Combinations I - Earth-Sun Signs

As you have likely already realized, both your Sun and Moon signs play an enormous role in determining your personality traits. Given the popularity of Sun signs, there is a good chance you already know how they affect your personality, but things can take a turn when you also consider your Moon sign.

Suppose you are an earth Sun sign, Taurus, Virgo, or Capricorn, looking to understand how your personality can change when you take your Moon sign into account. In that case, this is the chapter for you. We will look at the different Sun-Moon combinations, including each sign's good and bad traits, and figure out the perfect partner for each one. We will also offer advice to help you interact with people with these signs.

Taurus Sun-Taurus Moon: The Down-to-Earth Hand-worker

People with sun and moon in Taurus are usually hard workers.
https://unsplash.com/photos/k_T9Zj3SE8k?utm_source=unsplash&utm_medium=referral&utm_content=creditShareLink

People with both their Sun and Moon in Taurus are down-to-earth, dedicated, and hardworking. They have extraordinary focus and maintain a grounded outlook on life. They are relatively conventional and aren't fans of change. However, at the same time, they are also not easily ruffled by stressors and are solid, steadfast friends.

Good Traits: Hardworking, Persistent, Diplomatic

Taurus Sun-Taurus Moon individuals are dedicated to each activity they attempt. They are extremely eloquent, and people attentively listen when they talk. They are also calm and easygoing and can put other people at ease. They are trustworthy and reliable in their relationships and are loyal and honest with their loved ones.

Bad Traits: Materialistic, Conventional, Intolerant

People with this Sun and Moon combination often find themselves overly focused on money which may not be the best option when dealing with high-risk financial situations. They want the safety of money too badly, which can lead to them becoming materialistic. Additionally, they are highly conventional – and may find it challenging to adapt to change. They can also be intolerant towards other people, especially those with other perspectives.

Perfect Partner: Taurus Sun-Taurus Moon people are loyal and dedicated partners with a deep desire for physical and emotional intimacy. However, they can also become comfortable in routines, which can bore air and fire signs. On the other hand, water and earth signs work well with them. Their perfect partner should be able to bring a spiritual side to the relationship. High-conflict individuals are a bad match.

Advice for Taurus Sun-Taurus Moon People:

- Try to open up more to your partner. You can come across as closed off and withdrawn, especially when you keep negative feelings bottled up.
- Talk about your feelings more. Allowing frustrations to pile up can lead to emotional outbursts.
- Keep other perspectives in mind. It can be difficult to see why other people cannot find solutions to problems as easily as you, but trying to understand them will serve you well.

Advice for Dealing with Taurus Sun-Taurus Moon People:

- They are slow to adjust to change, so you should be prepared to give them the time they need.
- They appreciate consistency, steadiness, and loyalty in their personal relationships, both romantic and otherwise.
- While they are hard workers, this will not be at the cost of their personal relationships. They generally have a great work-life balance and will be able to give time to their loved ones.

Taurus Sun-Virgo Moon: The Charming Pragmatist

People with this Sun-Moon combination have a good deal of common sense and a scrutinizing mind. They are astute judges of character and err on the side of caution in whatever they do. They are naturally appealing, making it easy to charm the people around them.

Good Traits: Studious, Responsible, Observant

When given responsibilities, they can be relied on to accomplish their tasks. They have quick minds and love to read and retain material that others may find insignificant. They are very observant and analyze each decision thoroughly before committing to it.

Perfect Partner: Taurus Sun-Virgo Moon people are often attracted to people with a more happy-go-lucky personality. They are considerate, supportive, and loyal partners but look for people with similar goals and desires. They want long-term relationships and stability and are drawn to people they can shape.

Advice for Taurus Sun-Virgo Moon People:

- Do not get distracted by perfection; it can stop you from taking any kind of action.
- Remember to manage your stress. You can take your stress out on your partner without realizing it, so you should develop management strategies to prevent this from happening.
- Plan your tasks ahead of time; a routine will help you focus.

Advice for Dealing with Taurus Sun-Virgo Moon People:

- Provide them with challenges. A lack of challenges can lead to them procrastinating and falling behind on tasks.
- Be prepared for criticism. Taurus Sun-Virgo Moon individuals are perfectionists who criticize others and themselves. This can benefit their own growth but can be disturbing to others.
- They may occasionally isolate themselves from others due to their perfectionist tendencies and worries about their own skills. You will have to push them to interact with the people around them.

Taurus Sun-Capricorn Moon: The Role Model

People with this Sun-Moon combination are stable and decisive and do not waste time daydreaming. They are dependable, practical, and responsible. They are also ambitious and determined, which will help them succeed in life. They often seek to be positive role models and are honest and reliable.

Good Traits: Cautious, Humble, Reliable

Taurus Sun-Capricorn Moon people appreciate the efforts of the people around them. They are cautious, only act after thinking things through, and often have a backup plan to fall back on if things go wrong. They are very supportive and are great friends.

Bad Traits: Materialistic, Narrow-Minded, Workaholic

While they are not the most materialistic of all Taurus Sun-Moon combinations, they are still focused on achieving monetary success and afraid of poverty. This can lead to them becoming workaholics and ignoring personal relationships. They are also conservative to the point of being narrow-minded and need to feel in control of every situation.

Perfect Partner: These individuals need partners who understand their stubbornness. They are looking for a committed partner who is a doer instead of a speaker, and they enjoy providing and being provided for. They appreciate partners who let them take charge, but they also appreciate the security boundaries offer.

Advice for Taurus Sun-Capricorn Moon People:

- Remember to let people in and open up to others when you are feeling stressed.
- Be careful about how much you work. If you are not careful, you will become a workaholic.
- Be careful when working with other people. You can occasionally come across as pushy and overbearing.

Advice for Dealing with Taurus Sun-Capricorn Moon People:

- If a Taurus Sun-Capricorn Moon is stressed, ensure you do not leave them alone, as this can lead to them bottling up their emotions.

- Do not provoke these individuals as they can be very stubborn and occasionally quite nasty when crossed.
- They are hardworking and industrious. However, be careful that you do not take advantage of that as they will often do more than expected. Make sure the Taurus Sun-Capricorn Moon in your life takes breaks and focuses on themselves from time to time.

Capricorn Sun-Taurus Moon: The Gentle Critic

Capricorn Sun-Taurus Moon people are calm and eloquent and are determined to deal with their problems efficiently. They are realistic but have a positive outlook, and people find their advice about life's problems effective and reassuring. Their calm personality means their criticism is gentle but firm, and they offer a realistic judgment of the situation.

Good Traits: Uncomplaining, Determined, Persistent

These people have a dedicated mind and will never waste time complaining or feeling sorry for themselves. They work toward their goals with determination and will continue to work towards them even if life puts up obstacles in their way. They are ambitious and hardworking and make for good leaders and CEOs.

Bad Traits: Stubborn, Repressed, Rigid

While they work hard, sometimes this may devolve into stubbornness. They find it difficult to be flexible and adapt to changes in their life. They are also closed up and have difficulty expressing their emotions. This can lead to a buildup of negative emotions, eventually leading to an emotional outburst.

Perfect Partner: Capricorn Sun-Taurus Moon people appreciate the finer things in life and are looking for a partner who shares this appreciation. They want security and a stable partner, but their ambitious nature means they also want someone who improves their social status. Additionally, they need a partner who understands their way of doing things.

Advice for Capricorn Sun-Taurus Moon People:

- Remember to open up to people. A buildup of negative emotions will never go your way.
- Take time to have fun and relax. Your focus on success can lead to you forgetting to take downtime.
- Consider other options. Your lack of flexibility means you may lose out on opportunities, so look for ways to be more adaptable.

Advice for Dealing with Capricorn Sun-Taurus Moon People:

- If you are in a romantic relationship with a Capricorn Sun-Taurus Moon person, you may have to take the reins and be the spontaneous and imaginative one, as they are unlikely to take that role.
- Work with them and help them express their emotions. You should also be willing to open up simultaneously if you want to form a strong bond.
- When angered, these individuals can be ruthless, so it is best not to question their honesty or challenge their pride.

Capricorn Sun-Virgo Moon: The Reserved Scholar

These individuals tend to be shyer and more reserved than extroverted. They are rational and analytical and always work toward their goals with determination. They are skilled at grasping facts, which makes them suited for scholarly aims, and they do best when they have a single goal to focus on.

Good Traits: Logical, Practical, Loyal

Capricorn sun-Virgo moon people are great friends.
https://www.pexels.com/photo/anonymous-man-writing-on-chalkboard-near-group-of-diverse-students-at-table-6238020/

Capricorn Sun-Virgo Moon people are practical and down-to-earth. They do not waste time fantasizing and instead take action towards achieving their goals. At the same time, they are great friends and are always available to help when needed. They will not hesitate to complain about their issues but generally only need an ear to listen to them.

Bad Traits: Insecure, Self-Critical, Reserved

These individuals can be aloof and cautious, making them challenging to speak with. They are highly self-critical and insecure, and some of their cold and distant demeanor results from worries over the future. Their self-critical nature leads to a tendency to nervous disorders, always thinking of failures in place of successes.

Perfect Partner: Partners to Capricorn Sun-Virgo Moon individuals need to understand that work comes first for these individuals. They are devoted to their relationships and will always look for ways to help. To complement them, they need a neat and organized partner who understands that this sign is not the most romantic of individuals.

Advice for Capricorn Sun-Virgo Moon People:

- Take the time to be self-indulgent and focus on your successes instead of your failures. Without acknowledging your achievements, you will never be happy.
- Make sure that your focus on work does not become an obsession.
- Be willing to understand your partner's needs and focus on them instead of simply on work.

Advice for Dealing with Capricorn Sun-Virgo Moon People:

- These individuals appreciate being neat and organized, so ensure they are not surrounded by your clutter.
- Take the time to listen to them. These people are loyal and steadfast to their friends but require the same in return.
- These individuals can be picky and difficult to please, so you should know how to address their concerns without feeling bad or denigrating yourself.

Capricorn Sun-Capricorn Moon: The Serious Authoritarian

Double Capricorns are reserved and determined. Though they are not imposing, they can be too stubborn to take other opinions into account, giving them an authoritarian streak. At the same time, they are dependable; a double Capricorn's word is as good as gold.

Good Traits: Honest, Responsible, Dryly Witty

Double Capricorns are concerned with the facts. They are realistic and honest and not shallow in the least. They have been handling responsibilities since a young age, and it is something they enjoy. They also have a unique sense of humor that is both dry and sarcastic. While not everyone enjoys that, those who do enjoy their company.

Bad Traits: Distant, Ambitious, Controlling

These individuals are rarely satisfied with their achievements and always need more. This can lead to them becoming workaholics, and they need to open up and be more compassionate. Additionally, their inability to understand other opinions can lead to them becoming stubborn and, in some relationships, controlling.

Perfect Partner: The perfect partner to a double Capricorn will need to understand their need to be in charge. Additionally, they will need to understand that Capricorn Sun-Capricorn Moon individuals are reserved about their emotions and do not display them often. Double Capricorns need a partner who is not too needy and as ambitious as they are.

Advice for Capricorn Sun-Capricorn Moon People:

- Remember to open up to others and spend time socializing; otherwise, you risk becoming a workaholic.
- Understand that people often have different ideas and goals than your own.
- Open yourself to different perspectives to avoid becoming stubborn and defensive.

Advice for Dealing with Capricorn Sun-Capricorn Moon People:
- Double Capricorns have strong walls, but compliments can help you get past them, especially sincere ones.
- These individuals are afraid of getting hurt, making them seem cold and closed off. You will have to get them to trust you before they open up to you.
- Their desire for control means they often cannot see things from the right perspective. You will have to step in and act as a restraining influence on occasion.

Virgo Sun-Capricorn Moon: The Independent Realist

People with a Virgo-Capricorn Sun-Moon combination are independent individuals who dislike being restrained or controlled by others. They are also analytical and rational, able to set high goals and plan for the future and still approach things realistically. While their goals may be high, they are never impossible to reach.

Good Traits: Composed, Caring, Hardworking

These individuals are hardworking, dedicated to their goals, and motivated by success. They enjoy the limelight, and public recognition is important to them. At the same time, they are composed and caring in their personal relationships and are attentive to the needs of the people around them.

Bad Traits: Imposing, Distant, Erratic

When crossed, these individuals have a fearsome temper. Even though they think they are being composed, they can have volatile emotions they take out on the people around them. They do not understand people who are not as ambitious as they are and can even distance themselves from them. Additionally, while they try to be fair to others, their demeanor can be rude, imposing, and even tyrannical.

Perfect Partner: Virgo Sun-Capricorn Moon individuals need a partner with whom they can be their true selves. This includes understanding that, while they can be critical, it comes from a place of trying to help. They also need someone who can understand their need for independence, allowing them to retain it even in a romantic relationship.

Advice for Virgo Sun-Capricorn Moon People:

- Stay away from negative, pessimistic people. You will find it challenging to deal with them, leading to conflict.
- Be open to change, both at work and at home. Taking others' needs into account may be challenging, but it will improve your interpersonal relationships.
- Take the time to be open about your emotions with your partner. You can come across as closed off, which can cause conflict in your relationship.

Advice for Dealing with Virgo Sun-Capricorn Moon People:

- Do not cross them. They have sharp tempers, and it is difficult to control them once they are angered.
- Keep an eye out for procrastination. If they are procrastinating, it is because they are not ready to start working, and you may need to intervene.
- They are looking for stable relationships and not short-term flings. If you get into a relationship with a Virgo Sun-Capricorn Moon, be prepared for things to get serious.

Virgo Sun-Taurus Moon: The Dependable Pragmatist

These individuals are solid and trustworthy with calm personalities. They rarely react emotionally unless under significant stress. They are patient and pragmatic, making them good managers and at business.

Good Traits: Loyal, Calm, Honest

Individuals with Virgo Sun-Taurus Moon are honest and own up to any mistakes they make. They can be relaxed and firm at the same time and are loyal in their relationships, both romantic and platonic.

Bad Traits: Judgmental, Eccentric, Reserved

These individuals think being sensitive and compassionate is a weakness. This can make them come across as both judgmental and reserved. They hide their emotions from everyone but their closest friends, and they dislike change. They can also be very erratic and difficult to deal with when stressed.

Perfect Partner: Virgo Sun-Taurus Moon individuals value security and look for that in a partner. Their perfect partner will be faithful and dependable like them but should be able to deal with their sometimes obsessive need for perfection.

Advice for Virgo Sun-Taurus Moon People:

- Open up to the people around you. While you do not have to, let them see as much as you show your closest loved ones, as being less reserved will help you make friends.
- Take the time to look at the bigger picture. If you do not, you may slip up without even realizing it.
- Do not fall for the misconception that compassion equals weakness. Take the time to understand the people with whom you are interacting.

Advice for Dealing with Virgo Sun-Taurus Moon People:

- They give great advice and are good people to consult when you need help.
- These individuals can fall into the trap of becoming complacent in their personal relationships. Do not take it personally; be prepared to shake them up if needed.
- They are not great with change, so if you hope to get them to try something new, be prepared to work for it.

Chapter 8: Sun-Moon Combinations II: Air Sun Signs

Have you ever wondered what it would be like to have the qualities of two different astrological signs? Suppose you are an air sign with your Sun in Gemini, Libra, or Aquarius and are interested in knowing more about your astrological personality. In that case, this is the chapter for you.

In this chapter, you will learn about the different Sun-Moon combinations and what each says about a person's personality. We will also look at the good and bad traits of each combination and the perfect partner for each one. Finally, we will give some advice on how to deal with each personality type.

Gemini Sun-Libra Moon: Social Butterfly

This combination is also known as the "social butterfly." People with this combination are known for their charm, wit, and intelligence. They are natural communicators and are always the life of the party. They are also very diplomatic and fair-minded and always see both sides of every issue.

Good Traits: Charismatic, Witty, Intelligent

If you were born with the Sun in Gemini and the Moon in Libra, you are a very social person who loves to communicate. You are also very fair-minded and have a strong sense of justice. You always want everyone to get along and are willing to compromise to maintain harmony.

Bad Traits: Indecisive, Gossips, Flirtatious

If you have a Gemini Sun and a Libra Moon, you might sometimes find yourself stuck between two different worlds. This can make it difficult for you to commit to anything, as you always second-guess yourself. You may also find yourself gossiping more than you should.

Perfect Partner: Gemini Sun-Aquarius Moon

Gemini Sun-Aquarius Moon is an excellent match for Gemini Sun-Libra Moon. These two signs share a strong intellectual connection and a love of freedom and independence. As long as they can respect each other's need for space, this relationship can be very fulfilling.

Advice for Gemini Sun-Libra Moon People:

If you have a Gemini Sun and a Libra Moon, here are some things to keep in mind:

- You need to balance your need for change and stability.
- Try not to be too indecisive. You need to learn to trust your instincts and make decisions quickly. Otherwise, you will miss out on opportunities.
- Stay loyal to your friends. They are the people who truly know and love you, and they will always be there for you.

Advice for Dealing with Gemini Sun-Libra Moon People:

If you are dealing with a Gemini Sun-Libra Moon person, here are some things to keep in mind:

- They are very social creatures, and if you want their attention, you need to be interesting.
- They are also very curious. Do not tell them if you do not want them to know something.
- Finally, they can be a bit flirty. If you are in a relationship with them, make sure to keep them in check.

Gemini Sun-Aquarius Moon: The Intellectual

This combination is also known as the "intellectual." People with this combination are known for their quick wit, intelligence, and originality. They are natural communicators and are always the life of the party. They are also very independent and have a strong need for freedom.

Good Traits: Quick-Witted, Original, Independent

If you have a Gemini Sun and an Aquarius Moon, you are probably one of the most quick-witted and intelligent people around. You are always coming up with new ideas and are not afraid to be different. You are also very independent and need your own space to grow and thrive.

Bad Traits: Detached, Arrogant, Unemotional

Those with this combination may find themselves being a bit detached from their emotions. You have difficulty understanding why people get so worked up about things, and you might find yourself withdrawing from emotional situations.

Perfect Partner: Cancer Sun-Pisces Moon

Cancer Sun-Pisces Moon is the perfect match for you as they will understand your need for space and freedom. In addition, they are very creative and imaginative, so you will always have something new and exciting to do together.

Advice for Gemini Sun-Aquarius Moon People:

If you have a Gemini Sun and an Aquarius Moon, here are some things to keep in mind:

- You need to find a balance between your intellectual side and your emotional side.
- Try not to be too detached from your emotions. You need to learn to understand and empathize with other people's feelings.
- Do not be a know-it-all. Sometimes, it is better to listen than to talk.

Advice for Dealing with Gemini Sun-Aquarius Moon People:

If you are dealing with a Gemini Sun-Aquarius Moon person, here are some things to keep in mind:

- They are very independent, so do not try to control them.
- They are also very intelligent. If you want their attention, you need to be interesting.
- Finally, they can be a bit unemotional. Do not take everything they say or do personally.

Libra Sun-Gemini Moon: The Communicator

This combination is also known as the "communicator." People with this combination are known for their communication skills, social nature, and ability to see sides of every issue. They are natural diplomats and are always able to find common ground.

Good Traits: Social, Diplomatic, Balanced

If you have a Libra Sun and a Gemini Moon, you are probably one of the most social and diplomatic people around. You are always able to find common ground, and you are very good at mediation. You are also very balanced and fair-minded and always see both sides of every issue.

Bad Traits: Indecisive, People-Pleasing, Superficial

Those with this combination might find themselves being a bit too indecisive. In addition, you can be a bit of a people-pleaser, and you may need to learn to stand up for yourself. You may also be superficial because you are so good at diplomacy that you never seem to take a firm stand on anything.

Perfect Partner: Aries Sun-Capricorn Moon

Aries Sun-Capricorn Moon is the perfect match for you as they will be able to help you with your indecision. They are also very independent and strong-willed, so you will never have to worry about them trying to control you. In addition, they are very down-to-earth and practical, so you will always have someone to rely on.

Advice for Libra Sun-Gemini Moon People:

If you have a Libra Sun and a Gemini Moon, here are some things to keep in mind:

- You need to find a balance between your social side and your more introverted side.
- You need to learn to make decisions. Indecision can be a real problem for you.
- You also need to learn to stand up for yourself. Do not be a doormat.

Advice for Dealing with Libra Sun-Gemini Moon People:

If you are dealing with a Libra Sun-Gemini Moon person, here are some things to keep in mind:

- They need their space. Do not try to force them into anything they do not want to do.
- They are very independent. Do not try to control them.
- They can be a bit indecisive. You must be interesting and make things happen if you want their attention.

Gemini Sun-Gemini Moon: The Chameleon

This combination is also known as the "chameleon." People with this combination are known for their adaptability, versatility, and resourcefulness. They are natural communicators and are always the life of the party. They are also very independent and have a strong need for freedom.

Good Traits: Adaptable, Resourceful, Versatile

If you have a Gemini Sun and a Gemini Moon, you are probably one of the most adaptable and resourceful people around. You can always find new solutions to problems and are not afraid to try new things. You are also very independent and need your own space to grow and thrive.

Bad Traits: Scattered, Inconsistent, Flaky

Those with this combination may find themselves being a bit scattered and inconsistent. You may have difficulty sticking to one thing for a long time, and you may find yourself changing your mind a lot. You also need a lot of freedom, so you might not do well in situations where you feel trapped.

Perfect Partner: Aries Sun-Aquarius Moon

Aries Sun-Aquarius Moon is the perfect match for you as they are also adaptable and independent. They are not afraid of change and will always be up for trying new things. In addition, they are very spontaneous and exciting, so you will never be bored when you are with them.

Advice for Gemini Sun-Gemini Moon People:

If you have a Gemini Sun and a Gemini Moon, here are some things to keep in mind:

- Find a balance between your need for freedom and your need for stability.
- Try not to be too scattered. Focus on one thing at a time and see it through to the end.
- Do not be afraid to try new things. Life is full of surprises, so embrace them!
- Finally, be flexible. Things will always change, so learn to go with the flow.

Advice for Dealing with Gemini Sun-Gemini Moon People:

If you are dealing with a Gemini Sun-Gemini Moon person, here are some things to keep in mind:

- They are very adaptable and resourceful, so they can usually find a way to get what they want.
- They need their freedom, so do not try to control them.
- They can be a bit scattered and inconsistent so try to be patient with them.

Libra Sun-Aquarius Moon: The Visionary

Libra Sun and Aquarius Moon are highly creative and visionary combinations. You are drawn to the arts and have a strong sense of intuition. You see the world in terms of potential and possibilities and are always searching for new ways to express yourself.

Good Traits: Creative, Visionary, Intuitive

If you have a Libra Sun and an Aquarius Moon, you are probably one of the most creative and visionary people around. You are always searching for new ways to express yourself, and you have a strong sense of intuition. You are always seeking knowledge and understanding and are not afraid to challenge conventional thinking.

Bad Traits: Scattered, Disconnected, Unpredictable

The downside of this combination is that you can sometimes be seen as scattered or disconnected. You may have trouble finishing things, and you can be very unpredictable. You may also find it difficult to relate to people, as you always see the world differently.

Perfect Partner: Gemini Sun-Aquarius Moon

If you are a Libra Sun and Aquarius Moon, your perfect partner is a Gemini Sun and Aquarius Moon. This combination is the perfect match for your creative and visionary nature. In addition, you will always have someone who understands your need for freedom and independence.

Advice for Libra Sun-Aquarius Moon People:

If you have a Libra Sun and an Aquarius Moon, here are some things to keep in mind:

- You need to learn to focus your energy and use your creative power for good.
- You need to find a way to express your unique perspective to the world.
- You also need to learn to be more organized and focused. Indecision can be a real problem for you.

Advice for Dealing with Libra Sun-Aquarius Moon People:

If you are dealing with a Libra Sun and Aquarius Moon person, here are some things to keep in mind:

- Be patient with them. They might take a while to make up their mind.
- Encourage them to express their unique perspective. It is one of their greatest strengths.
- Finally, do not try to control them. They need their freedom and independence, so let them be.

Libra Sun-Libra Moon: The Idealist

This combination is known as the "idealist." People with this combination are known for their idealism, compassion, and diplomacy. They are natural peacemakers who are always looking for ways to unite people. They are also very fair-minded and have a strong sense of justice.

Good Traits: Idealistic, Compassionate, Diplomatic

If you have a Libra Sun and a Libra Moon, you are probably one of the most idealistic and compassionate people around. You are always looking for ways to help others and are very quick to forgive. You are also very fair-minded and always see both sides of every issue.

Bad Traits: Indecisive, Manipulative, Gullible

Those with this combination might find themselves being a bit indecisive and manipulative. You may have a hard time making decisions, and you may find yourself trying to control others. You also tend to be very gullible and can be easily taken advantage of.

Perfect Partner: Gemini Sun-Aquarius Moon

Gemini Sun-Aquarius Moon is the perfect match for you as they are also idealistic and independent. They are not afraid of change and will always be up for trying new things. In addition, they are very spontaneous and exciting, so you will never be bored when you are with them.

Advice for Libra Sun-Libra Moon People:

If you have a Libra Sun and a Libra Moon, here are some things to keep in mind:

- Try to be more decisive. Indecision can lead to missed opportunities.
- Do not try to control others. Everyone has a path to follow.
- Be wary of people who try to take advantage of your gullibility.

Advice for Dealing with Libra Sun-Libra Moon People:

If you are dealing with a Libra Sun-Libra Moon person, here are some things to keep in mind:

- They are very idealistic and compassionate, so they might not be realistic.
- They need their freedom, so do not try to control them.
- They can be a bit indecisive and manipulative, so try to be patient with them.

Aquarius Sun-Gemini Moon: The Thinker

Aquarius Suns with Gemini Moons are known for their quick wit and intelligence. They are natural-born leaders with a sharp mind for strategy. But they are not just all talk; these folks are also *doers*. When they set their sights on something, they go after it with determination and tenacity.

Good Traits: Intelligent, Leader, Innovative

People with an Aquarius Sun and Gemini Moon are some of the most intelligent and innovative people around. They are always searching for new knowledge and have a strong desire to make a difference in the world. They are natural-born leaders who are always looking for new ways to grow and express themselves.

Bad Traits: Scattered, Impatient, Unpredictable

The downside of this combination is that you can sometimes be seen as scattered or disconnected. You may have trouble finishing things, and you can be very unpredictable. You may also find it difficult to relate to people, as you always see the world differently.

Perfect Partner: Aries Sun-Gemini Moon

If you are an Aquarius Sun and Gemini Moon, your perfect partner is an Aries Sun and Gemini Moon. This combination is the perfect match for your intelligence and drive. You will always have someone who understands your need for freedom and independence. In addition, you will never get bored, as your partner is always full of new ideas and energy.

Advice for Aquarius Sun-Gemini Moon People:

If you have an Aquarius Sun and Gemini Moon, here are some things to keep in mind:

- Focus your energy and use your intelligence for good.
- Find a way to express your unique perspective to the world.

- Organize your thoughts and be more focused. Indecision can be a real problem for you.

Advice for Dealing with Aquarius Sun-Gemini Moon People:

If you are dealing with an Aquarius Sun and Gemini Moon person, here are some things to keep in mind:

- Keep an open mind. They are always searching for knowledge and new perspectives.
- Encourage them to express their unique ideas. It is one of their greatest strengths.
- Finally, do not try to control them. They need their freedom and independence, so let them be.

Aquarius Sun-Libra Moon: The Idealist

Individuals with this Sun-Moon combination are hardworking idealists who strive for balance and harmony. People born under this influence are natural peacemakers and mediators, always looking for ways to bring people together. Overall, those with an Aquarius Sun and Libra Moon are kindhearted souls who work tirelessly to make the world a better place.

Good Traits: Altruistic, Mediator, Idealistic

If you have an Aquarius Sun and Libra Moon, you are probably a very altruistic and idealistic person. You always strive for balance and harmony and are quick to lend a listening ear or a helping hand. In addition, you are probably a very hardworking person looking for ways to improve the world.

Bad Traits: People-Pleaser, Indecisive, Overly Idealistic

The downside of this combination is that you can sometimes be seen as a people-pleaser. You may have trouble making decisions as you always try to find the best solution for everyone. In addition, some people may see you as too idealistic.

Perfect Partner: Gemini Sun-Libra Moon

If you are an Aquarius Sun and Libra Moon, your perfect partner is a Gemini Sun and Libra Moon. This combination is the perfect match for your altruism and idealism. You will always have someone who understands your need for balance and harmony. In addition, you will never get bored, as your partner is always full of new ideas and energy.

Advice for Aquarius Sun-Libra Moon People:

If you have an Aquarius Sun and Libra Moon, here are some things to keep in mind:

- Do not try to please everyone. Focus on what is best for you and your partner.
- Make decisions based on logic, not emotion.
- Be careful of being too idealistic. It can sometimes lead to unrealistic expectations.

Advice for Dealing with Aquarius Sun-Libra Moon People:

If you are dealing with an Aquarius Sun and Libra Moon person, here are some things to keep in mind:

- Do not try to change them. They are who they are and will never try to be someone they are not.
- Encourage their idealism. It is one of their greatest strengths.
- Be patient with them. They may take longer than others to make decisions, but they always try to find the best solution for everyone involved.

Now that you know about the different Sun-Moon combinations, you should better understand the different personalities out there. Remember, this is just a general guide. Not everyone will fit perfectly into one of these categories. The most important thing is to be yourself and to find someone who accepts you for who you are.

Chapter 9: Sun-Moon Combinations Ill: Water Sun Signs

Water Sun signs are often described as being "in their feelings." If you have a water Sun sign such as Pisces, Cancer, or Scorpio, you may find that you are especially tuned in to the emotional energies of those around you.

If you have a water Sun sign and a water Moon sign, this chapter will explore some of the potential traits and qualities you may possess. It will also provide insight into how to use your emotional sensitivity to your advantage.

Pisces Sun-Scorpio Moon: The Intense Idealist

The combination of Pisces Sun and Scorpio Moon creates an intense, idealistic, and compassionate individual. Those with this combination are often deeply in touch with their emotions and may find themselves drawn to helping others. They may also be highly intuitive and have a strong connection to the spiritual realm.

Good Traits: Passionate, Loyal, Intuitive, Spiritual

Pisces Sun-Scorpio Moon individuals are often passionate about their beliefs and very loyal to those they care about. They may also be highly intuitive and strongly connected to the spiritual realm. With their intense emotions, they understand and relate to others on a deep level.

Bad Traits: Distracted, Secretive, Jealous, Possessive

Pisces Sun-Scorpio Moon combinations tend to be easily distracted.
https://unsplash.com/photos/BNrlDv8w07Y?utm_source=unsplash&utm_medium=referral&utm_content=creditShareLink

Pisces Sun and Scorpio Moon individuals can be easily distracted, and their imaginations can sometimes run wild. They can also be quite secretive and often have a dark side they may not show to others. They may have a dark side that they do not show to others and are often drawn to the mysterious and the unusual.

Perfect Partner: Taurus Sun-Cancer Moon

The perfect partner for the Pisces Sun-Scorpio Moon is the Taurus Sun-Cancer Moon. This pairing is ideal because they share similar emotional needs and desires. Both signs are loyal, compassionate, and protective of those they love. They will also understand and support each other on a deep level.

Advice for Pisces Sun-Scorpio Moon:

If you have a Pisces Sun-Scorpio Moon, here are some tips that may help you make the most of your combination:

- Try to stay focused and ground yourself in reality.
- Be careful not to get too caught up in your own emotions.

- Don't be afraid to express your emotions.
- Be honest with yourself and others.
- Try to stay calm and centered on your emotions.

Advice for Dealing with Pisces Sun-Scorpio Moon:

If you know a Pisces Sun-Scorpio Moon, here are some tips that may help you deal with them:

- Be patient with them.
- Try to be understanding and compassionate.
- Do not try to control or manipulate them.
- Be honest with them.
- Allow them to express their emotions.

Pisces Sun-Cancer Moon: The Nurturing Mystic

The Pisces Sun-Cancer Moon is a unique and special combination. Those with this combination are often very intuitive and in touch with their emotions. They are also deeply compassionate and caring, always ready to lend a shoulder to cry on. If you know someone with this combination, consider yourself lucky. You have a true friend for life.

Good Traits: Caring, Nurturing, Compassionate

Pisces Sun-Cancer Moon individuals strongly connect to the spiritual world and often possess psychic abilities. This combination gives them a natural ability to nurture and care for others. They are gentle healers who often go out of their way to help those in need.

Bad Traits: Needy, Moody, clingy

Pisces Sun-Cancer Moon individuals may occasionally come across as needy or clingy. They may also be quite moody, and their emotions can sometimes get the best of them. However, these individuals are usually well-meaning and just need some understanding and compassion.

Perfect Partner: Virgo Sun-Capricorn Moon

The perfect partner for the Pisces Sun-Cancer Moon is the Virgo Sun-Capricorn Moon. This pairing is ideal because they share similar emotional needs and desires. Both signs are loyal, compassionate, and protective of those they love. They will also understand and support each other on a deep level.

Advice for Pisces Sun-Cancer Moon:

If you have a Pisces Sun-Cancer Moon, here are some tips that may help you make the most of this combination:

- Try to stay in touch with your emotions.
- Don't be afraid to express your feelings.
- Be patient with yourself and others.
- Try to stay calm and centered.
- Allow yourself to be nurtured and cared for.

Advice for Dealing with Pisces Sun-Cancer Moon:

If you know a Pisces Sun-Cancer Moon, here are some tips that may help you deal with them:

- Let them know that you are there for them.
- Be understanding and compassionate.
- Encourage them to express their emotions.
- Respect their need for space and privacy.

Pisces Sun-Pisces Moon: The Compassionate Dreamer

Pisces is the gentle dreamer of the zodiac, and those with a Pisces Sun and Pisces Moon are especially in tune with their emotions and intuition. Pisces are natural healers, and their ability to connect with others on a soul level is what makes them so special. If you know Pisces, be sure to cherish them, as they are truly one of a kind.

Good Traits: Compassionate, Intuitive, Caring

Pisces Sun-Pisces Moon individuals are some of the most compassionate and caring people you will ever meet. They are also highly intuitive and in touch with their emotions. Pisces have a natural ability to heal and comfort others, and they are often drawn to professions that involve helping others, like counseling or social work.

Bad Traits: Overly Sensitive, Moody, Escapist

Pisces Sun-Pisces Moon individuals may occasionally come across as overly sensitive or moody. They may have a tendency to escape from their problems instead of facing them head-on. However, these individuals are usually well-meaning and just need a little extra understanding and compassion.

Perfect Partner: Cancer Sun-Scorpio Moon

The perfect partner for the Pisces Sun-Pisces Moon is the Cancer Sun-Scorpio Moon. This pairing is ideal because they share similar emotional needs and desires. Both signs are loyal, compassionate, and protective of those they love.

Advice for Pisces Sun-Pisces Moon:

If you have a Pisces Sun-Pisces Moon, here are some tips that may help you make the most of your combination:

- Channel your compassionate and intuitive nature into helping others.
- Create a safe and comfortable space for yourself to relax and dream.
- Get in touch with your emotions and allow yourself to feel them fully.
- Do not be afraid to express your feelings.

Advice for Dealing with Pisces Sun-Pisces Moon:

If you know a Pisces Sun-Pisces Moon, here are some tips that may help you deal with them:

- Look for ways to help them channel their compassionate and intuitive nature.
- Give them space to relax and dream.
- Encourage them to get in touch with their emotions.
- Respect their need for privacy and solitude.

Cancer Sun-Pisces Moon: The Sensitive Homebody

Cancer is the nurturing homebody of the zodiac, and those with a Cancer Sun and Pisces Moon are especially sensitive and in touch with their emotions. Cancer is a natural caregiver, and their ability to create a warm and loving home is what makes them so special. If you know Cancer, make sure you cherish them, as they are truly one of a kind.

Good Traits: Sensitive, Nurturing, Caring

Cancer Sun-Pisces Moon individuals are some of the most sensitive and nurturing people you will ever meet. They have a natural ability to care for others, and their homes are usually warm and inviting. Cancer is loyal and protective of those they love, and they often make excellent parents.

Bad Traits: Overly Sensitive, Moody, clingy

Cancer Sun-Pisces Moon individuals may occasionally come across as overly sensitive or moody. They may also have a tendency to be clingy or needy at times. However, these individuals are usually well-meaning and just need a little extra understanding and compassion.

Perfect Partner: Virgo Sun-Taurus Moon

The perfect partner for the Cancer Sun-Pisces Moon is the Virgo Sun-Taurus Moon. This pairing is ideal because they share similar emotional needs and desires. Both signs are loyal, reliable, and patient. They also have a shared love of security and stability.

Advice for Cancer Sun-Pisces Moon:

If you have a Cancer Sun-Pisces Moon, here are some tips that may help you make the most of your combination:

- Channel your nurturing nature into caring for others.
- Create a warm and inviting home that is a haven from the outside world.
- Get in touch with your emotions and allow yourself to feel them fully.
- Do not be afraid to express your feelings.

Advice for Dealing with Cancer Sun-Pisces Moon:

If you know a Cancer Sun-Pisces Moon, here are some tips that may help you deal with them:

- Look for ways to help them channel their nurturing nature.
- Give them space to relax and dream.
- Encourage them to get in touch with their emotions.
- Respect their need for privacy and solitude.

Cancer Sun-Scorpio Moon: The Sensual Survivor

Cancer Sun-Scorpio Moon is a potent and passionate combination. Those with this combination are highly sensitive and have a strong intuitive connection to the emotions of others. They are also natural survivors who can overcome any obstacle. Cancer is loyal and protective of those they love, and they often make excellent parents.

Good Traits: Sensitive, Intuitive, Passionate

Cancer Sun-Scorpio Moon individuals are some of the most sensitive and intuitive people you will ever meet. They have a strong connection to the emotions of others, and they can use this knowledge to their advantage. They are also passionate and intense. They are natural survivors.

Bad Traits: Jealous, Possessive, Manipulative

Cancer Sun-Scorpio Moon individuals may occasionally come across as jealous or possessive. They may also tend to be manipulative or controlling at times. However, they are usually well-meaning and just need some understanding and compassion.

Perfect Partner: Pisces Sun-Cancer Moon

The perfect partner for the Cancer Sun-Scorpio Moon is the Pisces Sun-Cancer Moon. This pairing is ideal because they share similar emotional needs and desires. Both signs are loyal, reliable, and patient. They also have a shared love of security and stability.

Advice for Cancer Sun-Scorpio Moon:

If you have a Cancer Sun-Scorpio Moon, here are some tips that may help you make the most of your combination:

- Channel your intuitive nature into understanding the emotions of others.
- Use your passion to drive you toward your goals.
- Never give up, no matter how hard things get.
- Allow yourself to be vulnerable with those you trust.

Advice for Dealing with Cancer Sun-Scorpio Moon:

If you know a Cancer Sun-Scorpio Moon, here are some tips that may help you deal with them:

- Encourage them to channel their intuitive nature into something positive.
- Help them to find an outlet for their passion.
- Be there for them when they need someone to lean on.
- Respect their need for privacy and solitude.

Cancer Sun-Cancer Moon: The Emotional Caretaker

Cancer Sun-Cancer Moon is a deeply emotional and compassionate combination. Those with this combination are natural caretakers who are always there for the people they love. They are also highly intuitive and have a strong connection to their emotions. Cancer is loyal and protective of those they love, and they often make excellent parents.

Good Traits: Emotional, Compassionate, Intuitive

Cancer Sun-Cancer Moon individuals are some of the most emotional and compassionate people you will ever meet. They strongly connect to their emotions and are always there for the people they love. They are also highly intuitive and have a strong sense of intuition.

Bad Traits: Overly Sensitive, Moody, Possessive

Cancer Sun-Cancer Moon individuals may occasionally come across as overly sensitive or moody. They may also tend to be possessive at times. However, these individuals are usually well-meaning and just need some understanding and compassion.

Perfect Partner: Pisces Sun-Pisces Moon

The perfect partner for the Cancer Sun-Cancer Moon is the Pisces Sun-Pisces Moon. This pairing is ideal because they share similar emotional needs and desires. Both signs are loyal, reliable, and patient. They also have a shared love of security and stability.

Advice for Cancer Sun-Cancer Moon:

If you have a Cancer Sun-Cancer Moon, here are some tips that may help you make the most of this combination:

- Use your emotional nature to your advantage.
- Take care of yourself so you can be there for the people you love.
- Make sure to nurture your relationships.
- Allow yourself to be vulnerable with those you trust.

Advice for Dealing with Cancer Sun-Cancer Moon:

If you know a Cancer Sun-Cancer Moon, here are some tips that may help you deal with them:

- Let them know that you appreciate their emotional nature.
- Encourage them to take care of themselves.
- Make sure to nurture your relationship.

Scorpio Sun-Cancer Moon: The Passionate Protector

Scorpio Sun-Cancer Moon is a passionate and compassionate combination. Those with this combination are natural protectors who are always there for the people they love. They are also highly intuitive and have a strong connection to their emotions. Scorpio Sun-Cancer Moon individuals often make excellent parents.

Good Traits: Passionate, Compassionate, Intuitive

Scorpio Sun-Cancer Moon individuals are some of the most passionate and compassionate people you will ever meet. They strongly connect to their emotions and are always there for the people they love. Scorpio Sun-Cancer Moon also has a strong sense of intuition.

Bad Traits: Overly Sensitive, Moody, Jealous

Scorpio Sun-Cancer Moon individuals may occasionally come across as overly sensitive or moody. They may also tend to be jealous at times. However, these individuals are usually well-meaning and just need some understanding and compassion.

Perfect Partner: Pisces Sun-Pisces Moon

The perfect partner for the Scorpio Sun-Cancer Moon is the Pisces Sun-Pisces Moon. This pairing is ideal because they share similar emotional needs and desires. Both signs are loyal, reliable, and patient. They also have a shared love of security and stability.

Advice for Scorpio Sun-Cancer Moon:

If you have a Scorpio Sun-Cancer Moon, here are some tips that may help you make the most of your combination:

- Break out of your comfort zone and try new things.
- Prepare for the worst but hope for the best.
- Take your time when making decisions.
- Learn to trust your intuition.

Advice for Dealing with Scorpio Sun-Cancer Moon:

If you know a Scorpio Sun-Cancer Moon, here are some tips that may help you deal with them:

- Appreciate their passion and compassion.
- Encourage them to take care of themselves.
- Make sure to nurture your relationship.

Scorpio Sun-Pisces Moon: The Jealous Lover

Scorpio Sun and Pisces Moon are a great match. These two signs are both associated with water, making for a very emotional and intense connection. Scorpio is known for being jealous and possessive, but Pisces is also very loyal and devoted. This can create a very intense and passionate relationship, as both partners will be extremely committed to one another.

Good Traits: Passionate, Loyal, Devoted

Scorpio Sun-Pisces Moon individuals are some of the most passionate and loyal people you will ever meet. They are also very devoted to the people they love. Scorpio Sun-Pisces Moon individuals often make excellent parents.

Bad Traits: Jealous, Possessive, Overly Sensitive

Scorpio Sun-Pisces Moon individuals may occasionally come across as jealous or possessive. They may also have a tendency to be overly sensitive at times. However, these individuals are usually well-meaning and just need some understanding and compassion.

Perfect Partner: Cancer Sun-Cancer Moon

The perfect partner for the Scorpio Sun-Pisces Moon is the Cancer Sun-Cancer Moon. This pairing is ideal because they share similar emotional needs and desires. Both signs are loyal, reliable, and patient. They also have a shared love of security and stability.

Advice for Scorpio Sun-Pisces Moon:

If you have a Scorpio Sun-Pisces Moon, here are some tips that may help you make the most out of this combination:

- Create a safe and secure environment for yourself and your loved ones.
- Do not let your emotions overwhelm you.
- Try to be patient with yourself and others.
- Learn to trust your intuition.

Advice for Dealing with Scorpio Sun-Pisces Moon:

If you know a Scorpio Sun-Pisces Moon, here are some tips that may help you deal with them:

- Appreciate their passion and loyalty.
- Encourage them to take care of themselves.
- Make sure to nurture your relationship.

Scorpio Sun-Scorpio Moon: The Intense Investigator

People with a Scorpio Sun and Scorpio Moon are one of the most intense combinations. They are the detectives of the zodiac, always probing and looking for answers. They feel deeply, and their emotions run high. They can be quite dramatic at times.

Good Traits: Sharp, Passionate, Resourceful

Scorpio Sun-Scorpio Moon individuals are some of the sharpest and most resourceful people you will ever meet. They are also very passionate and can be quite persuasive when they want to be. They have a sharp intellect and are not afraid to use it.

Bad Traits: Jealous, Possessive, Controlling

Scorpio Sun-Scorpio Moon individuals may occasionally come across as jealous or possessive. They may also have a tendency to be controlling at times. However, these individuals are usually well-meaning and just need some understanding and compassion.

Perfect Partner: Cancer Sun-Cancer Moon

The perfect partner for the Scorpio Sun-Scorpio Moon is the Cancer Sun-Cancer Moon. The emotions of these two signs are in sync. When one is happy, the other is happy. When one is sad, the other is sad. They understand each other's need for security and stability. It is a very nurturing and supportive relationship.

Advice for Scorpio Sun-Scorpio Moon:

If you have a Scorpio Sun-Scorpio Moon, here are some tips that may help you make the most of your combination:

- Get to know yourself and your emotions.
- Learn to control your emotions.
- Be honest with yourself and others.
- Find a partner who understands you.

Advice for Dealing with Scorpio Sun-Scorpio Moon:

If you know a Scorpio Sun-Scorpio Moon, here are some tips that may help you deal with them:

- Appreciate their passion and intensity.
- Encourage them to get to know themselves.
- Make sure to nurture your relationship.

Each Sun-Moon combination is unique and has its own set of strengths and weaknesses. This chapter has only scratched the surface. To really understand yourself or someone else, it is important to look at the whole chart. However, the Sun-Moon combination is a good place to start. Look up your combination and see what it has to say about you.

Chapter 10: Sun-Moon Combinations IV: Fire Sun Signs

Now that we have covered the Sun-Moon combinations for the earth, air, and water signs, the next step is to look at the fire signs. If your sign is Aries, Leo, or Sagittarius, your Sun sign is a fire sign. In this chapter, we will take a look at the different Sun-Moon combinations, including each option's good and bad traits. We will also figure out the perfect partner for you and offer advice you can use for yourself or when interacting with an individual who belongs to one of these signs.

Aries Sun-Aries Moon: The Charismatic Visionary

Dual Aries have truly magnetic personalities. They can fiercely express themselves when needed. Intelligent and brilliant, they are driven by a need to be challenged at all times and are interested in change. A lack of change will leave them bored, and they are the type to be drawn to subjects like science, medicine, and social studies. Their minds are always busy, making them effective leaders.

Positive Traits: Action Oriented, Responsible, Multifaceted

These individuals need to have a range of hobbies to keep them busy. They are always ready to act when needed but will also never express an opinion unless they are certain of the veracity of their words. Full of energy, they invest much effort into each situation.

Negative Traits: Blunt, Impatient, Egocentric

These individuals express their opinions freely, which can be positive, but it can also result in causing harm to people around them. Additionally, they cannot understand other perspectives and consider what they need. To be satisfied, they need things to keep moving or risk boredom. Additionally, they are reckless, and they react to the slightest provocation.

Perfect Partner: Dual Aries individuals need someone who will always challenge them. At the same time, their perfect partner should be a calming influence on their dynamic and energetic nature, and they get along well romantically with Taurus Moons. Dual Aries individuals are too egoistic to be involved in a long-distance relationship. They need events to happen in the here and now, and long-distance relationships do not afford them that.

Advice for Aries Sun-Aries Moon People:

- Remember to set attainable goals. You tend to chase after moon-shot dreams to the detriment of the people around you.
- Take the time to understand people around you. Your focus on yourself can affect your interpersonal relationships.
- Think things through. Being too reckless can easily backfire on you.

Advice for Dealing with Aries Sun-Aries Moon People:

- Try not to provoke or cross them. They can be reckless and volatile when tested.
- They like to fight for the people they love, so give them a challenge and a reason to fight.
- Take time to work with them. They are huge individualists, and it will take some time before they are willing to open up to you and see both of you as a singular

team.

Aries Sun-Leo Moon: The Exuberant Egotist

These individuals are highly energetic and magnetic. They love interacting with people and have a deep desire for social interaction. They enjoy the limelight and know how to showcase themselves in the most flattering light. At the same time, they can be stuck in their ways and hate giving up control to others.

Good Traits: Imaginative, Affectionate, and Sociable

They love interacting with people and are warm and generous. They are moved by the suffering of others and will always be the first to share their time and resources to help others. While stuck in their ways, they also have great, innovative ideas, which will see them become successful.

Bad Traits: Trusting, Impulsive, Attention-Seeking

Their desire for social interaction shows them developing a histrionic, attention-seeking personality to the point where they become captives to their own vanity. They lack good judgment and may fall prey to those with negative intentions. They easily get into relationships but never know how to end them well.

Perfect Partner: Aries Sun-Leo Moons need someone who admires them and is happy to take care of them. They get bored easily, so you must keep them entertained. They also need attention as being ignored will result in unhappiness. When in the right relationship, however, they are generous and devoted romantics who are great at long-term relationships when motivated to do so.

Advice for Aries Sun-Leo Moon People:

- Look for ways to stay interested when you feel your attention slipping, or else you may miss out on important moments
- Consider other options. Being stuck in your way may lead to you missing out on better solutions
- While cynicism is not something to aim for, being slightly wary about strangers' comments will serve you well

Advice for Dealing with Aries Sun-Leo Moon People:

- Keep an eye out for them to ensure they do not get scammed. As mentioned above, their intuition is not the best.
- When they are successful, make sure to admire and celebrate them, as their desire for public accolades is quite high.
- In frustrating situations, they can be impatient and short-tempered, so make sure you have solutions ready before breaking bad news to them.

Aries Sun-Sagittarius Moon: The Philosopher

Patient, thoughtful, and determined, these individuals have a philosophical approach to life and will never take action for no reason. They are strident believers in the truth and are led by their personal ideals. They have a wanderlust driven by the desire to find out what life is really about.

Good Traits: Independent, Enthusiastic, Determined

Aries Sun-Sagittarius Moon will never give up once they have decided on a course of action. Their enthusiastic, dynamic personality means they love challenges and living in the moment. They enjoy being in charge and making decisions for themselves instead of on behalf of others.

Bad Traits: Authoritative, Impulsive, Stubborn

Their dynamism also means that they do not think through their decisions. While each action has a reason, it is not necessarily well-reasoned, which can get them into trouble. Additionally, while they are independent, their desire for control can make them authoritative and autocratic.

Perfect Partner: The perfect partner for these individuals is as passionate about life as they are and will be direct and open with them. Their way of expressing themselves may occasionally veer into the hurtful, so their partners should have thick skins. Their desire for travel means they seek out sociable people who will travel with them.

Advice for Aries Sun-Sagittarius Moon People:
- Consider giving others a bit of control. This will improve your interpersonal relationships and allows you to get to know different perspectives
- Make sure you are patient and thoughtful and fight impulsivity and agitation.
- Train yourself not to fall for generalizations and snap judgments.

Advice for Dealing with Aries Sun-Sagittarius Moon People:
- Variety is the spice of their lives, so constant change and the opportunity for new discoveries are a must to keep them interested.
- They are straightforward and see things in black and white, so be ready for direct, frank conversations.
- You will need to help them understand others' perspectives, emotions, and opinions, as they can often be self-absorbed and forget about those around them.

Leo Sun-Aries Moon: The Alpha

These individuals are extremely forthright in their opinions. They can come across as aggressive but are also highly esteemed, and their opinion is greatly valued. They are born leaders and need to be in control of things to be truly happy.

Good Traits: Passionate, Confident, Productive

When a Leo Sun-Aries Moon sets their mind on something, they will achieve it. These individuals need to be involved in everything happening, and they will fight for people and causes that they think are worthwhile. Their enthusiasm means they burn brightly and turn their aggression into productivity.

Bad Traits: Aggressive, Controlling, Self-Centered

These individuals love the limelight and enjoy attention from others. If they decide they deserve something, they will work to get it, to the detriment of others. Their leadership skills can often manifest as aggression and overt control, while their reactive nature means they often act without thinking.

Perfect Partner: These individuals need a partner who challenges them every step of the way. Their perfect other half needs to be honest and trustworthy and able to shower them with the praise they crave. They desire passion and excitement in their lives and look for it in the people they enter into romantic relationships with.

Advice for Leo Sun-Aries Moon People:

- Remember to think of others. Letting your emotions rule you can turn you into a selfish person lacking in empathy, which can affect your interpersonal relationships.
- Be humble about your successes. Making waves in the world is an achievement, but refraining from crowing about it will bring you more respect.
- Remember to listen to and incorporate the advice of others in your life.

Advice for Dealing with Leo Sun-Aries Moon People:

- Try not to take their bluntness to heart. They are like this with everyone, and their bluntness comes from a place of kindness.
- Appreciate them for their successes. Verbal affirmations are essential for their happiness.
- Be prepared for the risk of emotional tantrums, as these are simply signs that they fully trust you.

Leo Sun-Leo Moon: The Noble Leader

Focused and determined, dual Leos are self-controlled natural-born leaders. They are willing to fight for themselves and others and can be compassionate and warm when in charge. They enjoy attention and admiration and can be jealous, possessive, insecure, and authoritarian without it.

Good Traits: Friendly, Generous, Charismatic

These individuals are cheerful and good-natured and get along well with people while still retaining their independent streak. They are generous and easygoing in their friendships, and their strong charisma means that people flock to them and their good nature.

Bad Traits: Authoritarian, Ruthless, Vain

A dual Leo's vanity can only be satisfied with admiration and praise from the people around them. Their natural leadership tendencies can occasionally become authoritarian, damaging their personal relationships. When crossed, they are absolutely ruthless in their response.

Perfect Partner: These individuals need a partner to give them the attention they crave. They need to be the center of the world for the people around them, but especially for their other half. The more they feel they are important to their partner, the more attention they will pay to them in gifts, romantic gestures, and time.

Advice for Leo Sun-Leo Moon People:
- Look for measures of success beyond the material.
- Though you are social, take care when choosing who your inner circle of friends and confidants is.
- Remember to bring yourself to the level of the people around you. Acting as if you are in charge when around friends can result in broken friendships and bitterness.

Advice for Dealing with Leo Sun-Leo Moon People:
- More than anything, these individuals need to be showered with attention. The more you give them, the closer they will be to you.
- They can be jealous and possessive in romantic relationships, so their partners should know how to react.
- Do not cross them. They treat anyone they see as enemies ruthlessly, and you will never be able to develop any relationship (let alone a friendship) with a dual Leo once you provoke them.

Leo Sun-Sagittarius Moon: Bluntly Independent

These individuals are extremely straightforward and honest, to the point of bluntness. They do not mind that speaking the truth can make them unpopular; they will still say what is on their minds. They are extremely independent and are unhappy when tied down or restricted from doing as they please.

Good Traits: Principled, Passionate, Caring

They are highly passionate and enthusiastic about meeting their goals and succeeding in life. They are charming, energetic, have a vivid imagination, and believe strongly in honesty and truth. They look to inspire others, and while they can be blunt, they are also well-intentioned.

Bad Traits: Flighty, Selfish, Restless

These individuals are often motivated by inspiration instead of hard work, making it challenging for them to stick to a single job or relationship. They are impatient and always looking for a change and are extremely restless when they feel tied down or at the beck and call of others.

Perfect Partner: Their perfect partner should love change and adventure and should love to travel as much as these individuals do. They also need constant attention. Lack of it can result in them losing interest, so their perfect partner should be willing to provide enough of it. Additionally, their other half should be okay with their honesty, as being unable to express themselves can be stifling.

Advice for Leo Sun-Sagittarius Moon People:

- Look for ways to constructively channel your passion for achieving great things.
- Be patient with others, and keep their potential reaction to your words in mind before being blunt.
- While your optimism is a strong trait, temper it with a dose of realism, or you risk becoming reckless.

Advice for Dealing with Leo Sun-Sagittarius Moon People:

- Give them the attention they crave. If they feel ignored, they will turn their attention away from you.
- They can find patience challenging, so you may have to be patient with them instead.
- Try not to give them too many orders as this can make them unhappy and tied down.

Sagittarius Sun-Aries Moon: The Adventurer

Freedom-loving, honest, and outspoken, these individuals love adventure and are always on the lookout for action and excitement. They love to be challenged and often cannot stay in one place for long. However, this can also lead them to act on impulse instead of thinking things through.

Good Traits: Intelligent, Humorous, Charming

These individuals are great at satire and make brilliant comedians. Their humor and positivity make them charming and, combined with their energetic personality, make people constantly drawn to them. Despite their occasionally reckless nature, they are also extremely intelligent and can be very profound when speaking to others, and it is their inquisitive mind that pushes them to constantly seek new challenges.

Bad Traits: Reckless, Restless, Impulsive

Their desire for adventure and challenges means they find it difficult to stay in one place for long. As soon as they learn something new, they need to have an opportunity to put it into practice. Their courageous and adventurous nature means they are always looking for further excitement, which can make them careless and reckless.

Perfect Partner: Their perfect partner will be someone who is patient with them as they can often forget to listen to their other half's needs. At the same time, their easygoing nature means their partner should be ambitious and give them the push they may need to go ahead with their plans. Though they have a temper and fiery personalities, they do not hold grudges. Because of this, their other half should be calm. A partner who loves arguing can bring out the worst in them.

Advice for Sagittarius Sun-Aries Moon People:
- Remember to give your partner the attention they need and let them occasionally take charge.
- While your direct nature is part of your charm, not everyone will appreciate it.

- Take the time to think your decisions through before you make them. If you do not, you risk making a major mistake.

Advice for Dealing with Sagittarius Sun-Aries Moon People:
- Their love for satire can occasionally lead to them making fun of the people around them, and you should be direct with them if you are uncomfortable with this.
- They can be insensitive in their personal life but expect a lot of attention in turn. Again, being direct with your feelings will help.
- Their positivity can result in them seeming a bit naive. However, they are unaware of the dark side and simply choose to look at the best parts of life.

Sagittarius Sun-Leo Moon: The Honorable Intellectual

People with this sign constantly pursue the mysteries and knowledge of the universe. At the same time, they value tolerance and honor, and once they give their word, they will not break it. They give their reputation a lot of importance and treat everyone with integrity and kindness.

Good Traits: Curious, Friendly, Energetic

These individuals are constantly searching for more information and are always willing to share this knowledge with others. Their eagerness and honesty make them great friends, and when their idealistic nature and desire to help are channeled properly, they can be great leaders.

Bad Traits: Vain, Stubborn, High-Maintenance

Sagittarius Sun-Leo Moon individuals love being in the spotlight and must be told they are special. They enjoy the attention, which can make them appear vain and high-maintenance, especially in their personal relationships. They are also extremely stubborn, and they dislike accepting advice or admitting they made a mistake.

Perfect Partner: Their perfect partner must understand that their easy-going nature comes with a constant desire to achieve more in life. They need someone who sets goals that are as lofty as theirs, someone who is always willing to attempt the impossible. They also need a partner who gives them the appreciation they crave, which can take the form of attention, gifts, time, or all of them together.

Advice for Sagittarius Sun-Leo Moon People:

- Your love for humanity will make you extremely successful in the social service field, and it is where you will find happiness.
- Remember to take the time to appreciate others just as they appreciate you.
- Be flexible and listen to the advice offered to you. What you do with it is your decision.

Advice for Dealing with Sagittarius Sun-Leo Moon People:

- Give them the attention they crave. Without it, they can become extremely dramatic.
- Remember that, while their honesty and integrity are praiseworthy, they are still human. Many see them as perfect people, and placing them on a pedestal can sometimes bring out the worst in them.
- Do not try to convince them that something is impossible. As far as they are concerned, *impossible* does not exist.

Conclusion

In this book, you have learned that your zodiac sign can indicate much more than just potential prospects for your future. Once you master the language of astrology, you will be able to reveal the secrets behind the stars, namely, how they affect your birth chart. Along with the four cardinal elements, the astrological planets exert enormous power over each zodiac sign. Each planet transits between the signs, and the one ruling over a sign at the time you were born will determine your core personality. The Sun and the Moon have the most prominent influence. The Sun determines your outer personality and can help you reveal how your inner light shines over the different areas of your life, whereas the Moon defines your soul's desires, wants, and needs – which you often hide from the outside world. Since the Sun does not move, its energy is distributed over the rest of the astrological planets, anchoring them and guiding them through the zodiac signs. Your journey toward discovering your personality starts by revealing your Sun sign.

That being said, the fine traits of your personality will always come from the energy zodiac sign present on your birth chart. Each sign is influenced by one of the four cardinal elements and their qualities. According to the element they are ruled by, the 12-star signs are divided into four triplicities, which are Fire signs, Water signs, Air signs, and Earth signs. These are further split into quadruplicities defined by the quality associated with the element at the time you were born. Quadruplicities change seasonally and typically indicate how stable specific personality traits were in the season you were born. The energy of the star signs manifests differently in each zodiac house, further narrowing down how it will influence your personality traits.

So, essentially, your entire personality is determined by the combination of your Sun sign, Moon sign, zodiac sign, and the element that influences the latter. Each group of combinations (the Earth-Sun-Moon signs, the Water-Sun-Moon signs, the Fire-Sun-Moon signs, and the Air-Sun-Moon signs) carries a set of unique personality traits. While your zodiac sign can reveal your positive and negative traits, the Sun-Moon combination can help you define these further. This will allow you to understand your emotions, thoughts, and actions more. It can also enable you to understand people born under a particular star combination and connect with them despite the differences in your personalities. Last, but not least, it will help you find people with similar combinations and perhaps reveal your ideal partner.

Part 3: Rising Signs

What Your Ascendant Sign Reveals about Your Personality Type and More

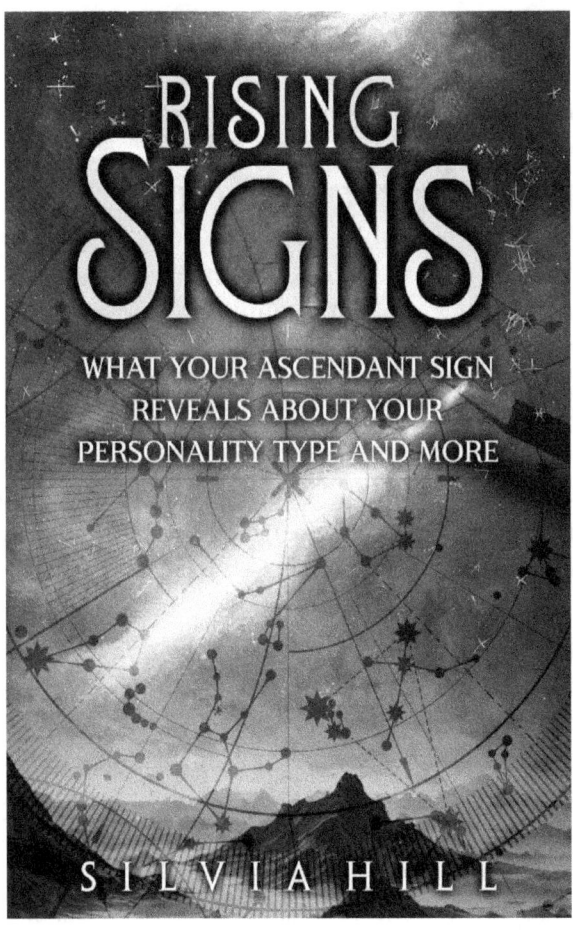

Introduction

Whether you're new to astrology or have been interested in astrological signs for a while, it's common to be confused regarding which zodiac signs affect you. Whether you believe it or not, your zodiac sign is not the only astrological entity affecting your life. Every single one of the planets, zodiacs, and celestial bodies affects you. Out of these, one of the most misunderstood placements is regarding the ascendant or the rising sign and how it impacts your life. If you're one of those who don't understand this, then this book is the perfect guide to help you learn how the ascendant works.

Understanding how the rising sign works paves the way to understanding the truth about yourself. The rising sign highlights the most important themes and patterns of your life and, thus, holds the key to understanding your natal chart. Therefore, it's essential that you clearly understand what the ascendant entails and that you are also able to identify your rising sign. After all, the rising sign establishes which planet is the chart ruler of your natal chart.

So, whether you want to be able to interpret your personal natal chart or help a friend understand their rising sign and zodiacs, this book will provide an in-depth description of each rising sign. Each of these comes with specific personality traits and mannerisms when approaching every challenge, difficulty, or situation. Understanding what motivates these approaches can help you understand an individual's mental psyche and behavior. Their rising sign and ruling planet explain much about their nature and why they act the way they do.

As a bonus, we have included an extra chapter on how you can embrace your rising sign. None of us has any control over when we're born, so we don't get to choose our ascendants and ruling planets. And while some people have no trouble accepting themselves for who they are, others find it very challenging to be happy with their true selves. The best way to deal with this is to first understand everything about your ascendant and then work toward accepting your sign and the traits that come along with it.

The placement of your ascendant is extremely sensitive, and understanding it is essential to understanding the entire astrological significance of your ruling planet. Therefore, it's best to first learn about the importance of the rising sign on your birth chart and then get into detail about all the traits that come with it. Knowing the difference between the sun and moon signs and the rising signs, as many people often confuse these with each other, is also key to a greater overall understanding of your chart and character. So, read on to discover everything about the ascendant and your particular rising sign traits and life patterns.

Chapter 1: Introducing the Rising Sign

An astrological birth chart holds the key to a unique cosmic signature based on the placement of planetary bodies, zodiac signs, and houses. At the time and place of your birth, your birth chart depicts the position of the planets, sun, stars, and moon. We can discover all sorts of things about ourselves and our place in the world within the structure of astronomy.

The rising, the moon, and the sun are the three main planetary points within the birth chart that define personalities. The sun sign is well known to most people, but the moon and rising signs are less familiar. Did you know that the question of birth signs is much more complex than simply stating a zodiac or star sign? We are not just one single zodiac aspect. We are talking about the entire universe and its changing planetary alignments. All planets, celestial bodies, and galactic coordinates occupied astrological signs when you were born, and each had a unique meaning. Introducing the Rising Sign, otherwise known as your Ascendant, is essential as it is one of astrology's most integral yet overlooked placements.

Even if you're aware of what your rising sign is, you may not be so sure of what it means for you. So, we're here to explain it, along with an insight into why you need it and how it differentiates from the sun and moon signs.

The Signs in Astrology

In astrology, there are plenty of symbolic representations to go around. Each sign has its own unique set of symbols, which practitioners often use as identifiers during a reading. These symbols provide additional insight into various attributes and characteristics in a person's birth chart. But what do these signs mean, and how do they come into play? Let's take a look...

Most people are familiar with their sun sign, also known as their star sign. What does a rising sign mean?

The signs of the rising sun on the day you are born are known as your rising sign or Ascendant. It is a subtle but powerful indicator of your personality and character. Utilizing their power through knowledge can help explain the rising signs in Astrology, their traits, and their compatibility with other signs. Peering into the future and analyzing horoscopes has been an indispensable part of our lives for many centuries now. Every human being on this planet has a set of stars and planets that influence their actions, thoughts, speech, habits, and every other action they undertake during their lifetime. The study of these celestial bodies and their effect on human beings is known as Astrology. The zodiac plays a considerable role in this field, with each star having its own particular significance and impact on people who are born under its domain.

Your first breath occurred at the moment of a unique configuration of all the planets. And when you get your natal chart drawn up, you'll see the sky as it appeared at the exact time, date, and location of your birth. These charts are potent tools astrologers use to understand and pass on information and insight into personal opportunities, personality, timing, identity, motivation, and recurring themes throughout life.

The birth chart includes it, along with the moon and sun signs - the foundation of your character.

- The moon sign symbolizes the inner you
- The sun sign symbolizes your essence
- The rising sign represents the outer you

Your rising sign determines what people think of you when they see you for the first time. Your rising sign may also explain why people might perceive you as a fickle Aquarius despite you being a serious Virgo.

The Rising Sign

Your rising sign reveals a great deal about your personality and outlook on life. A birth chart's angle determines the alignment of the zodiac wheel, and it depends on the time of your birth. Here's your chance to better understand this part of you!

It is also called the ascendant because it rises over the eastern horizon at the time of your birth. Despite appearing static to the naked eye, the scene overhead actually moves extremely quickly. Ascendant and rising sign placement is also very sensitive. You need to know your exact (not approximate) time of birth to calculate your rising sign.

This is one of the most important aspects of a birth chart, one of the most defining and representative aspects within you, and it expresses your natal energy. Your natal energy is your life trajectory and personality. It is also one of the most misunderstood angles in the birth chart. Because we tend to think of the ascendant as how we appear to people or how we look, it is a projection of ourselves. But the ascendant is so much more and affects more in the birth chart than merely your outward appearance. Using your rising sign can be a great way to understand others' energy and personalities and show the same enlightening aspects of yourself.

Knowing how and why your signs are the way they are will help you understand them better. By understanding another person's ascendant, you can better understand their energy, preferences, and outlook of that person. It's an excellent way to get a sense of their birth chart. As a result, you can use it to work on things you need to improve in yourself, and understanding someone's ascendant helps you to understand their outlook.

How Does the Rising Sign Affect Who We Are?

So, a rising sign represents how you appear. You give an impression to others based on how you project yourself, how you look, and how you behave. This angle on the birth chart depicts the impressions we give out of ourselves and others. This makes it an exciting part of your birth chart to explore, to know who you are to other people. This is because the rising sign, the ascendant, is the first self-impression determining factor of the birth chart. Despite differences in the placement of the planets, the rising sign is the one that sets and calibrates the zodiac wheel in our chart.

The rising sign indicates which sign is on the horizon at the time of birth. It determines our houses and what signs rule over our houses. The house system is a study of its own and is covered in other books. We need to know that a person's astrology chart is divided into 12 houses, each representing a different side of their life. The ascendant position in a chart establishes house systems. The rising signifies who you are, what you look like, and the words you use as you enter the first house. In other words, it represents a person's character and exterior, which are the first things that are noticed in them.

This then completely changes the personality type, and as it changes each sign, it will trail through different degrees depending on the degree of your ascendant. Therefore nobody is the same. Because every second of every day, through the celestial planetary movements, there is a slight shift in degree. This is known as the zodiac wheel. So, if people are born even one second apart, they will have very different personalities.

In contrast to the sun sign, which represents your inner core, is the moon sign, which symbolizes your center. Thus, rising signs are the masks you wear to the world.

Why Are Rising Signs Important?

Rising signs are vital because they give us information about people's personalities, character traits, and future. These zodiacal positions directly impact your life and influence who you are as a person. They also give insight into how other people may perceive you. How you view the rising sign will tell you a lot about your self-image and self-perception, especially concerning matters of the heart. Rising signs are also linked to elements such as the sun, moon, and earth. Understanding these connections can help you better understand how their position impacts your life moving forward.

The subtleties and complexities of the change aspects of astrology and ascendants dictate our energies and what we hold true in our lives. It creates different archetypes in each of our lives. Things like money, relationships, health, outlooks, and philosophies all have different houses (rising signs) ruling them. The ascendant determines our houses, and which sign rules over which house is a definitive aspect of understanding ourselves and other people.

Rising Signs in Practice

By knowing how to read rising signs, we can get a better understanding of why it is necessary to know this part of the puzzle. As already mentioned, the rising sign in your birth chart represents the planets ascending on the Eastern horizon when you were born. So, we can decipher what others think of us and a person's gut-level and spontaneous reaction to things. For example, during a difficult situation, a Leo rising will end things with a tremendous impact, and everybody will know about it. In contrast, a Pisces rising will leave more quietly. It is an essential part when determining personality type.

Rising signs determine how to deal with difficulty and come out of the shadow.
https://pixabay.com/images/id-3151869/

Our rising sign determines how we deal with things in our lives, coming out of the shadows and hardships. Ascension and spirituality are popular concepts, and your ascendant will show you what that looks like and how it works.

How the Rising Sign Is Different

Whenever people ask about your star sign, they're referring to your sun sign or where the sun was when you were born. With more people becoming interested in astrology, rising signs are also becoming better known. Due to the rapid changes in the horizon, it is essential to know your exact birth time when looking for your rising sign.

Astrologically speaking, the sun sign, the moon sign, and the rising sign are the three most important signs. By meeting someone's rising, sun, and moon signs at different life stages, you will learn more about their character.

Generally, sign discovery on a person will work like this:

- Your first discovery will be the rising sign, which acts as a social guardian
- A sun sign personality follows
- Then, when trust is gained, the moon sign will appear

As the exterior representation of who you are, your rising sign corresponds to your outer self, your sun corresponds to your core self, and your moon corresponds to your inner self. If you're ready to dive deeper into personal astrology, take a moment to learn about rising, moon, and sun signs.

The Sun Sign

The sun sign is the premise of many horoscopes, so when someone asks you what your sign is, it is generally related to the sun sign. You can determine your sun sign based on birthday information.

Sun signs are honored in astrology for a good reason. The sun sign defines who we are, just as the universe is defined by the sun. Knowledge of your astrological natal chart is necessary because it represents intellect, identity, vitality, and spirituality.

Astrology has been practiced for thousands of years. Around 2,100 years ago, the Babylonians developed their own form of horoscopes, and astrology soon spread to the Mediterranean. As we know them today, horoscopes were first introduced in the 1700s by astrologist William Lilly. Reading horoscopes became mainstream in the 1930s when British astrologer R.H Naylor started publishing birth chart predictions for the royal family. Naylor simplified his readings by focusing on sun signs for readers curious about their own astrological forecasts.

What Can We Learn from the Sun Sign?

You will inherit a set of character traits and qualities that will help you achieve what you desire in life based on your sun sign. Zodiac signs each have their own rulings that guide and influence the personalities of those born under that sign. For example, it is known that Mercury is the planet of communication, which governs the Virgo sign. Therefore, you'll probably find you have yet to meet a Virgo who doesn't have excellent communication skills and the ability to handle any situation.

In astrology, the sun sign represents our highest expression of self, so it's no surprise that it's given added importance. Sun signs represent how we present ourselves to the world and are associated with specific sides of our personality. In a chart, the sun's place can indicate how someone expresses themselves, whether that is creatively or verbally.

Although your sun sign, determined by the sun's position on the day you were born, may be an essential part of your identity, it is not always comprehensive. On the other hand, your rising sign offers a lot more. Knowing your rising sign symbolizes integrating all the elements of your life and chart.

The Moon Sign

After the sun sign, the moon sign is regarded as the next critical influencer on your horoscope. Sun signs represent the ego, while moon signs represent the inner self.

A person's moon sign corresponds to the moon's position at the time of their birth. About two and a half days pass between the moon's visits to each zodiac sign. Because an individual's personality and emotions are greatly influenced by their moon sign, according to the astrological universe, moon signs provide an insight into the inner self. Those deepest desires, thoughts, and fears we keep hidden from others can be identified by understanding the moon sign.

What Can We Learn from the Moon Sign?

The moon sign separates us from people who share sun signs in terms of personality traits and qualities. You may also find that this lunar sign balances out the extremes of the sun sign. Alternatively, you may have a deeper understanding of yourself and others when both the sun and moon belong to the same zodiac. Essentially, the lunar sign is a gateway to emotions, the subconscious mind, and the inner voice. You can uncover much more about your individual potential if you use it.

In astrology, the moon is associated with maternal influence. It represents basic reactions and habits hidden deep within us. It corners the subconscious side of our thoughts and feelings that may lay dormant even to ourselves. The moon sign governs our inner self, bringing our fragility, sensitivity, and deepest desires face-to-face.

Even though the sun and moon signs can predict specific characteristics of your personality, astrology isn't an exact science, and your astrological profile is made up of various factors. Your horoscope is most accurate when all the placements in your chart are acknowledged.

The Rising Sign

One of the most crucial points in a natal chart is the rising sign since it governs the first house of the ruler chart (when you were born).

On a symbolic level, it represents the spot where the sun rises each day and the point at which the earth and sky meet. In the chart ruler, wherever the rising ascendant degree falls, it sets up the rising sign, which is the foundation for all the houses. Houses describe the areas of life where the alignments of the planets fall. This is why the rising sign of the incident is so vital because it sets the stage for the rest of the chart.

In reality, a chart is more than just your internal world; it is a map of your life. Don't consider it the most prominent facet of your personality. Aside from the fact that it incorporates both internal and external dynamics, it is also the most technically important point in the chart, not because it carries more than the other components but because it is crucial to where the other components end up.

Rising signs reflect our external characteristics, including appearance, immediate responses, relationships, and attitude. In other words, it represents the appearance and persona of the self. Your rising sign energy may lead you to dress or look differently than your moon or sun sign energy does. In addition to guarding our deepest selves, rising signs can be used to increase insight and help us adjust to new situations with new people.

The Different Components of the Three Signs

To find out about anyone's signs, you must know the exact place, time, and date of birth. There can be many rising signs among people born on the same day, making things very interesting.

- The place of birth determines the moon sign
- The rising sign is determined by the time of birth
- The sun sign is determined by the date of birth

The ascendant, also known as the rising sign, is associated with our social personalities, so it is possible that if someone is guessing your sign, they may get your ascendant before your sun sign. This is because our rising sign encompasses the characteristics of our outward appearance.

You can't just say you're a Virgo since that would mean your personality is the same as everyone else born in Virgo season. The Virgo sun may land in the tenth house of achievement and public roles, making them more of a public figure instead of the stereotypical homebody Virgo personality you may read about online. In the next chapter, we will discuss houses in more detail.

Whether you're new to the three signs or new to the rising sign, knowing it can make all the difference between knowing someone and truly knowing them - or even yourself! This is because there is a lot more to a person than the typical sun-only signs can provide.

Chapter 2: Identifying Your Rising Sign

The astrology birth chart has captured your imagination, so you have decided to explore it for yourself. There's a saying that postulates that we don't come with an instruction manual. Let's think again about that! We can understand our personality and path by looking at our astrology chart. Our horoscopes can provide insight into our everyday lives and help us make life changes based on the planets' movements. What is the formula for interpreting the movements and locations of planets? Why do the planets affect the zodiac signs, and what is the definition of a zodiac sign?

To be able to read a birth chart, also known as a natal chart or astrology chart, we need to first understand these questions. A birth chart shows where the planets were at the time of our birth. It also provides information about our preferences, aims, and character. A birth chart gives the reader significant insight into a person. In this chapter, we will discuss what a birth chart is and detail its crucial component of one. We will then go on to discuss how you can identify your rising sign using a birth chart.

What Is an Astrology Birth Chart?

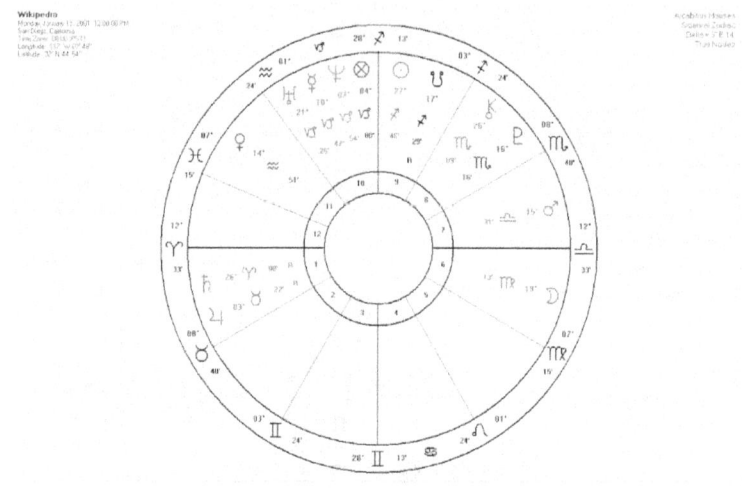

Sample Birth Chart.
https://commons.wikimedia.org/wiki/File:Wikipedia_Sidereal_Birth_Chart.gif

A birth chart may initially seem confusing, so let us explain what it is. It shows the sky at the exact moment and place when you were born as a two-dimensional map. It may seem like a confusing circle of glyphs and symbols when first laying eyes on one. There is no denying that a birth chart has its language. To decode it, you'll need patience, energy, and time. But once you become aware of what the symbols and lines mean, you'll soon ask for the birth information of everyone you know to discover their rising signs.

All of us have an astrological chart that identifies who we are. A birth chart can show you who you and others really are by calculating the astrological particulars of your birth. You can find out about your assets and liabilities and future growth prospects by analyzing your birth chart.

What Does an Astrology Birth Chart Do?

Virgos are stoic, and Geminis are crazy. In general, these are some of the generalizations about the sun signs of the zodiac. The sun sign may be the most well-known feature of a birth chart, but there are other things to consider. Multiple planets are placed in 12 different houses in a birth chart. There is no such thing as a duplicate birth chart, just as there is no such thing as a duplicate person.

They reveal the positions of the planets at the time of birth for people, including insight into circumstances, connections, and ambitions. Even your pets will have their own specific astrology charts. For now, though, we will concentrate on yours.

Natal charts can give clues about someone's character and reveal significant events in their lives based on their placement of planets at birth. So, birth charts offer insight into our lives, pointing us in the right direction and helping us become the best version of ourselves. Most people see astrology as a way of participating in the world while shaping their futures rather than fate.

As an example, consider the following. If someone has a Uranus Pluto placement, they tend to never settle-always look for the next thing to try or place to go. But, if they understand that, it can help them to become more aware of what they're doing. You can gain insight into why you act the way you do in all aspects of your life by studying your birth chart. Positive behaviors are amplified, and negative behaviors are highlighted. Knowing why they happen will help you to prevent them from happening again.

Why Is an Astrology Birth Chart Important?

A birth chart is a map of your life's purpose, just as a map shows rivers, directions, and places from our point of view. Similar to a map, it outlines precisely where things are, how to get there, and how things have evolved over time. Our very own life story is outlined, along with instructions on how to complete it. A birth chart can provide fascinating information about personality traits and behaviors. Using them can help you understand unseen areas and shape your perception. By doing so, we can improve ourselves and grow as individuals. The growth of your abilities can be improved by understanding your capabilities and shortcomings.

Astrology Birth Charts: What We Can Learn

- Venus's zodiac signs and houses, as well as the sun and moon's
- Aspects or angles of the planets
- Each planet's house and zodiac sign
- There is a high concentration of energy if more than one planet is in a sign (stellium)
- Balance of the four elements (planets in fire, earth, water, and air signs)
- Balance of the chart (planets in changing, stable, or seasonal signs
- Patterns of planets
- Jupiter is the planet of fortune, Saturn is the planet of preservation

Element and quality scores can be calculated by adding them together. If there is a deficit of one characteristic or dominance in another, we can learn to achieve equilibrium in our lives.

Key Components of an Astrology Birth Chart

A birth chart takes the shape of a 360-degree circle. We position ourselves in the circle as if we were at its center instead of looking down from above. For example, West would be on the left, not on the right, and vice versa. As a result, the directions are flipped since we categorize it as if we are on the inside, looking out.

We discussed the sun sign in chapter one. Our horoscopes are based on this. The essence of who we are can be found in it. Further on, we discussed how we can know our emotional self through our moon sign and how we were raised. As an adult, it relates to our relationships and needs. At the time of our birth, we were born under a constellation, which gives us our rising sign, essentially indicating how we present ourselves to other people.

An astrology birth chart can provide insight into every facet of our existence.

The Zodiac Signs

A birth chart consists of 12 sections around the outer rim. There will be a section that corresponds to your birth date. The Zodiac sign you were born under is determined by your birth date. Each sign of the Zodiac represents a distinctive personality.

- Capricorn (December 22- January 19)
- Sagittarius (November 22- December 21)
- Scorpio (October 23- November 21)
- Libra (September 23- October 22)
- Virgo (August 23- September 22)
- Leo (July 23- August 22)
- Cancer (June 21 - July 22)
- Gemini (May 21 - June 20)
- Taurus (April 20- May 20)
- Aries (March 21- April 19)
- Pisces (February 19- March 20)
- Aquarius (January 20- February 18)

You can read an astrology chart in more than one way, depending on how you read your Zodiac sign. A variety of factors influence the way your sign is read, so to do it successfully, understanding an astrology chart means putting all this knowledge together to get a true reading.

The Houses

It is through horoscopes that we get a deeper understanding of astrology. The more we follow them, the more familiar we become with our birth charts and the more interested we become in them. Signs and planets are well known, but what on earth is a house?

Several areas of one's life are affected by a planet's energy, such as a person's relationships, profession, and sense of self. In the first house, the planet Mars represents individuality and motivation, and

Aries governs this house. No matter what sign we are, we can use this method to define everything that makes us special.

Each celestial point, planet, or asteroid has its own house, and its placement provides valuable insight into our personal characteristics and how we live with the world around us. Different external and internal events are activated by the movement of the planets in the sky. Each house has its own sign.

There are 12 houses in the birth chart, just as there are 12 zodiac signs. For example, the 7th house of health symbolizes relationships, bonding, and romance, which corresponds with Cancer's energy, which is all about caring and emotions.

The Twelve Houses

1. The self, body, temperament, appearance, and vitality (Ascendant level on the birth chart)
2. Possessions, resources, livelihood, and value
3. Community, relationships, communication, expression
4. Home, domesticity, foundations, and blood relationships (The Imum Coeli level (bottom) on the birth chart)
5. Creativity, children, pleasure, and romance
6. Routine, health, environment, well-being
7. Perspective, relationships, bonding, and romance (Descendant level on the birth chart)
8. Intensity, death, animalist, and desire
9. Philosophy, travel, exploration, curiosity, and open-mindedness
10. Image, appearance, achievement, and public roles (The Midheaven (top) level on the birth chart)
11. Support, friends, ideas, and joy
12. Inner self, emotions, secrets, and dreams

In case you still feel unclear about the difference between houses and signs, keep in mind that the moon passes through a sign in two to three days. During a 24-hour period, the Moon passes through every house in your birth chart. Every planet follows the same rule. The passage of Pluto through a house takes 24 hours but will take 12-31 years to pass through a sign.

The Planets

You can interpret your reading based on the planets that pass through your chart's different houses. Different symbols represent the planets throughout the chart. Various energies are influenced by the placement of planets in your astrological chart that influences daily life.

- Neptune and Uranus combine to form Pluto. Two interlocking lines on either side form a female glyph
- In the form of an upside-down female glyph, two lines curve away from Uranus on either side
- An upside-down cross appears on Neptune with two lines curved skyward
- Mars represents males, while Venus represents females
- Two lines protrude from the top circle of Mercury, which is the female symbol
- The sun is represented by a circle with a dot in the center
- The moon is a small half-crescent moon shape
- The symbol for Jupiter is similar to the number four
- A symbol resembling five represents Saturn

Two types of planets exist within the birth chart: outer planets and personal planets.

The outer planets include Neptune, Jupiter, Uranus, Pluto, and Saturn.

- Neptune - spirituality, imagination, intuition, dreams
- Jupiter - philosophy, personal growth, wisdom, and luck
- Saturn - bonding, responsibilities, habits, and partnership
- Uranus - revolution, growth, learning, and change
- Pluto - passion, change, transformation, and evolution

Personal planets include mars, the sun, Venus, mercury, and the moon.

- The moon - intuition, privacy, memories, and reaction
- Mercury - communication, perception, information, and

efficiency
- The sun - identity, ego, truth, and individuality
- Venus - finances, comfort, enjoyment, and love
- Mars - passion, will, confidence, and energy

The planets play an important role in understanding the house's energy. For example, Venus within the fifth house is creative, while mercury within the first house is talkative.

The following information will help you better understand where things are on the birth chart.

The Imum Coeli (IC)

Imum Coeli, or the IC, is situated in the Northern Hemisphere. This is the midnight of the chart, where our private lives are.

The Midheaven (MC)

High noon on the chart corresponds to the midheaven in the Southern hemisphere. We are most visible in this part of the chart, where the Sun peaks in the sky.

The Ascendant (AC)

The rising sign, or the sign of the Sun, in the birth chart is situated in the Eastern hemisphere (left side of the chart). When we are born, our ascendant degree represents us most intimately since it rises at the moment of our birth.

The Descendant (DC)

The birth chart's setting (descending) sun is situated in the Western hemisphere. This point in the chart represents our close relationships.

The signs can help you better understand the chart now that you have examined the houses and the planets. Identify the house signs by looking at their ruling signs. You can then check which planets are in which houses and signs. Knowing your birth chart in this way will enrich your understanding. For example, a person with an Aries ascendant will be outspoken and confident, as Mercury is positioned here.

How to Use an Astrology Birth Chart to Find Your Rising (Ascendant) Sign

Finding out your sun sign is easy enough to do these days. Simply unfold a newspaper, magazine, or Google search, and you'll find your horoscope anywhere. Finding the rising sign is going to be a little bit different. Remember, if you really want the best reading possible, we must do a few extra things first. When astrologers are doing a full birth chart, they'll often emphasize the ascendant or the rising sign more than the sun sign. And, in some instances, the importance of the rising sign is taking precedence more than it used to. Many new horoscope columns are written in many instances with the rising sign or the ascendant sign in mind rather than the sun sign.

For beginners, it is best to find out what sign their planets are in (e.g., are you a Virgo sun with a Capricorn moon?) and which house those planets fall in their birth chart.

Collecting information about your birth will be necessary to determine your rising sign. You can find an online rising sign calculator or visit an astronomer once you have this information. But there's nothing better than a good old DIY project. You may have learned all you know about astrology so far by yourself, so you may as well go one step further. Below you find all the information you need to discover your rising sign. Knowing your sign will help you understand what each planet represents when you interpret it. More of that is in chapter three!

Your Date of Birth

Record your birth date, month, and year. This should already be obvious to you. Your birth certificate or parent can provide this information if you are unsure.

Find Out About Your Time of Birth

It is important to know your time of birth to get an accurate answer because the rising sign changes every two hours.

But this can be tricky to do as not all of us know this detail of our birth. Sometimes, neither will our parents! Or they're not around for us to ask them. Ask some member of your family to give you a rough estimate. Your birth certificate may contain your date of birth. Knowing your precise time of birth will help you identify your rising sign. If possible, limit the time to at least two hours in the morning or evening.

The Location of Your Birth

Taking into account your birth location will also be crucial, primarily because of time zone differences. If you're unsure of this information, ask your parents or check your birth certificate.

Calculate the Time Difference

Time intervals are two hours apart on a rising sign chart. You may need to make some adjustments to certain areas since the sunrise could be after or before 5:30 when you were born. The chart may not work unless your date of birth is modified. Daylight savings time may also need to be considered.

- Subtract 1-2 hours from your birth time if the sunrise was earlier than 5:30
- You should add 1-2 hours to your birth time if the sunrise was much later than 5:30
- Deduct an hour from the time you were if your date of birth was during daylight saving time

A Farmer's Almanac, published during your birth year, is a great place to find this information.

Find Your Sun Sign

Identifying your rising sign requires knowledge of your sun sign. Probably the most familiar Zodiac sign to you. Depending on what day you were born, your Sun sign can reveal a lot about your personality.

- Capricorn (December 22- January 19)
- Sagittarius (November 22- December 21)
- Scorpio (October 23- November 21)
- Libra (September 23- October 22)
- Virgo (August 23- September 22)
- Leo (July 23- August 22)
- Cancer (June 21 - July 22)
- Gemini (May 21 - June 20)

- Taurus (April 20- May 20)
- Aries (March 21- April 19)
- Pisces (February 19- March 20)
- Aquarius (January 20- February 18)

Check out a Rising Sign Chart

On a rising sign chart, the twelve sun signs are displayed horizontally. Two-hour windows are displayed on the vertical axis. Navigate through the sun signs until you find yours. Calculating your birth time requires consideration of your local sunrise.

Below is a guide to your rising sign, the planets, zodiac signs, and houses so you can begin to piece together a complete chart.

ZODIAC	GLYPH	PLANET	GLYPH	HOUSE
ARIES	♈	MARS	♂	1ST
TAURUS	♉	VENUS	♀	2ND
GEMINI	♊	MERCURY	☿	3RD
CANCER	♋	MOON	☽	4TH
LEO	♌	SUN	☉	5TH
VIRGO	♍	MERCURY	☿	6TH
LIBRA	♎	VENUS	♀	7TH
SCORPIO	♏	PLUTO/MARS	♇/♂	8TH
SAGITTARIUS	♐	JUPITER	♃	9TH
CAPRICORN	♑	SATURN	♄	10TH

AQUARIUS	♒	URANUS	⛢	11TH
PISCES	♓	NEPTUNE	♆	12TH

* Another glyph for Pluto is ♇

Astrology is complicated, and no matter how much we simplify our sun-rising horoscopes, learning our rising signs can still be quite complex. Nonetheless, with this comprehensive guide to discovering your rising sign, you will soon be well on your way to discovering more about yourself and others. There is more to understanding your rising signs in the next chapter.

Chapter 3: Understanding Your Rising Sign

There is something frightening about identifying the unknown. This is why many people find identifying their rising sign challenging. The reason is that this aspect of astrology offers so much potential. So much of what we don't know about ourselves and others are hidden beneath the swirling glyphs, conflicting symbols, and confusing birth charts.

The best way to look at it is to remember that no matter how far back you go, through your adult life, angsty teenage years, carefree childhood, all the way back to your birth - your rising sign has always been there waiting for you to discover it. And why might that be? Knowing your rising sign can provide essential insight into who you are. There is no better place to delve deeply into the crevasses of who we really are than here.

Through chapter one, we went into the specifics of what constitutes a rising sign and why it is an essential aspect of astrology and the discovery of the self. In chapter two, we took a hopefully not-too-confusing look at a birth chart and how using one can help you identify your own rising sign. In this chapter, we will go through some of the more pertinent reasons why knowing your rising sign is necessary and what it can offer you in the long term. Then we'll take an exciting look at each specific rising sign and its characteristics.

Benefits of Knowing Your Rising Sign

Astrology studies the position of the sun, moon, and planets in relation to one another in time and space. You can learn a great deal about yourself, your future life, and your place in the world by learning your rising sign. The rising signs are a treasure chest of knowledge. They reveal our hidden potential and uncover the secrets of our personality. They also give us insight into our compatibility with other signs in the birth chart. In fact, knowing your rising sign can be especially helpful because it offers you unique insights into your character. If you're interested in knowing more about your rising sign, we have all the details for you! Keep reading to learn about the benefits of knowing your rising sign.

Discover the True Self

If you're aware of your rising sign and all that it means, you'll be less surprised by negative events in your life and more likely to deal with them positively. You'll also be better able to control your emotions and cope better with stress-inducing situations. In other words, our rising signs are like the guidebook of our entire lives, taking us through life's ups and downs, repeating cycles and themes. Eventually, making us aware of the patterns we will encounter in our lives.

Better Reading

The problem with clinging to your sun sign as the only truth is that accurate sun sign horoscopes concentrate on the bigger picture. They are not tuned into the specifics. Reading for your rising sign will give your horoscopes a degree of accuracy you just can't find from sun signs alone. Sun sign predictions are almost always tailored to the current moment, which is why they aren't as accurate.

Know Your Most Compatible Signs

If you know your rising sign, you can use it to find out which other signs are most compatible with you. This can help you decide who you should date and who you should avoid. For instance, if you have a Leo rising, you are most compatible with Cancer, Taurus, and Pisces signs. Similarly, if you have a Taurus rising, you are most compatible with Cancer, Pisces, and Virgo signs.

The Bigger Picture

Undoubtedly, the rising sign plays a role in personal astrology. Besides influencing the way, we present ourselves to the world, it is also the basis for our entire birth chart (also known as the ascendant). Identifying your rising sign can help you understand your personality and become more aware of how others perceive you.

Discover the Unknown

You can gain a deeper understanding of yourself and your inner intricacies by understanding your rising sign. You can also defend yourself against those who insist horoscopes are simply generalizations. Basing your reading on the rising sign is more reliable than the sun and moon signs we see in popular media today.

Signs of the Rising (Ascendant)

Rising signs symbolize our personalities on a social level. It is the internal and external parts of ourselves. For example, understanding our rising sign helps us to understand the type of energy that drives life philosophy.

Having learned what rising signs are and how to locate yours, let's take a look at what each sign means. This is only a small glimpse of the zodiac rising signs, as a more in-depth feature will follow in the next few chapters.

The rising sign is one of the most helpful tools for understanding your personality. And knowing your rising sign can be especially helpful because it offers you unique insights into your character. Now that you know how your rising sign impacts your personality, you can use this knowledge to improve your life.

NOTE: As shallow as it may seem to characterize the physical appearance of rising signs, we have already established that the rising sign heavily influences an individual's appearance and outward manner. This can give us a better determining feature when interpreting the rising signs of others.

Aries

March 21- April 19

First Impressions

Direct, confident, courageous, and strong.

In the Chart

Mars, the god of war, rules this planet. As the rising sign of the zodiac, Aries is a courageous fighter. You are the first fire sign of the zodiac, and you are intensely competitive in nature.

You lack tact and sensitivity and can be oblivious to others' needs, preferring to act self-sufficiently. You don't rely on social approval and reinforcement as much as others do and may act on impulse and with little forethought and precision.

You see yourself as a warrior and are eager to get into action as soon as possible. Consequently, Aries lacks patience and is careless with details.

Characteristics

Walking and moving swiftly is a hallmark feature of Aries rising. As well as prominent facial features, people born with this rising sign will have visible marks or scars. Aries' features are muscular, and they have an athletic physique.

Taurus

April 20- May 20

First Impressions

Slow, attractive, sensual, and dependable.

In the Chart

As the most beloved goddess of love, and prosperity, Venus rules you. You can't help but be influenced by your sensual nature. This means you love to be active and creative with your hands.

Your Taurus rising means others view you as a rock of strength – dependable and consistent. You do things methodically, and you are extremely stubborn.

Despite appearing unfazed and collected, Taurus Rising reveals tremendous strength underneath. Due to your tenacity, you often prevail in disagreements. Your need for security is very strong, and you will not willingly change your present conditions unless forced to do so. Your home and job are all examples of tangible security.

Characteristics

In general, Taurus ascending relates to solidity, strength, and stability. Taurus rising personalities tend to weigh more because of their propensity to indulge. The most common physical attributes include broad shoulders and a stocky neck.

Gemini

May 21 - June 20

First Impressions

Adaptable, social, intelligent, witty.

In the Chart

Mercury, the divine emissary, rules a Gemini. You are destined for immense success as a public speaker because you are charming and have excellent speaking skills. Having Gemini Rising in your sign also means you learn quickly but are susceptible to being easily distracted. You value variety and an active social life.

Others like interacting with you due to your humorous and intelligent nature. Your Gemini Rising makes you social, no matter how bad you feel. Because of this, you never appear somber.

Gemini risings are generally very social and witty.
https://www.pexels.com/photo/two-women-sitting-on-white-bench-1549280/

Serious people might find your behavior silly. By not taking life to heart, you keep a lighthearted attitude and a positive outlook. Gemini Rising is a restless sign, so consistency and reliability are not your strong suits. A slow pace makes you fidgety and nervous.

Characteristics

People with Gemini rising signs are typically slim and seldom suffer from excess weight (unless they have a lot of Taurus or Cancer planets in their natal chart). They are usually always active and busy and don't enjoy staying still for long periods.

Cancer

June 21 - July 22

First Impressions

Emotional, Maternal, sensitive, nurturing.

In the Chart

The intuitive moon rules cancer rising, so you appear kind. Having a deep desire for stability and connection, your friends and family are very important to you. Cancer Rising can make it challenging for you to accept new ideas or change from the familiar.

As someone who sees the world through a deeply individual viewpoint, it can be challenging to separate yourself from assumptions and stereotypes.

Your Cancer Rising gives you a caring personality, which shows itself in your dedication and support of the people you love. The ability to understand others' emotions makes you an empath. Given your caring and understanding nature, you are easily moved by others' distress.

Characteristics

An individual with Cancer rising has a round, moon-shaped face. People with cancer also tend to gain weight, particularly on their hips. Legs are usually slim and short. Cancer Rising females are voluminous and curvy.

Leo

July 23- August 22

First Impressions

Dramatic, playful, affectionate, creative.

In the Chart

Having the powerful sun as your ruling planet makes you destined for the spotlight if you have a flair for it. You are not shy or meek, and you rarely settle for having to play second fiddle. Having a Leo Rising makes you a leader by nature, not one to like to be dictated to.

Once you become friends with someone, you are extremely loyal and will do anything to make that person happy. You are kind and generous but don't want your generosity to go unnoticed; you always expect acknowledgment and appreciation.

When you have a Leo Rising, you always present the best possible face to the world, and you rarely show anyone when you are hurt or discouraged.

Characteristics

A Leo rising's hair is often their dominant feature and resembles a lion's mane. The head and facial features of these people are also strong. Having a regal disposition makes them a person who demands respect. Exaggerated mannerisms are characteristic of the Leo rising individual.

Virgo

August 23- September 22

First Impressions

Innocent, humble, shy, helpful.

In the Chart

Mercury is the governing planet of Virgo risings, so they are inquisitive and expressive. As a protector of the zodiac, Virgo is extremely compassionate and will take a supporting role rather than the lead. You are modest, unobtrusive, and often quiet or shy.

When it comes to your own assessment of yourself, you are often very critical of yourself because of your humility; you strive for perfection. Often, when you doubt that you can live up to your own expectations, you won't try. You cannot express your spontaneous nature when you are not confident in yourself and your abilities. Yet, what you do, you do very well.

You deeply understand right and wrong due to your Virgo Rising. This unflappable disposition you display is evident to others. In spite of your kindness and caring, your lack of evident sympathy may prevent others from seeing your helpful qualities.

Characteristics

The Virgo ascendant is associated with small, well-shaped facial features and fair, smooth skin. A Virgo rising has high nervous energy and is extremely sensitive. Presentable and well-groomed, this individual is usually well-dressed.

Libra

September 23- October 22

First Impressions

Indecisive, charming, peacemaker, graceful.

In the Chart

Those born under Libra rising are flirty and ethereal, as Venus is Libra rising ruling planet. Conflicts are settled by finding common ground and similarities rather than focusing on the points of disagreement.

The Libra Rising expresses a strong desire for harmonious relationships and a willingness to be fair. Others' opinions easily influence young Libra risings because of your desire to be liked. Beauty is something you appreciate, and style and art are important to you in everything you do.

You are not an independent loner due to your Libra Rising; you enjoy being part of a close couple. The problem, though, is that you are prone to being overly dependent on your partner and struggle with developing an identity away from your relationship.

Characteristics

Libras rising generally have a strong body, and the details of their face are distinct. When they reach middle age, however, their bodies get heavier. Their politeness and elegance are evident in their behavior.

Scorpio

October 23- November 21

First Impressions

Powerful, magnetic, mysterious, intense.

In the Chart

Scorpio rising is ruled by Mars, the warrior, and Pluto, the ruling planet of the underworld. You have been through some things which made you guarded, especially if your chart includes other Scorpio influences. Despite your reserved demeanor, you are enthusiastic and driven.

Getting something requires quiet persistence and dedication. You don't fear danger or challenges because you're driven and enthusiastic.

Immediate intuition usually determines whether a reaction is favorable or unfavorable.

When you devote your emotional life to a relationship, you are deeply committed and dedicated, expecting loyalty in return. When someone has wronged you, you may respond with the same passion you once felt for them.

Characteristics

One of the most distinguishing characteristics of Scorpio-rising individuals is their large, penetrating eyes. It is common for the skin to be shiny or sallow, with sharp features. The body usually has a lot of muscle, strength, and thickness. Lack of emotional expression is a typical characteristic of this personality type.

Sagittarius

November 22- December 21

First Impressions

Inspiring, cheerful, restless, and optimistic.

In the Chart

Due to Jupiter's rule over Sagittarius, you consistently come out on top. A lot of the time, you dream about future possibilities and long for an experience more fulfilling than what you've had till now. Having your ascendant in Sagittarius, you like to have goals, but once you reach them, you move on.

This rising sign cannot withstand long-term confinement, and those close to you must respect your desire for independence.

There are times when you tend to exaggerate your excitement. Usually, you speak a lot, make lots of promises, and are pretty persuasive. A generous spirit permeates every aspect of your life.

Characteristics

The most distinguishing features of a person are their facial roundness and a wide smile. Sagittarius risings are often awkward and clumsy. Their gestures are excessive and grandiose. An individual rising in Sagittarius is usually energetic but dislikes exercise and tends to overeat.

Capricorn

December 22- January 19

First Impressions

Determined, reserved, refined, and serious.

In the Chart

You often approach the world with caution and reservation since you don't see it as do not a welcoming or secure place. You also have a wild side, which can be addictive to lovers. When young, you were already worldly and cynical.

In Capricorn Rising, you plan carefully to make the most impact with your activities. It takes dedication and persistence to achieve what you want. Some of the time, you don't ask for or need help from others.

When it comes to softer feelings, you dislike sentimentality. Instead of buying goods as fleeting indulgences, you invest in long-term, profitable investments. It is easy for you to live without because you are disciplined and self-controlled.

Characteristics

Those with this rising sign tend to be lean and thin with bronze skin tones and sharp features. The rise of Capricorn can make this person seem distant.

Aquarius

January 20- February 18

First Impressions

Funny, creative, quirky, independent.

In the Chart

As eccentric as you are, Uranus governs your horoscope. You are usually passionately dedicated to the community or philanthropic causes.

Fairness and equity are integral parts of Aquarius Rising's philosophy and outlook on life. The collective good matters as much to you as your own health.

In your interactions, you express impersonal goodwill. Many of your close relationships are based on shared ideals and principles rather than emotional ties, and you probably have many acquaintances but few close friends.

Characteristics

There is usually a quickness and unpredictableness to their mannerisms and walk. The way they behave or dress leans towards the unusual, causing others to notice. Their features are distinct and aesthetically pleasing.

Pisces

February 19- March 20

First Impressions

Sensitive, easygoing, impractical, imaginative.

In the Chart

You are ruled by the mysterious Neptune, which makes you alluring. This rising sign is compassionate and empathetic, with a positive perspective on life. Due to your distaste for confrontation and your timidity, you are likely to retreat in these situations.

In light of your Pisces Rising, your emotional balance and well-being need to spend time in quiet solitude in a peaceful environment. As a child, you frequently retreated into fantasy whenever life got too stressful or repetitive.

In Pisces Rising, people feel attracted to you because they sense your sympathetic nature. In many situations, Pisces rising will give to others even when they realize they are being exploited.

Characteristics

Individuals born under the Pisces rising sign are relatively small and well-proportioned. This sign is also associated with large, dreamy eyes and long, thick lashes on the ascendant. It is common for the feet and legs to be small and the arms and legs to be short. Usually, they speak softly and are shy.

This short breakdown of the rising signs should give you a better indication of what to look for on a birth chart. They are also quite useful when doing a reading. So, if you're interested in getting deeper into astrology, knowing the characteristics of the individual rising signs as they relate to a person can open up a wealth of knowledge.

Continue reading about the rising signs in the following chapter to discover even more.

Chapter 4: Aries Rising and Taurus Rising

Now that you know what rising signs are, how they affect your personality, and how to identify yours, we'll discuss all the rising signs and their different personality traits in this part of the book. This chapter will focus on Aries rising and Taurus rising signs. We will discuss their mindsets and how a person born under these signs acts in the different areas of their lives like work, relationships, home, etc.

Aries Rising Sign

Aries Rising's Glyph

Aries symbol.
Bruce The Deus, CC BY-SA 4.0 <https://creativecommons.org/licenses/by-sa/4.0>, via Wikimedia Commons: https://commons.wikimedia.org/wiki/File:Deus_Aries.png

Aries Rising's Personality

Aries is a fire sign, and a person with Aries as their ascending sign can feel its fiery hotness in their attitude and even appearance. They are bold and hotheaded, which can be great qualities in most cases. However, at times, it can overwhelm those around them. Mars, the planet named after the god of war, is Aries's ruling planet, and Aries rising individuals can feel its impact on their personality. There is always a fire burning inside them that drives them to fight for what they want and always come out on top. These individuals are very energetic and enthusiastic, especially at social events. They are the life and soul of the party. Excited and passionate, everyone enjoys their lively conversation. However, boredom is their biggest enemy. They enjoy living an active life and like to have something to do.

As a result of the fiery energy inside of them, they don't like to sit on the sidelines, and they are always the first to take action. Impatient and impulsive, they would rather do something than sit and wait. However, they usually act before they think. Aries rising is a competitive sign; it is all or nothing with them. Although there is nothing wrong with being competitive in certain areas in life, they usually put themselves under a lot of pressure. Failure or losing is never an option.

People born under an Aries rising sign are independent individuals. The only person they rely on is themselves. Although there is nothing wrong with being independent, Aries can take it too far. They won't ask for help even when they need it the most. They usually depend on their inner strength and resilience. There is no denying that they can handle anything life throws at them, but they need to understand there is no shame in asking for help.

These individuals are straightforward and say it as it is. They don't care if people judge them or mistake them for being aggressive. They don't have ill intentions or want to hurt people; they are simply direct, honest, and blunt. They don't struggle with making decisions because they would rather act quickly than waste time thinking things over. However, some decisions require patience and time. As a result of their impatience, they usually don't finish projects and tend to flit from one project to the other.

They are brave risk-takers and are not concerned about consequences. The ambition of an Aries rising knows no bounds. They will do whatever it takes and will not stop until they reach their goals. At times, Aries rising can be selfish and insensitive to other people's feelings. However, they are kind and considerate when it comes to the people they care about. Aries rising individuals like to always look their best which is why they focus on their appearance. Their love for life is contagious, as is their passion and cheerful personality. Ruled by Mars, Aries rising usually has a short temper. However, they tend to cool down quickly and don't hold grudges.

Aries Rising's Mindset

We can summarize the Aries rising mindset in three words: new beginnings, emergence, and creativity. They are always in a hurry, and everything must happen right now. They happily venture out to the unknown because they see the advantages of taking risks. They never shy away from taking chances, especially on things most people would be reluctant to try.

Aries Rising at Work

When Aries rising walks into a room, everyone will notice them because they have a very strong presence. However, they are usually stable and grounding. They are critical thinkers and have strong work ethics, which help them advance in their careers. They don't let adversity get to them. If a plan doesn't work, they make the necessary adjustments and get the job done. Aries rising excel when working alone; however, they can work well with a team. They are born to lead, not to follow, which is why they usually seek leading and management positions at work. They are people who get the job done without making a fuss. These natural-born leaders excel in positions like CEOs or having their own businesses.

Aries Rising in Relationships

Because they are usually competitive and extremely focused on their work and projects, some people may think that an Aries rising person may not have time for relationships. However, it doesn't matter how busy they are. They find ways to show those closest to them that they are also important. They will never make the ones they care about feel like they don't matter. They are always there for them, especially when they need help. They aren't the type of people to change their priorities for others. However, if they make someone a top priority, then they must mean a tremendous amount to them. They aren't the type of people to be hung up on being in relationships. They will come through for the people they love, and if they make a promise or a plan, they will always keep them. Aries rising individuals are known to be loyal in a committed relationship.

Aries Rising in Friendships

It doesn't matter if someone is a casual friend or a close friend; an Aries rising will always be supportive and help others with any problems they have. Even if a person simply needs someone to listen, an Aries rising will never get tired of listening to someone talk and will show them nothing but understanding. In fact, they are very empathetic individuals and will go above and beyond for the people they love. Their fighting nature doesn't only apply to them and their goals; they will also fight for people close to them. They are very private individuals that could be mistaken for being aloof. However, they are an "open book" with those close to them, like their partners and their best friends.

Aries Rising in Love

When Aries rising is in love, they may not stop talking about their partners to others. They will want to show their loved ones off to the whole world because they know they are amazing and want others to see it too. They also want everyone else to know how important and special this person is to them. If there is an important event, whether professional or personal, they will ensure that their partner is by your side. That said, an Aries rising doesn't let their lives revolve around their partner, but they will still be there for them no matter what.

Aries Rising at Home

Aries rising people love their family and include them in all special events. Their home is always open to their family members and the friends they consider family as well. Their home is their safe haven, so they make sure it is a comfortable and relaxing place where they can unwind after a long day at work.

Taurus Rising Sign

Taurus Rising's Glyph

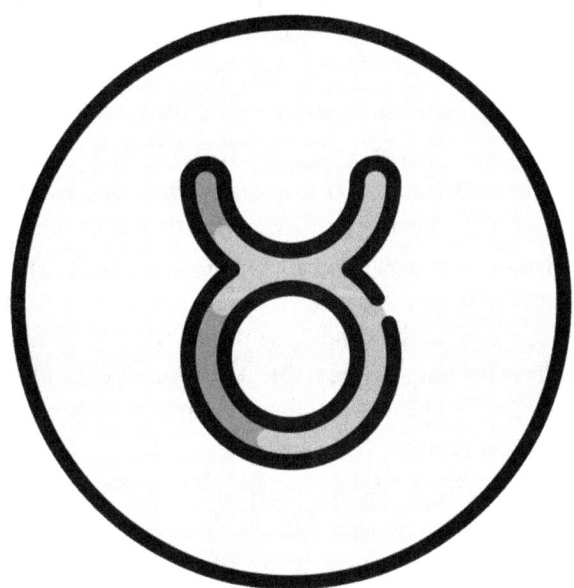

Taurus symbol.
Bruce The Deus, CC BY-SA 4.0 <https://creativecommons.org/licenses/by-sa/4.0>, via Wikimedia Commons: https://commons.wikimedia.org/wiki/File:Deus_Taurus.png

Taurus Rising's Personality

Taurus rising individuals are organized, hard-working, loyal, and patient. They have expensive tastes and an appreciation for the finer things in life. However, they can also be jealous, lazy, and stubborn. They are usually traditional individuals who prefer structure. They are productive and perfectionists. They avoid drama, which is why they are usually quiet in social situations. Whether it is their work or love life, they know exactly what they want and aren't afraid to go after it. They like the simple things in life and thrive in a quiet environment away from any tension or disturbance. For this reason, they always surround themselves with like-minded people who like to spread positivity. They are very stable and focused when it comes to achieving their goals.

Taurus rising individuals are loyal to a fault to their family and friends. They will always show up for the people they love offering unconditional love and support. People tend to gravitate toward them because of their agreeable and easy-going personalities. They are extremely consistent and rarely ever change their mind about something. It is almost impossible to sway or influence their opinions. However, this trait can have its disadvantages. They are stuck seeing things from one side and refuse to consider other perspectives. These individuals can be extremely rigid when it comes to their ideas, and they are resistant to change.

For this reason, Taurus rising individuals are considered very stubborn. If they set their mind to do something, nothing and no one can change it. Occasional stubbornness can be a good quality, but it can also have disadvantages as it prevents them from taking a different approach or going after new opportunities and experiences. These individuals are extremely focused and do things at their own pace. They don't appreciate being rushed or distracted. If they step out of their comfort zone, they will be surprised by what is out there.

Taurus rising individuals are extremely cautious with how they approach certain life situations. Unlike Aries' rising sign, they don't take risks or jump into things without thinking. They like to play it safe and weigh all their options first. However, not everyone appreciates this quality, especially these days when most people make decisions on the go. Although they are sensible individuals, others may see them as conservative or stand-offish. There is nothing wrong with being practical but remember to enjoy yourself every time.

Ruled by Venus, the planet of love and beauty, Taurus rising individuals are extremely sensual and feminine, although their practical and rigid personalities may make them seem otherwise. They know how to celebrate life's simplest pleasures like good food or hot sex. However, they may overindulge and value material possessions at times. They are also physically affectionate and love to greet the people they love with a warm hug. Another similarity they share with Aries is that they usually pay close attention to their appearance. They are creative, skilled, and disciplined, which makes them excel in whatever field they choose.

Taurus Rising's Mindset

Young Taurus rising individuals may seem older and more mature than their age because they have figured out a few things in life. As a result of having Venus as their ruling sign, they want to enjoy life and surround themselves with beautiful things. They like nice scents, a beautiful environment, and a serene atmosphere. When someone wants to win their heart, they can take them out into nature to see beautiful scenery like the mountains. In fact, they thrive in natural and quiet settings when they can be at peace and hate it if someone disturbs them. They would rather stay at home and watch movies than engage in someone's drama. They want to lead a peaceful and quiet life without any complications. However, some people may mistake them for being boring, but they are far from it. They just like to live a drama-free life and don't concern themselves with small matters. In fact, they can be the life and soul of the party if they can have interesting and fun conversations with others.

Taurus Rising at Work

Taurus-rising individuals thrive when they are part of a community which is why they do well when working in a team. However, if someone disagrees with them, their stubborn and headstrong personality takes over. They are very creative individuals and enjoy sharing their ideas with other people. If someone has a different idea, they will happily listen to it. They may even experiment with new things but eventually, they will go back to their familiar tried and tested. They are very curious about people, especially in the work environment. They are interested in discovering the motivation behind other people's actions and what drives them to act a certain way. If they find someone acting differently, they won't pass judgment. They will give advice when necessary or challenge people to help them see things from a different perspective.

Taurus Rising in Relationships

Taurus rising individuals can be jealous and possessive in relationships and find it difficult to end things. They are very loyal when they are in love, but they can also be very intense. These individuals are very sensual and thrive in stable relationships. Their calmness hides their very passionate nature. They are usually very private within relationships. However, they don't intend any malice; they simply value their privacy. These individuals would rather have light-hearted conversations than engaging in heart-to-heart or serious conversations. They don't like showing their vulnerable side because they want to appear charming in front of their loved ones.

Things are different when they start trusting someone, as they find it a lot easier to get close to them. However, they will still not open up or share their innermost feelings. They are great listeners and make other people feel comfortable enough to open up to them. Thanks to their loyal nature, these people's secrets are usually kept safe. They prefer to listen than to talk as this can help them learn more about the people in their lives.

Taurus Rising in Friendship

As a result of their private nature, they may confuse their friends at first. They usually don't share anything with them, making it frustrating to be a Taurus rising's friend at first. However, once a person gains their trust, they will reveal their truest self. However, they will still keep a part of themselves hidden from the rest of the world.

Taurus Rising in Love

Taurus rising individuals make great partners when they are in love. In fact, love is the only thing that can make them venture out of their comfort zone because they are willing to do anything for their loved ones. Although they are very thoughtful and giving, they struggle with opening up or expressing their feelings. They need to trust the other person before showing their weakness or vulnerability. Romantic and charming, they will show they care in their own way, like remembering certain details about the person or their birthday. They will be emotionally reserved initially, but only because they like to take things slowly. They will express their love only when they are 100% sure about their feelings.

Taurus Rising at Home

Think of a Taurus rise like Monica Gellar from Friends. A person can't just move around their furniture. Because they have expensive taste, they usually have high-quality furniture or unique pieces of art. They basically have the best in everything because they enjoy the attention and showing off. However, since they crave stability, they will make sure to choose long-lasting things. They will also focus on their home's lighting as it sets the vibe for the place.

Quiz

Is your rising sign Aries or Taurus? Take this quiz to find out.

1. Do you make fast decisions?
   - Yes
   - No
2. Would you quit your job to start your own business?
   - Yes
   - No
3. Do you work on more than one project at a time and rarely finish any?
   - Yes
   - No
4. Do your friends often tell you that you need to be more patient?
   - Yes
   - No
5. Do you lead an active and fast-paced life?
   - Yes
   - No
6. If someone asks you to go bungee jumping tomorrow (or on any adventurous experience), will you go?
   - Yes
   - No
7. Do you get frustrated when you have a lot of free time on your hands?
   - Yes
   - No
8. Do you have a hot temper?
   - Yes
   - No

9. Do you say things as they are without sugar-coating your words?
   - Yes
   - No

Results

If you answered "Yes" to most questions, your rising sign is Aries. If you answered mostly "No," then your rising sign is Taurus.

Taurus and Aries zodiac signs have a few things in common. For instance, their work ethics, loyalty to their partner, stubbornness, appreciation for privacy, and paying attention to their appearance. However, they are different in other aspects. Aries rising individuals are risk-takers and like to do things fast, while Taurus rising individuals are calm and like to work at their own pace.

Chapter 5: Gemini Rising and Cancer Rising

Following the pattern of the previous chapter, this one breaks down another two similar rising signs - Gemini and Cancer. You'll learn about each sign's personality, how their mind works and how they relate to people around them -whether it comes to professional or personal relationships. And, if you are curious about whether your rising sign is Gemini or Cancer, you'll also be able to find out at the end of the chapter.

Gemini Rising Sign

Gemini Rising's Glyph

Gemini symbol.
Bruce The Deus, CC BY-SA 4.0 <https://creativecommons.org/licenses/by-sa/4.0>, via Wikimedia Commons: https://commons.wikimedia.org/wiki/File:Deus_Gemini.png

Gemini Rising's Personality

Ruled by the planet of communication and intellect, Gemini rising is characterized by an inquisitive and sharp personality. They are known to be open-minded and vivacious, often surrounded by an air of mischief.

They always have something exciting to add to their conversations, whether that is an interesting piece of information they've recently learned or simple gossip. This sign finds everything so fascinating that they can't help but ask questions, especially if they're in a new setting. They notice everything, right down to the last detail make sure they don't miss anything interesting. Since not many people possess this ability, it gives Gemini rising a clear advantage as they'll now have even more information to share. However, keeping up with their conversations can be a grueling task. When excited, Gemini rising will speak fast and jump through topics so quickly that they must be reminded to slow down. They usually respond well to this and will try to listen to others as well. This sign will soak up everything they hear. If you tell them something and forget about it, they will certainly remember it and will be happy to recite it to you.

Due to their adaptable nature, they thrive on variety and are happy to experiment. While they are often criticized for this type of behavior, it helps them see things from a different perspective - which not many people are capable of doing. Together with these traits, the free-flowing personality of the Gemini rising sign also makes them easily influenced by the other signs. Since their individual characteristics will vary depending on other influences on their chart, people born under the Gemini rising signs are the hardest personalities to pin down. And sometimes, it even creates difficulties for Gemini rising themselves when trying to analyze their own behavior.

Gemini Rising's Mindset

Since communication is so important to this sign, the easiest way to analyze the mindset of Gemini rising is through their social interactions. They use their wit and intellect to win people over. While this may not be a conscious act initially, they will want to keep them around as soon as they come across an interesting person. This is because the more interconnected they are within different communities, the more likely their chances are to explore new horizons. They know that listening is just as key to successful communication as speaking, so they will make a point of being good listeners. Because of this, they can absorb an enormous amount of information they can use to their advantage. They have curious minds and will find a purpose for everything they learn. They are constantly analyzing their environment, which lets them find creative solutions to every problem they encounter. Their inventive mind often drives them to take on projects they don't finish simply because they lose interest and find something more exciting to do.

Gemini Rising at Work

Gemini rising constantly needs change, which is also reflected in their career choices. They'll opt for professions where they'll have plenty of opportunities to grow and develop new skills. And when they've learned everything they can at their current workplace, they'll move on to another job that lets them expand their mind even further. They also prefer working in an environment where they can communicate with people regularly. They can adapt quickly to any changes in the circumstances and love to find solutions to problems. The more chaotic the atmosphere is, the better. It will stimulate their mind, which works even better under pressure. Gemini rising may want to work with children because they can keep up with kids better than most people. They can also work in any creative field, as their mind is always filled with ideas.

Gemini Rising in Relationships

Because of their tendency to constantly seek novelties, Gemini rising isn't exactly known as someone who settles into relationships easily. They will constantly seek new acquaintances but may abandon them just as quickly when they lose interest. This is not to say they don't want to establish a committed relationship. It just means they are waiting for the perfect match or someone who challenges them and keeps up with their adventures and fast-paced life. Gemini rising will be a fiercely loyal partner when they find this person, even putting aside their closely guarded interests. They will go out of their way to spend time with their partner and give them everything they need.

Gemini Rising in Friendships

Gemini risings thrive on social interactions. They'll master the art of navigating multiple conversations and keeping up with everyone around them without even trying. They do put effort into keeping up with the friendships they value. The fact that they have a large social circle doesn't mean they are close to all those people. Despite this, people seem to gravitate towards them and will try to make friends with them. Of course, Gemini rising will be happy to talk to them and form new friendships though they'll choose who they associate with. This sign will be playful when they are with close friends and display incredible wit. They like to inform their friends about everything they've recently learned. Depending on their zodiac placements, Gemini rising may or may not share their opinion through other means. Introverts with this rising sign may feel more comfortable sharing everything they learned through art. Either way, their friends will always feel comfortable talking to them about anything.

Gemini Rising in Love

Unlike some other rising signs, Gemini is not exactly subtle about their love life. They are typically very blunt about their intentions and will use shocking statements and jokes to pique the interest of a potential partner. They are interested in people who can keep up with their intense communication. They show interest by asking as many questions as possible as if they were conducting a job interview. With a potential romantic partner, Gemini may also put conscious effort into maintaining eye contact - which is not something they usually do as their minds are too busy to focus. They also show affection by touch and offer a sincere friendship, which takes a significant effort on their part.

Gemini Rising at Home

Thriving in fast-paced environments, Gemini rising isn't exactly the domestic type. They don't feel the need to seek out the comfort of their home life, at least not if they don't have a trustworthy person to share it with. If they establish a stable home life, they want it to be dynamic, bright, and welcoming to the many guests they'll be receiving. However, even in this case, they look at home as a temporary setting, as they will most likely move on to a different one as soon as they hear the call of a new adventure. For them, home is more about who they surround themselves with and not a place to spend time in.

Cancer Rising Sign

Cancer Rising's Glyph

Cancer symbol.
Bruce The Deus, CC BY-SA 4.0 <https://creativecommons.org/licenses/by-sa/4.0>, via Wikimedia Commons: https://commons.wikimedia.org/wiki/File:Deus_Cancer.png

Cancer Rising's Personality

The core personality of a Cancer rising is built on values like resilience and being attuned to people around them. They constantly interact with the world and care about how they are viewed. This sign isn't afraid to launch into new ventures, driven by their emotions or by someone else. While some would consider being so emotional a weakness, Cancer rising learns how to make the most of it by turning it into their greatest strength. Their shining personalities are a balm to others, but they can absorb other people's energies. If this other person has a sensitive personality, the loyal Cancer rising will display the same traits. These displays of loyalty often only last until the person leaves the room. As soon as a different type of energy surrounds the Cancer, their personality will change to match it. Their personality is also affected by the moon's cycles - which probably explains why their moods shift so often. One minute they feel peachy and act with empathy, and the next, they will close off and retreat into their figurative shells. And just as the moon goes through different cycles, so will a Cancer rising sign. This allows them to experience a multifaceted life many people only dream of having.

Not only do Cancer rising have highly intuitive personalities, but they don't hide it either. They won't shy away from expressing their opinion or sharing their emotions and personal information. They are happy to embrace different circumstances and will tell you what they think. And if they don't, their mood will signal whatever type of energy they are currently affected by. At the same time, they also like to control everything around them - including what they show to others of themselves. It doesn't always work, but they are much happier if they can share only positive thoughts and emotions. More likely than not, at your first meeting, you'll get the feeling that they are easy-going people with a friendly attitude when, in fact, they are probably just as nervous as the next person. They will certainly worry about what impression they'll make on you, even if you can't tell this at the beginning.

Cancer Rising's Mindset

Many of the Cancer risings' thought processes are ruled by their emotions. On the one hand, this sign values their emotions and will often tap into them when they are trying to make a decision. On the other hand, Cancer rising is also sensitive to other people's feelings, and being tuned into these emotional stimuli often overwhelms their thoughts. Despite this, their philosophy is to help out whenever they can, even if it costs them their stability. After all, they can always regroup and continue with their life later on. They also consider that the level of loyalty they give has to be earned. They would rather be cautious at the beginning, so they can let their guard down later, than go all in at first and be surprised by their mistake. Another trait of their mindset is that they love order in all aspects of their lives. If something is out of order, they will do everything they can to remedy the situation. Not only that, but they will offer to do this for others as well.

Cancer Rising at Work

People with a Cancer rising sign are natural-born leaders and love working in a fast-paced setting. They will constantly work toward new goals, and if they have to compete against others to reach them, even better. They are not ruthless or unfeeling toward their competition. They simply love to feel like they are moving forward with their professional lives. Since they thrive on a structured schedule, Cancer rising will choose self-employment. They'll even consider careers that many consider too risky, such as creative arts or running their own freelance businesses. If they believe they can do it, they will follow through, no matter what anyone else says. Depending on their zodiac placements, Cancer rising may prefer a career that keeps them on the move, or they may want to work with people. Their compassionate and tender nature makes them perfect for becoming a therapist.

Cancer Rising in Relationships

Starting a relationship with a Cancer rising isn't the easiest thing to do. They will be interested and even act friendly, but some of their cordiality will be superficial. And while they don't particularly worry that someone will hurt them, they are very picky about how they share their emotions. They will need to test their partner and get to know them before they are ready to form deeper emotional bonds. Partners shouldn't be surprised if they can't get much out of them on the personal front, either. Cancer rising is very aware of the importance of surrounding themselves with people who positively impact their life. The person they form a relationship with is someone who affects their life's course, so it's understandably crucial for them to be able to trust that person. In well-established relationships, Cancer rising is a partner who always motivates and challenges their partners to take on new adventures. They can only be happy with someone who shares their love for being in motion and helping others.

Cancer Rising in Friendships

Cancer rising is a very wise and dependable sign. Most of the time, they are the friend that cheers you up with a joke or two when you are feeling down or simply lets you vent about the stressful day you had at your job. However, this can be draining for their own emotional state, and Cancer rising isn't afraid to admit this. They will state that they need some time alone and expect everyone to respect their emotions just as they've respected anyone else. That's not to say they won't feel guilty for not being there for their friends 24/7. However, to avoid feeling overstimulated, they must take time off. Once they are recharged, they will return to looking out for their friends and showing their loyalty whenever needed. In fact, they are so good at matching their friends' energies that someone outside their social circle will never be able to tell whether a Cancer rising is expressing their opinion or just being loyal to their friends.

Cancer Rising in Love

Cancer rising is always looking for the mysterious and all-consuming love - but when they find it, they are careful how to approach this situation. They are protective of their feelings and rarely express them to their partner, which complicates their love life. They will show affection through other means, such as seeking physical proximity, asking about the partner's interests, and making silly jokes. Rather than telling someone that they are interested in them, they will drop little hints. However, expecting the other person to pick up their signal often backfires as their messages tend to be far less obvious than they think they are.

Cancer Rising at Home

Because of their nurturing nature, Cancer rising considers home life extremely important. They like to come home after their latest adventure and rest for a bit before moving on to the next one. Because of this, they want their home to be inviting and will take great care of it and who they invite into it. At the same time, they like things to be organized, as it helps them run everything smoothly.

Quiz

Is your rising sign Gemini or Cancer? Take this quiz to find out.

1. Do you often take on a broad point of view rather than a deep one?
   - Yes
   - No

2. Would you quit your job to travel around the world?
   - Yes
   - No
3. Do you constantly need to do something, even if it's only talking to someone?
   - Yes
   - No
4. Do you get bored easily in familiar settings?
   - Yes
   - No
5. Do you have an active and multifaceted social life?
   - Yes
   - No
6. Are you quick to adapt to changes in your life?
   - Yes
   - No
7. Is being an intelligent person with unique interests the first impression you leave?
   - Yes
   - No
8. Are you insecure about your skills and abilities?
   - Yes
   - No
9. Have you ever been told that you ask too many questions?
   - Yes
   - No

Results

If you answered "Yes" to most questions, your rising sign is Gemini. If you answered mostly "No," then your rising sign is Cancer.

Gemini has an active mind and a tendency to communicate and soak in knowledge any way it comes. They are social butterflies ready to embrace variety and will even seek it out. The reason lies in their own dual personality - Gemini is open-minded about other people's feelings and opinions, yet so insecure about their own. While Cancer rising is similarly affectionate and generous with their feelings, they require more stability. They also place more importance on past events and will seek refuge in familiar places from time to time.

Chapter 6: Leo Rising and Virgo Rising

Now that we've looked at the rising signs for Aries, Taurus, Gemini, and Cancer, we'll look at the Leo and Virgo rising signs. As in previous chapters, we look at the personalities and mindsets of individuals with these signs, as well as how they act at work, in relationships and friendships, at home, and when they are in love.

Leo Rising Sign

Leo Rising's Glyph

Leo symbol.
Bruce The Deus, CC BY-SA 4.0 <https://creativecommons.org/licenses/by-sa/4.0>, via Wikimedia Commons: https://commons.wikimedia.org/wiki/File:Deus_Leo.png

The word "Leo" means "lion." In Greek mythology, the constellation was associated with the legendary Nemean Lion. This glyph is a stylized representation of a lion's head and tail or its mane and spine.

Some versions of this glyph include curved shapes inside the circle. These shapes are interpreted as stylized representations of the two halves of a heart.

Leo Rising's Personality

Leo is a fire sign; people born under it burn as brightly as the sun. They are bright and friendly and are the life and soul of the party as soon as they step into a room. They are confident, optimistic, warm, and always ready to take a stand for things they truly believe in.

This attitude toward life earns them a lot of friends, and they're rarely seen alone. These individuals like to stand out and, like the sun, are bright and flashy, so you won't miss them when you see them in a group.

At the same time, they have a good helping of self-regard. While self-confidence isn't bad, people born under Leo Rising can occasionally take things to the next level and become arrogant and egotistic. This can have a negative impact on their personal relationships.

People born under Leo rising love to show off. This isn't limited to boasting about their own achievements – they also take pride in their loved ones, particularly their children. At the same time, they can be controlling. They consider their creations as extensions of themselves, including their spouses and children.

Because of this, these individuals will find it difficult to collaborate with or work under people with stronger personalities than their own.

At the same time, people with this rising sign have a natural tendency for leadership. As natural-born leaders, their charisma makes them even more attractive to the people they lead. They love nothing better than being visibly appreciated and cheered on, and a leadership position gives them exactly this opportunity.

These individuals have a powerful desire to feel important and gain the approval of others. If they feel they are receiving the appreciation that they deserve, they return to their fun, life-of-the-party personality. However, if they feel not enough people are noticing them, they can get stuck sulking until they get the attention they need.

Leo rising individuals also tend to have larger-than-life aspirations and attitudes. They are all about grand gestures, and they believe that, more than anything else, life is meant to be enjoyed to the fullest. These individuals live life royally, as implied by the symbol (lion) of their rising sign.

If the pride of these individuals is injured, their temper will flare easily. However, though Leo risings are quick-tempered, they're also inherently easy-going, which means their anger rarely lasts for long.

Leo risings are faithful to a fault and will never cheat or harm the people they consider their own. At the same time, their lives are bound to be dramatic, so the people close to them should expect that the Leo rising in their life will constantly demand attention, playing and discarding many roles until they find one that suits them.

No matter what traits the Leo rising in your life shows as prominent, one thing is for certain: living with these individuals is certainly never boring!

Leo Rising's Mindset

The Leo rising mindset can be best described as one of clear and strong intentions. These individuals take pride in clearly understanding where they want to go, and no matter where this journey takes them, they will not falter until they achieve what they want. In some ways, they can be described as having a one-track mind, though this isn't necessarily a fair description; it's closer to the truth to say that once they have decided on a goal, there's very little in the world that can sway them away from it.

This is because Leo Risings do not tolerate failure. They value having the comfort of a plan and don't do well when forced to deviate from it. Luckily, they also know the value of surrounding themselves with high-achieving people, so they're rarely unsuccessful.

Leo Rising at Work

As mentioned, Leo risings values have a plan to fall back upon. They won't be spontaneous and unexpected in their decisions, but this doesn't mean they don't take risks - it simply means they aren't fans of "winging" things. If they're forced to work without having a plan, they'll become stressed and irritated.

They value hard work and will always conduct themselves professionally - but, at the same time, their charm means their every action seems calm and leisurely. Don't be fooled by the façade, however - there's a reason Leo risings shine so brightly, and it's *not because of a carefree attitude to life and work.*

Leo Rising in Relationships

In relationships, these individuals are always willing to lend an empathetic ear and shoulder, especially if you're very close to them. However, they are natural charmers, so people often mistake their natural friendliness for actual friendship.

While Leo risings are friendly with most people around them, true friendship is reserved for a select few. This isn't to say they'll be rude or unpleasant to people; it simply means, in their mind, the distinction between friend and acquaintance is clear, and it's always best to know where you stand if only to prevent heartache for yourself.

Leo Rising in Friendships

If you're friends with a Leo rising, you have a true friend for life. These individuals give everything they have to the people they care about and are the most loyal friends you'll ever have.

From spending hours looking for a solution to your problems to being available for your important occasions, a Leo rising will do it all for the people in their close circle. Their hearts are as big as the sun, and when they share theirs with you, you'll know you have a friend for a lifetime.

Don't step on their friendship, however. These individuals are guarded because they have been burned before; if you take advantage of them, they will neither forget nor forgive.

Leo Rising in Love

Just as they are loyal to their friends and family, Leo risings are also loyal to their partners. They will never cheat on you, and with a Leo rising as a partner, you never have to worry about being betrayed.

These individuals are natural givers and will ensure you have everything you want and need. They love to care for their partners, and their way of showing their love includes cheerleading their partner, acts of service, and words of affirmation.

They love to show off the people they care for, and if you're in a relationship with a Leo, that will mean you, so be ready for their attention to be all yours! Leo risings will always show up for you, make you feel valued, and are great partners.

Leo Rising at Home

Leo risings know the value of appearances, which extends to their home. While they may not come from wealth, they appreciate life's finer things and will look for hours to find the perfect items to decorate their homes. Other people may think that a Leo rising's home is a bit too ostentatious for them, but it's undeniable that everything is of high quality.

At the same time, these individuals love their privacy. They do not easily let other people into their sanctuary and safe space, so if you're invited to their home, treat it as a gift for what it is. When you visit, make sure you complement their home as it's a surefire way to make them feel appreciated and score a return invitation.

Virgo Rising Sign

Virgo Rising's Glyph

Virgo symbol.
Bruce The Deus, CC BY-SA 4.0 <https://creativecommons.org/licenses/by-sa/4.0>, via Wikimedia Commons: https://commons.wikimedia.org/wiki/File:Deus_Virgo.png

The word "Virgo" means "maiden," and, in Greek mythology, the constellation was associated with various goddesses – generally either goddesses related to wheat (such as Demeter and Persephone) or virgin/maiden goddesses (such as Astraea).

This glyph comes from the Greek letters ΠΑΡ. These letters are an abbreviation of the word "*parthenos*," the Greek word for "virgin." Another interpretation of this glyph is that it represents a maiden carrying a shaft of wheat.

Virgo Rising's Personality

The Virgo rising individual is conscientious, well put-together, and organized. They are reliable and can be perfectionists, but they also have enormously trustworthy personalities. They are purposeful and can be obsessed with cleanliness and tidying up.

These people are logical and pragmatic and can be bluntly honest in their analysis of other people. This can make them come across as cold and aloof, but it's a quality they also use on themselves.

They are ambitious and self-motivated, so, unlike many other rising signs, they're not dependent on outside encouragement. They are humble, self-effacing at times, and have a drive towards being of service. They have a need to be productive, and their big heart means this will be shown by helping the people around them.

They are always looking for ways to improve themselves. They often struggle with insecurity, though their desire to fix things occasionally makes them seem negative and critical of the people around them. However, this couldn't be further from the truth. Rather, their struggle with insecurity means their criticism is usually directed inward at their own selves.

They enjoy patterns and balance around them and can be extremely disconcerted when faced with change, especially major change. Their need for balance also means they tend to worry a lot and become very anxious when faced with new and unexpected situations.

They are kind and good-tempered but, at the same time, enjoy their privacy. Their logical side will find it challenging to express themselves, especially if they haven't had time to mull over every possible outcome of their words.

At the extreme, they can become obsessive perfectionists, which often causes people to mistake them as being dull and boring.

Mercury rules a Virgo rising, the planet of communication, and, as a result, they are quick-thinking and curious about the world around them. However, the planet Chiron (a minor planet in astronomy) also influences Virgos, which is where their logical and guarded nature comes from.

These individuals are also considered to be the healers of the zodiac. While they're unlikely to let many people see the real them, their caring nature, call to service, and altruism means they are always willing to help people around them. They are loyal and supportive and will always be considerate of your emotions.

However, they are susceptible to falling prey to their more judgmental tendencies in extreme cases. They are not only critical of others. They are extremely critical of themselves as well. If they aren't able to complete tasks they have set for themselves to the standards they expect, they are very hard on themselves, to the point where their mental health could suffer.

Others can find their observant, perfectionist natures intimidating. However, once you get to know the Virgo rising, you'll soon realize that they're anything but intimidating, and your life will be all the richer for it.

Virgo Rising's Mindset

Though Virgo risings are fond of change, they're also well aware that the world is constantly changing around them. In some ways, this is what makes them so resistant to change. They are desperate to maintain the ground on which they have built their world, which can make them appear guarded.

However, this desire to prevent change does have a silver lining. Virgo risings know that relationships of all kinds need to be maintained, and they are always willing to put in that effort. At the same time, they crave peace and security, which means they always approach life with a plan. This can mean something as innocuous as stocking up on products for their home in advance of their needs, or on the other end of the scale, can make them hesitant to take action without considering every possibility, which often results in them missing out on important opportunities.

Virgo Rising at Work

Virgo risings are ambitious and self-motivated. They work tirelessly toward being successful at work, and their love of service means they are always willing to dedicate hours to things they consider to be worthy causes. If they can see the goal they've been aiming for in the mirror or the light at the end of the tunnel they want to reach, they're completely capable of speeding things up so they can reach their final destination without compromising the quality of their work.

While they might seem unapproachable, they thrive when working in a community of like-minded people. While they are working alone, being connected to people around them gives them additional incentive to keep going. So, if you work with a Virgo rising individual, make sure you get in touch with them often, as you'll find no better coworkers when you're working towards a common goal.

Virgo Rising in Relationships

If you can get past the intimidating hard shell often put out by a Virgo rising, you'll quickly find that they are pleasant and kind individuals. It may take them time to figure out the best way to connect with you, but they won't look back once they do. When they're close to a person, they are compassionate and understanding. All they ask is that you be there to match their energy and grow with them side-by-side.

Virgo Rising in Friendships

Virgo risings are dedicated friends and are often the first port of call when their loved ones are hurt. Though they can be hard to get to know, once they feel comfortable with you, they will always be there to help, no matter when you need them.

However, they can also be very private with their own emotions and often exclude close friends and partners from what is going on in their minds. This can sometimes cause issues in friendships, as some people will believe that a Virgo rising's inability to share parts of themselves unbalances their relationship. However, if you can be patient with these individuals and work with their need for logic and certainty, you'll soon find them opening up to you.

While their logical thinking can make it seem like they're unable to be affectionate toward their friends, they'll be loyal and present when you need them to be.

Virgo Rising in Love

Virgo risings are devoted partners. They enjoy being in love, even if they can seem a bit closed off and hard to get to know.

As the partner to a Virgo rising, it's essential to understand how they communicate nonverbally. Getting them to open up as much as you would like in a romantic relationship can often be challenging, but once you're in tune with what they're saying nonverbally, you'll quickly realize that they're quite expressive.

Keep in mind that, while they won't vocalize them, Virgo risings feel emotions deeply. This is especially true in romantic relationships, and they're unlikely to enter into a romance without having long-term expectations. So, if you're not serious about a relationship, don't step into one with a Virgo rising.

Virgo Rising at Home

Virgo risings are extremely curious and always looking for ways to bring the world into their homes. Even if they have not had the opportunity to travel extensively, they are always looking for ways to understand other perspectives, and their home décor and the contents of their bookshelves often reflect this.

They're always prepared for everything, which is reflected in their home. They want to have resources on hand, whether it is a well-stocked first aid kit or a comprehensive guide to topics they are interested in. At the same time, their home is their fortress and a way for them to reach their inner Zen, so if you're looking for a housewarming present for these individuals, a book on their current topic of interest or a therapeutic candle will not be unappreciated.

Now that we've looked at six of the 12 rising signs, the next step is to look at the other signs. Turn the page to learn more about the Libra and Scorpio rising signs. After that, we'll cover Sagittarius and Capricorn rising and Aquarius and Pisces rising.

Chapter 7: Libra Rising and Scorpio Rising

This chapter will focus on the Libra and Scorpio rising signs and discuss their personality traits and mindsets. Like in the previous chapters, you will get to understand how each of these signs deals with various parts of their lives, including work, relationships, friendships, love, and their homes.

Libra Rising Sign

Libra Rising's Glyph

Libra symbol.
Bruce The Deus, CC BY-SA 4.0 <https://creativecommons.org/licenses/by-sa/4.0>, via Wikimedia Commons: https://commons.wikimedia.org/wiki/File:Deus_Libra.png

Libra Rising's Personality

A Libra rising is the person to go to if you ever need a peacemaker. These individuals are excellent at maintaining peace and tranquility. They will do anything, even if it means they need to compromise, or even give up their own comfort if it means that everyone else will be happy. Their caring nature, even when dealing with strangers, is what makes them lovable and popular. They are great to be around.

Being the charming individuals they are, it should come as no surprise that Venus rules Libra risings. It is known for being the planet of love, passion, and everything beautiful. The older they get, the better they can master their captivating aura. They are naturally flirtatious and seductive. They know how to get in touch with their senses. When they are balanced and doing well, people find Libra risings very addictive. Influenced by Venus, these individuals are highly intoxicating. It can be very hard to stay away from them.

Libra is a cardinal sign, one of three astrological modalities or qualities. Cardinal signs are associated with the seasons since they start the seasonal cycles. Libra, the air sign, is associated with autumn. This means that Libra marks the start of the fall equinox. Cardinal signs are known for initiating change and their leadership skills. They like planning, visualizing, goal setting, and doing everything that brings them closer to their dreams. They are blessed with emotional and social intelligence, determination, and the important quality of self-initiation. But cardinal signs are susceptible to pessimism and absorbing negativity from others.

Libras are always on the go. They like to ensure that their voices are heard and their opinions are valued. The best thing about Libra risings is that they make their presence known with charm are grace. Libras are not loud. They don't seek attention, but instead, they earn it. This quality is very useful in a leadership role. The sign of Libra is represented by a scale, which shows how orderly this sign is. They like things to be symmetrical and seek balance in all areas of life.

Libra rising individuals are talkative and friendly. They have no problem walking up to anyone and conversing with them about anything and everything. If you struggle with social anxiety or often worry about awkward silence, a Libra rising can be the friend you never knew you needed. Libra risings are approachable and extroverted while maintaining respect and courtesy. They are very polite and are highly aware of those around them. They try to relate to others in all situations, encouraging people to warm up to them easily.

Libra risings are very intelligent. This is due to their open-mindedness and their ability to find compromises. They are problem-solvers and creative thinkers. They are also gentle and soft and approach all their interactions and tasks with care. Their delicacy shows in how they behave, move, think, and speak.

These individuals are also known for their kind-heartedness. Even though the inclination toward leadership sometimes makes them bossy, Libra rising individuals are generally sweet. They avoid conflicts and chaos whenever possible because balance and harmony are their priority. This is why they're very picky when it comes to who they choose to surround themselves with. They know better than to get involved in drama.

Even though they're very picky about those who make it into their circle, Libra risings are fun to be around. They are calm and joyful without even trying. It's best, however, if you always stay on their good side.

Libra Rising's Mindset

As mentioned above, Libra rising individuals are self-motivated; they don't need outside pressure to accomplish a task. A Libra rising's life mission is to experience endless happiness and good vibes. They want to maintain positive vibes and go with the flow of things. They don't like to over-complicate situations because they don't allow fear to hold them back.

Libra risings don't like staying in one place for too long. They are either up for changes or working on self-growth and development. If your ascendant is Libra, you probably don't dwell on unfortunate turns of events. You know that the world will go on, whether you like it or not. This doesn't mean you're emotionless, detached, or don't care. In fact, Libra risings are very in touch with their emotions. They just don't want to be stuck in them.

Libra Rising at Work

At work, you'll find Libra risings are the mediators of the team. They make compromises and find the middle ground in all interactions. This makes them great negotiators. This makes them great lawyers, judges, government officials, and diplomats in general. Libra risings are extremely ambitious and will go above and beyond to make its ideas happen. They're also very secretive regarding work, so they don't share the details with anyone. They know what they need to do, so they move in silence.

Their ambition and vast imagination allow them to succeed in creative fields. They also make good consultants. Since Libras are always on the move, sitting them down at a desk or giving them a strict timeline to stick to can be quite stressful and overwhelming. They thrive in work environments where they can enjoy a sense of freedom that enables them to work at their own pace. While this isn't necessarily bad, it can put them at risk of procrastination. Once they put their mind to it, they'll dive right into the task at hand. Libra rising like volunteer work, community building, and networking. They are often concerned with social causes and take on major activist roles.

Libra Rising in Relationships

Libra risings are very independent. They enjoy having people that they can trust and rely on in life. They like loving relationships and motivating connections that promote personal growth. Libra risings are lovers, not fighters. That said, they will only settle for people who are as self-motivated as the average Libra is. They appreciate emotions and the expression of love. However, they can't stand clinginess. They have strong boundaries in place.

Libra risings feel their best when like-minded individuals surround them. They love building relationships with optimistic, industrious, and inspiring people. They don't have any time to waste, so they won't give any chances to people who vibrate on lower frequencies.

Libra Rising in Friendships

Libra risings are very friendly and respectful. They may get a little flirty too. However, be careful not to take it too personally or feel flattered by their charm. They will go to great lengths to satiate the needs of the people they love. Libra risings are compatible with other rising air signs: Aquarius and Gemini. They are also compatible with fire signs Leo, Aries, and Sagittarius. Libra risings are least compatible with water signs, especially Scorpio rising and Pisces rising.

Libra Rising in Love

Libra rising individuals are natural-born activists. They are concerned with the greater good of the community, meaning that they will appreciate their partner being aware of the issues that impact the world. This is because Libra risings view love as an opportunity to share their passions, interests, and hobbies with the person they love. They will sit down and watch the football game with you if that's what you like to do.

Libra Rising at Home

Libra risings value order and structure. They are disciplined individuals who perform best when their home is clean and clutter-free. Their lives can get very busy, so having a home where they can relax is very important. Libra risings are known for their expensive taste. It can also take them a while to arrange their space exactly how they like it.

Scorpio Rising Sign

Scorpio Rising's Glyph

Scorpio symbol.
Bruce The Deus, CC BY-SA 4.0 <https://creativecommons.org/licenses/by-sa/4.0>, via Wikimedia Commons: https://commons.wikimedia.org/wiki/File:Deus_Scorpio.png

Scorpio Rising's Personality

Having the water sign, Scorpio, as your ascendant can make you appear quite mysterious. Everything about you, from your behavior to your appearance, can lead people to perceive you as a bit standoffish or unapproachable, at least when they first meet you. This is because Scorpios are very guarded and find it hard to open up to new people. They can't shake the fact that the world can sometimes be a dangerous place to live in, which is why they seldom let anyone into theirs.

Scorpio, like Aries, is ruled by Mars. One may think that this planet influences Scorpio the same way that it influences the fire sign, Aries. However, this isn't always the case. While a fiery temperament and rage do emerge at times, imagine a volcano, and you get the idea of the power of the energy exchange. Mars encourages Scorpio rising individuals to bottle up their feelings like lava. Unprocessed emotions sit seething in a sea of torment and self-criticism. Scorpio rising individuals continue to push their feelings down and torment themselves for their shortcomings until they erupt.

Scorpio's astrological modality or trait is fixed. The earth signs Taurus, the fire sign Leo, and the air sign Aquarius are also fixed signs. Each of them is associated with a certain season. Like Libra, Scorpio is associated with the fall.

Unlike the change initiator, Libra, Scorpio, and other fixed signs are natural traditionalists. They are believed to stabilize the zodiac. When we say that Scorpio rising individuals are traditionalists, we don't mean that they are boring or extremely uptight. Tradition here doesn't refer to a fixed routine or the rejection of modern tools and methods. It simply means that they value the meaning behind the actions they take and the things they do.

Scorpions, Taurus's, Leos, and Aquarians are known for their productive, loyal, and creative tendencies. They are also thought to be perfectionists. Fixed signs can get very stubborn. However, the exact manifestation of this trait varies depending on the astrological elements and dynamics of each sign. For instance, Taurus's are stubborn in maintaining structure in their lives. A Leo's stubbornness shows itself when they express the need to be the center of attention. Scorpions often let their emotions influence their ambitions, and Aquarians are stubborn when taking on leadership roles even though they enjoy their freedom.

Once they've set out on a decision or made up their minds about something, it can be impossible to get them to change their minds about it. They will never admit to being wrong or give up on their decision. While this gives them a sense of stability and consistency in their lives, it may also cause them to miss opportunities. Their stubbornness can keep them stuck in one place for too long. It may also cause them to walk down a path they now realize is wrong, just so they don't go back on their word.

Scorpio rising individuals are great at solving problems. They also have a strong eye for detail. They excel in areas that require critical thinking and deep focus. Sometimes, individuals with Scorpio ascending placement can feel out of place. They may feel disconnected from their environment. Their high intuition also causes them to appear somewhat robot-like. Engagement and communicating may not be their strong suit as they are not easy talkers. However, all their actions are highly calculated. They like to roam around the world purposefully and wisely. Going with the flow doesn't always work for them, meaning they always know their next move.

The best thing about a Scorpio rising individual is that they like to fight for the things they believe in. They are characterized by strong will and determination. Scorpio ascendants are known for their charm and allure, mostly from the air of mystery surrounding them. This sense of enigma makes them interesting and attractive to everyone around them. They hold some sort of power that attracts the attention of others. These individuals often seem unapproachable, yet the type of person that many wish to connect with.

People who are reluctant to approach a Scorpio rising individual end up being surprised by their charming personality; expecting a cold or aloof individual, people are often taken aback to find Scorpio risings to be delightful company. People with Scorpio ascendants master this charming aspect of their being because they wish to avoid numerous stupid questions. You will never entirely get to know them unless they let their guard down around you.

The delightful side to a Scorpio rising is not a mere facade. You may be surprised to learn that they are among the most generous and kind-hearted individuals out there. Their detachment and coldness is a protective mechanism.

Perfectionism and ambition run through a Scorpio rising's blood. They don't sit around after completing a task, nor do they take the time to admire or even rethink their work. They are ready to drive into another project right away. Scorpio risings are always on the lookout for great things to accomplish.

Scorpio Rising's Mindset

Scorpio rising individuals usually feel that no one understands what they're thinking or how they feel. They realize that they are quite complicated, and often, they struggle to understand the world around them too. They are passionate and strong-willed. However, the tiniest shift in their inner or outer balance can cause them to feel a little shaken and even disoriented. This is why they think a lot before they act. Because Scorpio risings spend most of their time being cautious and on edge, they deeply appreciate anyone with whom they can be themselves. They are risk-takers (calculated, of course!). They don't mind venturing – only if they think the experience, cause, or outcome is worth the risk.

Scorpio Rising at Work

The world of work feels like constant change, new ideas, and endless innovation. This is especially true for the demands placed on employees to be more creative, collaborative, and innovative. In this environment, what does it mean to be a Scorpio working in the world of work? As a sign associated with hidden depths and secretive nature, people who are born under the Scorpio rising are often seen as mysterious and aloof. Despite this common perception of them as loners or hermits, people born under the Scorpio zodiac sign are also known for their strength and courage – traits that will serve them well as they navigate their professional roles. The qualities of being a Scorpio professional are intense focus and dedication coupled with a deep-rooted intensity that can serve as both an asset or liability, depending on the situation.

Their diligence, critical thinking and problem-solving skills, and strong focus make them suitable for disciplines like law, writing, research, and finance. They will take on any challenge that comes their way, which allows them to thrive at work. The best thing about Scorpio risings at work is that their passion never fails to shine. Since they don't have a problem with taking risks, they stand out among their peers in the workplace. They also get things done quickly so they can hop onto the next tasks, making them an asset to the workplace.

Scorpio Rising in Relationships

These individuals like straightforward relationships. They like easy-going and manageable connections and will avoid dramatic people whenever possible. They value people that they instantly click. They are very intelligent when it comes to capturing subtle hints, clues, and overtones. However, interpreting hidden meanings is not something they want to do throughout the entire relationship. If they constantly must figure out what another person's gestures or words mean, they will quickly lose interest. Communication is not a Scorpio rising's best suit during periods of stress.

Scorpio Rising in Friendships

Their strong will and inclination to fight for everything that they stand for makes Scorpio risings incompatible with other individuals with Scorpio ascending signs. However, they are still compatible with the water signs Cancer and Pisces. Since they are equally sensual, Scorpio risings tend to be drawn by Taurus risings. They also get along well with Earth signs like Capricorn and Virgo.

Once a Scorpio ascendant reveals their authentic self to you, you will realize that they're the best friend that you've ever had. These individuals go to great lengths to protect the people they care for. They are very loyal and are ready to take your side even when you aren't on the same page. They will explain their point of view but will still defend you until their last breath. They greatly respect people who express their beliefs and speak their minds.

Scorpio Rising in Love

When it comes to love, Scorpio ascendants may unintentionally send mixed signals. Because of their aloof guise, which they use to protect themselves, they may appear to be head over heels one second and very distant the next. They fear appearing too clingy. However, once they've opened up to you, they can be. They like relationships with long-term potential. They have no interest in superficial connections. These protective individuals will always make you feel loved and safe. Scorpio rising is an intense and passionate sign. They're also secretive and guarded. But once they open up to someone, they have the potential to be one of the strongest and most loyal partners you will ever meet. The best partner for a Scorpio is someone who matches their drive and determination in life — not necessarily anyone with whom they fall in love at first sight. Knowing how to attract a Scorpio in love is important if you want to win their heart. Scorpios love deeply but cautiously. They are passionate about what matters most to them but distrust those who appear too eager to impress them from the get-go.

Scorpio Rising at Home

For a Scorpio Rising, their home is their safe haven. It's a den that they can use to escape the hustle and bustle of the real world. This is why they like to ensure that it has everything they could possibly need. They may decorate their home with house plants and paintings to give it a more relaxing feel. Scorpio risings are either into smart homes and futuristic designs or have very minimalistic tastes. Regarding the home, there are few other signs like Scorpio; they love the finer things in life and won't hesitate to spend their money on luxurious items that have special meaning to them. In addition, as we discussed previously, Scorpios spend a great deal of time in their homes. They are quite private individuals, so living in large homes might not be ideal for this sign.

Chapter 8: Sagittarius Rising and Capricorn Rising

This chapter expands on Sagittarius rising and Capricorn rising signs. It explains how the rising signs affect your life. People who were born during these periods display traits that make them different from other individuals. Sagittarius and Capricorn are two very different rising signs with very different outlooks on life. While Sagittarius is open, optimistic, and adventurous, Capricorn is reserved, cautious and realistic. As a result, when these two signs come together in the same person, the result is an interesting mixture of both signs' positive and negative traits. Depending on whether you have Capricorn or Sagittarius rising, this can have several implications for your character. Let's take a closer look.

Sagittarius Rising

Sagittarius symbol.
Bruce The Deus, CC BY-SA 4.0 <https://creativecommons.org/licenses/by-sa/4.0>, via Wikimedia Commons: https://commons.wikimedia.org/wiki/File:Deus_Sagittarius.png

People born when the Sun's horizon was in the same range as the sign of Sagittarius are usually found somewhere on a trip. To meet the Sagittarius rising, you need to travel since these people love traveling to learn history and are explorers at heart. They always try to move out of their comfort zone.

Sagittarius rising people are always interested in learning new things to expand their knowledge. They are optimistic and believe they can achieve great things that are often viewed as impossible. Their personalities are charming, and people are ready to help them realize their goals. They are also jokesters who make other people happy. Sagittarius Risings consists of people who love the truth. Although they may not realize it, they will use different means to attain the information they want. They don't want to live in the dark.

The Sagittarius Rising Mindset

Let's face it: We all have those days when it feels like the world is against us. Even though Sagittarius rising is known for its optimistic nature, even they can fall victim to occasional bouts of pessimism and self-doubt. But, as with all of us, what matters most is how we respond to these situations. Will we let them bring us down, or will we rise above them? The latter is what being a Sagittarius is all about. Let's take a look at why this sign is so optimistic and how we can stay that way on even the darkest of days.

Sagittarius risings focus mainly on growth, optimism, and positivity. The Sagittarius rising mindset reflects a risk-taking personality. They appreciate the things that belong to them but can go the extra mile to expand their knowledge by seeking answers to what they may not understand. Sagittarius energy is concerned with adventures and awareness that make them feel extraordinary. What they do not want is to feel misinformed or to ever appear mediocre.

Sagittarius Rising at Work

Sagittarius Risings can be a bit stubborn and are often over-ambitious. Most of them are talkative because Jupiter, their ruler, is primarily concerned with growth. As a result, the Sagittarius risings are interested in developing multiple talents and skills. Ironically, the Sagittarius risings are slow movers, although they are flexible when it comes to gaining new knowledge. Their method of work, while sometimes believed to be slow, is not a setback since they take pride in everything they do.

They are life learners and see each task as a wonderful opportunity to learn something new. The Sagittarius risings love to research and reflect on how the knowledge they acquire impact their life. These people are perfectionists and want to ensure In the workplace, they are focused and insightful. However, their biggest challenge is that they can be stubborn and judgmental, which may not go down well with co-workers.

Sagittarius Risings in Relationships

Sagittarius Risings find relationships easy since they have charming personalities. They are magnetic and attract many people. They can appeal to like-minded people who help them shape their opinions and ideas. The Sagittarius risings are careful when it comes to engaging with other people. They want to deal with smart people with whom they can meaningfully interact. They can also freely share their ideas when the right people surround them.

When the Sagittarius risings are with their close friends, they are conversational and open to different opinions. Many people admire their way of dealing with different situations. However, they can be a little blunt in some instances.

Sagittarius Rising and Love

In terms of love affairs, Sagittarius risings are practical. They are realistic and interested in dealing with reality to choose the appropriate people they can associate with. + They can be picky about the person they choose as a partner. These individuals can also fight for the people they are strongly attached to. When they look for a partner, they know what they are interested in, making them free to display an open mind.

Sagittarius risings like experimenting with different things and exploring new environments to improve their knowledge. At worst, these individuals can rush into love and often find themselves out within a short time. Many people struggle with tempo when it comes to relationships.

Home and Sagittarius Rising

With their natural thirst for adventure and love of travel, Sagittarian risings can thrive away from home. But they need to be in a home environment where they can thrive. The good news is that there are many ways you can feel at peace at home. You can do small things that will have a big impact on your life and happiness.

Sagittarius risings often feel at peace when they are at home. They do not consider every place they visit home because it may lack the facilities that give them total comfort. They feel at home if they find a comfortable space where they can perform their favorite hobbies. It can also be a local pub where they can enjoy their favorite drink and play a pool game. In other words, a home is a place that brings peace and tranquility.

Time of Excess

A Sagittarius rising's faith dwindles at some point, and they become despondent if they fail to find the answers they are looking for. Sagittarius risings are usually optimistic, but they need to be careful and avoid situations where they can set unrealistic goals that are difficult to achieve, which leads to disappointment. They also tend to overstep the mark or inflate their ego, but this does not always produce the desired results. This can lead to undesired behavior if you fail to achieve your goals.

The bad thing about over-optimism is that it can lead to recklessness, greed, or lack of due caution. If they go to extremes, they could end up believing they are invincible, which is not true, and the crash will be very hurtful when they realize the truth.

Truth Sharing

If Sagittarius is your Ascendant, you must explore different things that define your personality. Searching for teachings and philosophies that can satisfy your needs can take some time. You need to research different belief systems to gain insights and knowledge that can help you understand the world around you.

When you discover the right path, you'll develop a keen interest in it and become eager to share it. You will be more interested in helping others learn what you already know so they can develop. These people usually become excellent teachers and can also turn to preaching to share their belief systems with others. When you share your beliefs and ideas with others, ensure you respect their freedoms.

Capricorn Rising

Capricorn symbol.
Bruce The Deus, CC BY-SA 4.0 <https://creativecommons.org/licenses/by-sa/4.0>, via Wikimedia Commons: https://commons.wikimedia.org/wiki/File:Deus_Capricorn.png

If you are born with Capricorn Rising, you must love challenges. You can identify people who are committed to achieving their goals

The ruler of Capricorn is Saturn, which is shown through the power you have to master difficult tasks. At the same time, you will also have the patience to understand how elements like pessimism, fear, and negativity can affect your desire to reach your goals.

The qualities of your moon sign, sun sign, and house must also be considered. The time you were born determines your rising sign. The zodiac sign which was on the horizon during the time of your birth determines your sign. Capricorn Risings are usually ambitious, but the good thing is that Saturn makes them cautious. They don't rush into trusting something before they've taken the time to understand any situation before making any big decisions. Many Capricorn risings are calculated, and they don't rush into actions that can be disappointing in the end.

Another good thing about Capricorn Rising is that they focus on their future and take actions that will lead to long-term satisfaction. They know that trust is gained over a long time and is not an overnight event. For this reason, Capricorn risings carefully choose the people they can associate with. No haters and unmotivated people are allowed in the ring of Capricorn risings. If you want to be part of them, you'd better up your game, or you will be left behind.

Individuals belonging to this group are focused on money and determined to turn their dreams into reality. With their determination, few things get in their way. They are not bothered by the opinions and feelings of other people.

The Capricorn rising people are interested in working out the value of a relationship before opening up to others. For them, it's vital to understand other people's motivations before trusting other people. If you are lucky enough to be trusted, you will become a long-term investment to these people.

The Mindset of Capricorn Rising

The Capricorn risings are primarily concerned about money. They have realized that few things are worth sweating for besides making money. According to their doctrine, there is no need to waste energy on things they may not have in the next five years.

Capricorn energy focuses on dealing with issues that can last a long time. They first analyze the pros and cons of different situations before they involve themselves. They can drop specific actions once they suspect the end result might not be desirable. Although they can care about you or love you, they remain focused. If you are not part of them, then you are against them.

How to Make Your Way to the Top

Material resources are your prime concern when your ascendant is Capricorn. You may be strict, stern, or serious about achieving your goals. Some people are likely to respect you for your pragmatism and capability to work hard. You will learn from your past mistakes and other people's errors and try to turn everything into an opportunity.

Capricorn risings are interested in making decisions driven by their desire to attain long-term goals in life. Many people view these individuals as practical, goal-oriented, and pragmatic. They wait for the right time to reveal surprises to their peers. You need to make efficient use of the resources you have at hand to achieve your goals. This will help you become the master of your destiny. You can achieve this by carefully planning your approach to achieve your desired goals.

You must have self-respect and treat others as you would in a team situation. If the team makes a mistake, you are likely to remember and not repeat it. However, you need to focus on the things that you already have at the moment.

Capricorn Rising at Work

Capricorn risings are concerned with achieving their goals, which drives them to put their best efforts into whatever they are doing. They appear poised and quite solemn and serious and not the sort of people to play the fool at work. They are also quick and precise when undertaking their daily tasks. Capricorns have a gift for understanding and interpreting information quickly and easily. Other people often feel insecure when they are around the Capricorn risings because they will feel inferior.

The ascendant Capricorn is known for their determination and work ethic, so it's not surprising that this rising also has a lot of success in their careers. These ambitious individuals take their careers seriously, which is why Capricorns are often found in management roles. They're detail-oriented, strategic thinkers who take the time to plan out every step of a process before beginning it. This cautious, calculated approach makes them excellent project managers and team leaders who can see potential problems lurking around every corner. They enjoy working with facts and figures, which explains why many Capricorns choose STEM fields (science, technology, engineering, and math). They don't shy away from getting their hands dirty as an earth sign. Some common career paths for those born under the sign of the goat include architecture, accounting, civil engineering, and real estate.

Capricorn Risings and Relationships

When in a relationship, the Capricorn risings often reveal their positive characteristics. However, they usually take some time to show themselves to their partner. They tend to lead secretive lives and avoid sharing personal information with new people. They will open up at a later stage when they gain the trust of the new person involved.

Most Capricorn risings are hesitant to allow anyone into their close social circle to protect their privacy. They will let you know their feelings if you cross their path or even warn you to mind your business. These people are easily overwhelmed by emotions when in relationships and can easily shed tears. It is vital to understand them so you know how to deal with them.

Capricorn Rising and Love

Capricorn risings are genuine when they are in love, and they don't want a one-sided or conditional. When they love someone, there are no strings attached, and they expect the same in return. They make sure their partner is cared for, well-fed, and catered for. If you wonder whether the Capricorn rising loves you or not, this will usually answer your question - it means they don't love you or are not yet ready for you. The issue is that Capricorns cannot pretend to love someone they don't care about since they lead busy lives. If you find yourself in this situation, you should not waste your time. Instead, you should move on.

Capricorn Rising at Home

Home is where your heart is, right? So what does that say about you if your home is a mess and all you want to do is lock yourself in your room and escape from the rest of the world? A Capricorn rising at home means you're a reserved, practical person who loves order and structure. But this doesn't mean that you don't have any fun! The key to life as a Capricorn rising at home is finding a balance between work, rest, and play.

Capricorn risings love homes with enough space to include the things they cherish, like plants, paintings, a decent dining set, and other household items. Once the Capricorn rising finds a partner, they can improve the appearance of their home. They also want room for their athletic activities. You should not be surprised to see them with a yoga mat in their home. They treat their home as a special place where they can live in peace.

Patience and Endurance

Ambitions may not always go your way, but they will certainly become possible depending on your approach. If you are concerned about achieving something, you should know that perseverance and endurance pay off. You can read clues from your sign to gain insight into different things you can encounter in your life. Saturn is your ruler and is responsible for teaching your life lessons and how commitment and patience can help you achieve them.

Hardships are inevitable, and they can affect your desire to achieve your goals. However, you can overcome them by reviewing your objective and respecting the laws and other forces that can affect you. You need to exercise self-discipline to get what you want. It is vital to set realistic goals to make your life easier. With Capricorn rising, you should expect to experience hardships or limitations that can affect you at each turn. However, you must be careful about believing that life must be hard.

Indeed, challenges in life are inevitable, but it does not necessarily mean they are unconquerable. Learning to appreciate challenging work can set you apart from other people who subject themselves to fate. You need to put your ambitions into perspective and make sure your goals are achievable.

Pleasures of Life

Life is not only about discipline and hard work. You also need to recognize that you need to take time to relax and enjoy your life. Sensual pleasure is an integral component of our lives, so you should not deprive yourself of happiness and other activities that can make you relax. Self-repression can negatively impact your goals, especially if you are over-ambitious.

If you are responsive, this ascendant helps you work hard to achieve the goals you want. The best partner is someone who understands your aspirations and goals and supports you in achieving them. You also need to avoid things that can impede the pursuit of your goals. Follow the rules and regulations to avoid disappointment. In whatever you pursue, remember this sign is associated with earthly pleasures.

With Capricorn rising, balancing the desire to achieve your goals and downtime is essential; this also helps you recognize your capabilities and what you can achieve. Make sure you pursue happiness since it is good for your social well-being. Do not focus on material things alone since there are more things to life.

In this chapter, we explained the characteristics of people with Sagittarius rising and Capricorn rising signs, their qualities, and what makes them different from others. The next chapter focuses on Aquarius rising and Pisces rising.

Chapter 9: Aquarius Rising and Pisces Rising

In this chapter, we focus on Aquarius rising and Pisces rising signs. We explain different traits that characterize the people who belong to these rising signs. We'll highlight the characteristics that make these people who they are and what motivates their lives.

Aquarius rising and Pisces rising are two of the most challenging ascendants to have. With Aquarius as your rising sign, you'll be forever exploring new ideas and concepts and your unique identity. You may feel like an outsider for much of your life because you don't necessarily fit in with others around you. Similarly, with Pisces rising, you'll almost always feel misunderstood by those around you since they simply won't understand the way you think or see the world. Both of these ascendants require a lot of alone time, and a trusted few who can see past their oddities and get to know them at their core. Here we explore more about Aquarius rising vs. Pisces rising and how they affect your personality and outlook on life:

Aquarius Rising

Aquarius symbol.
Bruce The Deus, CC BY-SA 4.0 <https://creativecommons.org/licenses/by-sa/4.0>, via Wikimedia Commons: https://commons.wikimedia.org/wiki/File:Deus_Aquarius.png

Many years ago, people believed Saturn ruled Aquarius, but after recent research, it is agreed that Uranus now rules it. Aquarius has a dark history which means it is a sign not to play around with. Uranus is regarded as a planet of rebellion and chaos, and this extends to people who belong to Aquarius rising. They often experience a feeling of confusion and loss.

Therefore, the greater purpose of Aquarius rinsing's existence is mainly concerned with maintaining order. They also try to make as much sense to the world as possible. They will fight to protect their community because it is one of their greatest possessions. They also want peace so they can follow their interests.

The Mindset of Aquarius Rising

Aquarius risings trust their instincts, and they have an outstanding mindset. If they believe something to be true, they will follow their minds. Another notable characteristic about Aquarius risings is that if they oppose a motion, they will go in the opposite direction from other people. Like Aquarius suns, the Aquarius risings believe they are superior to everyone else.

Aquarius risings who are keen to learn new things can benefit by acknowledging their mistakes. This mindset promotes learning and knowledge acquisition, unlike people who mistakenly think they are always right. The water bearer represents Aquarius and reflects the rising's everyday life. They are always available to give a hand to the people they love and take their time to share anything that may affect their peers.

Aquarius rising people are reserved and often try to distance themselves from others as being the source of entertainment is stressful. They understand that one needs to be committed to being available to everyone. They believe that if you make a promise, you should keep it. When the Aquarius risings feel they no longer want to hang out with a certain group of people, they will fade away. They usually have good reasons for that kind of behavior.

Aquarius risings feel they have so many responsibilities they don't have time to attend to everyone. They also view other people who may not add value to their lives as vampires. However, these people have exceptional traits that make them excellent companions. For instance, if you intend to start a project, you can get inspiration from them to achieve your desired goals.

Aquarius Rising and Work

Individuals who belong to Aquarius rising signs are very hard workers and are determined to achieve all their goals. Once they commit themselves to a particular mission, they ensure it is accomplished. They are committed to achieving their mission instead of focusing on individuals. They know that people are not perfect and can make mistakes, which is why they commit themselves to the project, not the team members. Goal attainment is the main focus, which makes the Aquarius Risings unique from other groups in different societies.

They are concerned about how to reach structural equity, and they are leaders who stand by their beliefs. They do not suffer fools lightly and will walk away from nonsense if they get bored or people question their ideas. The Aquarius risings believe that individuals should trust their own instincts but respect the community.

Aquarius risings are excellent water bearers who become great professionals because of their outstanding community organizing skills. Their core values are focused on helping marginalized people and standing up for the rights of the less privileged members of society. They want to create a place where everyone can enjoy life and pursue their goals.

Aquarius risings always think of the bigger picture and want to reach bigger goals first. However, this does not necessarily mean they are obsessed with work. They also have other important things they want to achieve in their lives. This helps them structure their work and have a total commitment to any career path they are involved in. They believe a career is part of their identity. The good thing about Aquarians is that they have an appealing passionate nature that can motivate people to love their careers and anything they do for the benefit of others.

Relationships and Aquarius Rising

There is often a misconception that their Aquarius energy does not produce a perfect partner. However, if you believe this, you might be the one on the wrong side. Aquarius risings have great respect for their relationships, love, and friendship. They'll try to defend the people they love and do everything to understand their partners. They freely celebrate the achievements of their partners. They relish the company of others.

Aquarius risings are fun, easy-going, and light-hearted people. If they are in a relationship that gives them freedom and independence, they can thrive in whatever they are doing. If they seem to be down, this may be caused by pressure. So if you're in a relationship with one, give your partner plenty of space and don't take everything they say seriously.

To enjoy the best relationship with an Aquarius rising, you should focus on what you can give or do to make your partner happy. You should not always expect to get something from the person you love. Aquarius risings admire famous people, artists, and performers. They also have extensive networks that help them achieve their goals. The advantage of a strong network is to make tasks easier. Therefore, if you want to create links with famous people, ask an Aquarius rising to help you achieve your goal. They will probably know several people who are ready to volunteer their time for the benefit of other individuals.

Aquarius Rising and Love

Aquarius Risings are inquisitive and enjoy experimenting with different things to get answers to different problems. They are usually composed, and you can easily see if they are flirting. Signs like raised eyebrows and other facial expressions can tell you they are enjoying themselves.

They treat love as a fun experience, and they will develop interest along the way. Aquarius risings take their time to understand the person they are interested in. For instance, they will ask for personal details like hobbies, interests, and how you see different things in relationships. Your answers will determine if they feel you are the one they want to have a relationship with and how you'll be as a partner. If you feel you are under a microscope or are in an interrogation, don't worry, it's just Aquarius checking your character so they don't waste anyone's time in a dead-end relationship.

You will be very lucky to enter into a relationship with an Aquarius rising because they are genuine people. They will show their true personality if they know they can trust you. These are wonderful people who are easy to go along with.

If you want the Aquarius partner to show you love, always be honest and never deceitful - that will mean certain death to your relationship. They will drop you instantly if they feel they are being trifled with and messed around. Equally, don't play mind games with them, you won't win, and you'll risk a wonderful relationship.

Aquarius Rising and Home

Aquarius Risings prefer to live in comfortable homes where they can prepare their favorite dishes and listen to the best music. They treat the home as the best place to be, so they adorn it with the best things they can afford to make their lifestyle what they want it to be. However, they do not believe in spectacular mansions but in special places that make them feel like kings or queens.

Aquarius risings decorate their homes with plants, aquariums, and unique furniture. They incorporate different things that depict life in their homes. They create plenty of natural arrangements in their homes to show how they value nature. You should not be surprised to find that each room has a unique plant, and this is when you will discover that Aquarius risings love weird and strange things.

Once they choose a way of life, they do not backtrack and always find a way to their luxury. They are particular about their comfort and are not wasteful people. Additionally, they always try to find the means to perfect their art of living using the resources available to enjoy life to the fullest.

Pisces Rising

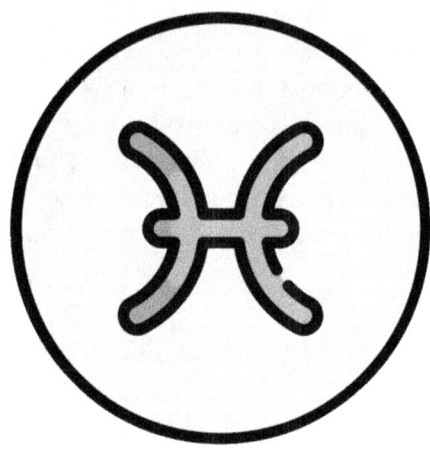

Pisces symbol.
Bruce The Deus, CC BY-SA 4.0 <https://creativecommons.org/licenses/by-sa/4.0>, via Wikimedia Commons: https://commons.wikimedia.org/wiki/File:Deus_Pisces.png

Your outer layer is the rising sign that determines how you appear to others. People who belong to Pisces often feel detached when young, but what they should know is that life is multi-dimensional. The Pisces rising is receptive, kind, and at times lost-looking.

Their persona may seem changeable, and if you belong to this category, you can morph into different masks to match the existing company. You are a chameleon; you can align your personality to match those around you. However, stronger personalities can easily overwhelm you. So you must be careful who you choose to be around you.

You thrive when you surround yourself with supportive friends who share your interests and vision. Pisces rising people can use their imagination and are talented in using symbols, sounds, and movement to reflect life. The most common ways of expressing themselves are through music, drama, dance, and visual arts. When Pisces is your rising sign, Neptune is the ruler of your chart.

Open Borders

Pisces rising people are compassionate and gather lost people and stray animals. However, you may be vulnerable to people who don't share your sentiments and are easily taken advantage of. When they look at you, they see potential prey. If you fail to pair critical thinking with your intuition, you may become a victim.

While you can lose yourself easily, you need to learn life lessons to set clear boundaries that will keep you away from people who may take advantage of you. In some cases, you may be on the wrong side by following the crowd, even if you see that it will be destructive. There are often sad stories of naïve of people who followed blindly and ended up in the deep end.

If you are Pisces rising, you are compassionate even about the dark forces among us. However, there is the risk of throwing yourself in harm's way. If you are intuitive, you can use that to save your life. This can only be possible if you heed your intuition. You need to take your time to study the people around you before you blindly trust them and bring them into your life. The more you observe and learn about people, the more confidence you will get in your decision-making about them, and the fewer mistakes you'll make by trusting the wrong people

In some cases, it is good for your soul to be alone. Staying away from people who may be a bad influence in your life can save you from many things. For instance, you may end up falling into the trap of addiction if you associate with bad company. This will affect your thinking and lead to bad decisions that can impact your life and overall well-being.

Mystic Attitude

The rising sign influences the way you move into the world. With Pisces rising, you are accustomed to things like dreams, good luck, and symbolic language. Too much socializing can overwhelm you, and enough time alone can be restorative. It is crucial to take some time to do the things you love most, like watching movies, reading books, or playing music. You also need to give yourself free time when you are not doing anything. When your mind is clear and you know what you want in life, you will grow strong.

Pisces Rising Mannerism and Appearance

People with Pisces rising are generally accommodative, kind, and prone to be dreamers. Most of them are soft and appear timid. They often present themselves in such a way that they can't cope with the struggles of the world and daily life because they seem weak. However, these are all mannerisms. Pisces rising mannerisms can be described as gentle, spiritual, sacrificial, dreamy, approachable, selfless, and empathetic.

Pisces Risings are compassionate and sensitive to others, but they always desire to escape reality. They often achieve this by turning to things like music, alcohol, drugs, or art.

Personality

The people with a Pisces ascendant behave like chameleons because they always change their personalities to adapt to different environments around them. However, few people realize this as they hide it so well. While most people will see the Pisces zodiac sign as being shy or timid, those with the Pisces personality are anything but. These individuals are incredibly intuitive and sensitive, which allows them to see past the surface of things. They're also incredibly compassionate and selfless, willing to give without expecting anything in return quite often.

High on Life

Pisces rising individuals appear to be on top of situations, which can be contagious. They want to create a rosy worldview and refuse to see its ugliness which makes them often live in fantasy. Because they're so giving, many assume that Pisces rising don't have a backbone or any real strength of character, but this couldn't be further from the truth. They have a quiet strength and courage that few other people can match. They know who they are and what they stand for and have no fear about going after what they want or speaking the truth as they see it. When you're on top of the world because you're so confident in who you are as a person and what you stand for as an individual, that's being high on life as a Pisces!

Depths of Despair

The Pisces Rising people are not always stable as ups and downs characterize their lives. Although they may have high hopes in life, they are quickly shattered if they fail to achieve their desired goals. As a result, they will turn to drugs and substances to drown their sorrows. In some cases, despair and loneliness can lead to suicide if it's left uncontrolled.

Pisces Rising and Relationships

The people with Pisces Rising are passive in a relationship, and they expect their partner to play the dominant active role. They idealize their partners and offer selfless love. These people are romantic and try to create emotional ties with their partners. However, they will suffer a disproportionate setback when the lover fails to live up to their expectations.

Pisces Rising Women, Men, and Children

Pisces rising women are attractive and very feminine. They also have several qualities that make them adorable. They love fashion and other things that can enhance their beauty.

Men with Pisces rising are charismatic, and they have big dreams. They are interested in pursuing their goals and want to keep them secret. They want their freedom and don't want people to interfere with their aspirations. In other words, they must be understood and encouraged to follow their dreams.

Children with Pisces rising are sensitive and delicate. They are loving, sweet, gentle, and cooperative such that their parents often find it difficult to believe that their children can do anything wrong. However, parents often fail to provide proper guidance to their children because they are overprotective. The kids often get away with anything since they can create convincing fairy tales when they are suspected of wrongdoing. Pisces rising kids need to be closely monitored; otherwise, they can grow up to be spoiled adults.

Hidden Talent

People with Pisces rising have hidden artistic talent. They can become a writer, musician, a dancer, an actor, or any other type of creative person. However, it is not easy to have Pisces on the ascendant. Great art comes from dedication and commitment.

In this chapter, we explained the traits of people with Aquarius rising and Pisces rising. The Aquarius rising people are unique and believe in their instincts and always think they are right. Pisces rising people are compassionate and possess a great love for others.

Chapter 10: A Guide to Embrace Your Rising Sign

The subject of astrology is fascinating to many people. And many more are intrigued by the discoveries that can be made by looking further into the subject. While the concepts of the rising sign have existed for thousands of years, a lot of what was once known has now been lost. But the primary concepts continue to exist along with unique interpretations.

When you learn how your rising sign influences different parts of your life and what the implications are, it becomes much less surprising when things happen the way they do. You are likely to be more focused, independent, and open-minded than others. In many cultures worldwide, people celebrate this illuminating aspect of astrology by taking an active role in realizing their full potential and developing their particular gifts.

The essence of such knowledge is an occasion for celebration. It brings a sense of empowerment and hopes to everyone. However, as any good astrologist and actualized person knows, *knowledge is always a caveat*. Certainly, you can stop your rune journey at this point and enjoy what you have learned and what you have crafted so far. There is still so much to learn if you want to progress further. Having a collection of runes isn't enough. You must understand how to handle your rising sign to take full advantage of your new status.

The rest of this chapter will provide you with information about how to embrace your rising sign and those of others. We will also cover how you can learn more about the craft and why it is essential to get the most out of this aspect of astrology and faith. Because when you realize the wealth of opportunities and benefits that your rising sign can bring, you will wonder how you ever lived with it.

Understand Rising Signs

Over time, we have become increasingly aware of the fact that there are thousands of other people out there who share the same interests and experiences. In response to this, individuals have found ways to reach out to one another to strengthen their sense of belonging. Those with a particular penchant for identifying with the rising signs can find solace in identifying as such and socializing with others who feel the same. Becoming involved in the world of astrology is an excellent way to strengthen one's identity while meeting new people and broadening one's horizons. However, this comes with its own unique challenges and pitfalls. The world of astrology is not everyone's cup of tea — those who identify as part of this subculture often face numerous misconceptions, difficulties integrating - and even discrimination, at times, because of it.

If you are aware and interested in learning more about astrology, you know that it is not something that simply rolls out of the heavens and aligns with positive influences in your life. To embrace astrology, you must work at it and understand the concepts behind it. To succeed, you must be willing to learn about the subject, see how it can support your thinking, and act based on what you learn.

For example, let's say you are a huge basketball fan and are excited about the upcoming season. However, every year your team misses the playoffs. What if there was another way to look at your season that doesn't focus on whether or not they will make the playoffs? What if you could look at it as an opportunity for growth instead of a time when everything goes wrong? Incorporating the rising signs into your life could be one of the best things you do for yourself.

Embrace the Magnitude

Astrology is often viewed as something mystical and unapproachable. However, this isn't the case. In fact, many people worldwide have a great love for astrology and what it has to offer. Many people are put off by the idea of exploring their own rising sign or horoscope because they think it sounds strange and creepy. However, being interested in your own personal traits is nothing weird or abnormal. And that's exactly why you should embrace astrology if you haven't already! Learning more about your zodiac sign can actually be really beneficial, especially when you combine it with other self-improvement techniques such as meditation and mindfulness.

Most people who enter into more advanced forms of astrology soon realize that astrology is not just about their Sun sign or the 12 signs but also about planets, houses, and birth information. It's amazing to know that the different signs of the zodiac can be aligned in different places in the sky, making them relevant to life's obstacles and offerings.

Everything is contained within your birth chart. Here you will find out what has been cast since the moment you were born. So, the time, date, and location of birth are necessary to generate an appropriate and comprehensive birth chart. This is at least a starting point.

You will find it confusing the first time you see one because when you learn astrology, you're essentially learning a new language. The symbols and glyph characters in this language will initially be unfamiliar to you.

Astrology is an ancient science that explores the connection between human and celestial bodies. It can be hard to understand something so abstract and mysterious, especially when you're first learning about it. But with time and practice, you'll learn to embrace astrology as another part of your life.

Never Stop Learning

To learn astrology, there are a few things you need to do. Despite their simplicity, each method can take a lot of time and energy, depending on how committed you are. You'll need to talk, study, practice, and read astrology and rising signs as much as possible.

- Online
- Books
- Websites
- eBooks
- Blogs
- Social Media
- Magazines

Astrology is an art, science, and philosophy all in one. Learning about astrology will help you gain a deeper understanding of the universe and your own life. The more you know about astrology, the more impressive your readings will be! Astrology is a vast and expansive field that can take an entire lifetime to fully understand. Even the most knowledgeable astrologers continue to learn more about their craft and its origins daily. And while there is no wrong way to learn astrology, certain methods are more beneficial than others. The best way to advance your knowledge of astrology is by reading books, taking classes or workshops, and practicing regularly. Astrologers have been writing books for centuries, and many of them can still be purchased today, either as print books or as eBooks. There are many good beginner astrology guides out there, so a good look around the internet, and you'll be able to pick up a couple of them.

Create a To-Do List

In this subsequent section, we will cover some ways to bring Norse magic into your life if you have no knowledge of astrology and the rising signs.

Here are some things you can do to learn more:

- Find an online course or meet with someone in person to receive formal training
- Read journals, blogs, books, and websites
- Search Google, Meetup.com, or NCGR (National Council for Geocosmic Research) for local groups
- Check out any astrology pages on social media (Reddit is best)
- Double-check your birth time

- Get a copy of or make your own birth chart
- Make your own or buy some runes
- Learn the symbols for the zodiac signs, planets, houses, etc.
- Take advantage of free online resources, such as blogs, websites, podcasts, YouTube, and Reddit
- If there are no meet-up groups in your area, then start your own
- The Astrology Dictionary
- Take a look at the birth charts of your friends, family, and famous people (you can find birth data online for many celebrities)
- Online or locally, you can take an astrology course
- Join an astrological organization and attend one of their conferences

Make Use of Online Sources

This is a no-brainer, but because knowledge of rising signs isn't usual and easy to find, you may feel alone in your new passion. But this couldn't be further from the truth. So, make use of free resources online. You can use them for simple things like learning the symbols for the signs, planets, and their meaning. Imagine if the runes' origin and power were documented in the way we document things today; online.

The internet is full of free resources. There is almost no end to it all. And the amount of free, quality information means there's no reason for small-budget enthusiasts not to study the craft. Look for the following:

- Astrology blogs and websites.
- PDFs of free astrological texts and other related things
- Podcasts and free episodes on Audible or Spotify
- YouTube has a wealth of information on all aspects of Norse magic, from techniques to topics

Talk to Others

You need to talk to other people. Communication is an underestimated learning tool. We need to interact with other people about the topic and language, the rising signs, astrology in general, as well as the faith aspects of it. Looking up local astrological groups on the web is important if you are considering meeting up with other astrology lovers. You can usually find many individuals around you looking for companionship in their interest in astrology, even if it is new to you. If you take a look, you may be able to locate a group to meet up with in person; if not, there are plenty of excellent online groups where people are very friendly and helpful.

Become a Student

One of the greatest things you can do is to take a structured course. However, people who start studying astrology don't realize that astrology becomes a lifelong job, passion, or interest for most people. It's very important, therefore, to obtain a solid base, a great foundation, or some great grounding in the basics if you can learn from a teacher or teachers.

Learning through a course with an astrologer will give you a great foundation.
https://unsplash.com/photos/jCIMcOpFHig?utm_source=unsplash&utm_medium=referral&utm_content=creditShareLink

Astrology is too vast a subject for one teacher to teach you everything you need to know. It's also too big a subject for one person to study alone. But being introduced to astrology by an astrologer will give you the foundation you need for the rest of your life. After this time, you can begin attending astrology conferences or dedicating yourself to a certain subfield, as long as you can speak the language.

Keep Your Feet on the Ground

Everything about astrology is about understanding yourself and the forces of nature. From the moment we are born, we can see our star charts and know where our path will take us in the future. Astrological knowledge is, however, much more than knowing our zodiac signs. It is about understanding yourself and how your personality aligns with nature's laws.

It can get very exciting when you finally meet someone who is on the same page as you. You may be shocked to learn that professional or long-term rising sign enthusiasts are not attracted to reading other people's birth charts or asking for readings, for example, at conferences. And in online forums, it is more pronounced. For example, this occurs if there is a new astrology forum, and a new astrologer appears and tries to get people to read their charts. Sometimes it is considered a faux pas when people only want to ask other people about their birth charts. However, astrologers will often ask each other about placements in their birth charts to get to know another person. So, someone may initiate a conversation, but generally, it's better to join in discussions that have already been started.

Be wary of asking other people astrological questions, and don't constantly bring up your own chart to generate discussion. Instead, offer to read other people's charts as a way to practice your skills. Not only will you learn more, but it will be a great way to interact with others.

The key to interacting with other astrologers is understanding the community's social norms. A professional astrologer usually focuses on their profession, so they don't necessarily read charts all the time. They don't just throw out statements about a person's life when a stranger pulls out a chart.

People who start astrology are either looking for information about themselves or want to learn more about the art. Therefore, you should think about your motivation. And it's okay to want to learn about yourself. We are curious creatures, after all. And if you want to learn about astrology itself, then you might go about it in a slightly different way.

Study the Rising Sign of Others

Speaking of reading birth charts, studying your own chart is not enough to learn astrology. You must also study other people's charts and transits as well. Even though your primary focus in astrology is likely to be you and your own life, one of the most entertaining things you can do is to use it to learn about the lives of others.

Study the charts of your friends, family members, or even famous people and others you are interested in to look for commonalities. Examine the chart itself or the data to determine how the locations of the stars in the chart are related to different life events and circumstances. You can study the positions of the Sun or other planets on the same day as an important life event to learn more about the person and discover how they are the way they are. Start studying the charts of other people and the planets' positions, and then apply the same process to your own chart.

Another thing you could try is comparing the birth charts of two people to see how they interact, even if you're not trying to determine their compatibility. You can also see whether the chart shows a connection between the two. For example, if you look at a composite birth chart (an advanced form of astrology) of a couple, you can see whether they are really connected.

It is when you start seeing other people's charts that you realize how diverse the study of astrology study really is. By understanding how much you can learn about other people by reading their birth charts, and other applications, you can see how ingrained it is in life exploration and personality.

Find Solace in a Professional

You will be eager to start learning as soon as you receive your first charms, runes, and birth chart. It might be worth your while investing in a reading with a well-established astrologer. Having the opportunity to sit down with a professional to discuss your chart can be one of the most valuable things a student can do for themselves. As a result, you will get so much out of it that is relevant, and it will be as if you are having a one-on-one tutoring session. Astrology is a great way to improve your understanding of human nature and provide insight into how people are likely to respond to various events or activities. If you're considering a career in astrology, it could be the perfect opportunity for you! Astrology professionals study the movement of celestial bodies and their impact on human behavior and affairs. Astrologers use knowledge of astronomy, the positions of planets and other stars, and their effect on individuals to better understand their client's life circumstances. These professionals may work directly with clients or in another capacity, such as within research organizations or the wider community. A career in astrology may also involve teaching students about astrological concepts and principles as part of a broader curriculum that includes other areas of astronomy.

Learn the Craft

Get started learning the zodiac signs, the planets, and the aspects of the chart by learning their symbolic representations. It has its own alphabet, representing planets and zodiac signs. This is your starting point.

The birth chart is a rich piece of information and insight, but you can only get into it if you understand the symbols. The best way to do this is memorization. Once you have these down, you'll never forget them. It will then become like a second language to you. Once memorized, you will know what Scorpio in Jupiter looks like just by identifying the symbol for Jupiter and identifying the symbol for Scorpio in the birth chart. You can understand specific placements in your birth chart and other charts as soon as you understand this.

When you are learning astrology, the emphasis is on keeping your eyes and ears open, as much as on learning the theory. This is because you are learning astrology on two levels: the theory or the way it manifests and how to add depth to your knowledge. For instance, if you want to learn astrology, you must first acquire a book on the subject, but reading and absorbing the book can also teach you a lot about the craft.

For example, knowing how to observe is a big part of learning, and astrology, in particular. Let's say you want to understand the houses better. So, you begin by tracking the sun or the moon through the houses. But, if you observe correctly, you will notice how the moon changes every couple of days. So will the outcome. And if you track the Sun through the houses, you'll notice how topics are repeated every time the Moon is in the seventh house.

You can chart the positions of the planets and the Moon to track their movements through the twelve houses of the zodiac, or you may track the Sun through the houses to see if the planets influence an aspect of your life. This observational method is rich in how it enhances your knowledge and learning.

Many things can help you embrace your rising sign and get the most out of this special element in your life. In some cases, it might just be as simple as realizing that you have a different view of the world when compared with other people. However, as with anything, you should use your rising sign to your advantage. There are various ways to do so, including learning more about other cultures and how their beliefs differ from yours. Be willing to try new things, but always be willing to stick to your guns when you do. Also, don't forget that you have very little control over what your rising sign shows you. This is just one of the many things the stars have aligned for you. So, make the most of it, and however you accept your current situation, you will likely find more peace than you have experienced in the past.

Learning about your rising sign is a process of discovery. As you journey through, you will learn more about yourself. You will also learn more about what's possible for you in the future and gain a deeper understanding of the general patterns that have impacted your life so far.

The rising sign will always be there. It is a core aspect of the astrological nature of each person. And it is a powerful influence on growth and change. You must be willing to explore and discover your rising sign, its meaning, and how it can benefit your life. The more you know about it, the more you will be able to appreciate its value, and the more likely you will be able to take advantage of it.

Conclusion

The rising sign is one of the most important astrological aspects that affects your natal chart readings. The rising sign is specific to everyone and decides their ruling planet. It basically refers to the zodiac sign that was rising on the eastern horizon at the time of someone's birth. This zodiac sign changes every two hours, and to identify your rising sign, you need to know the exact time of your birth.

It reveals the significant sides of your personality. While many think these traits reflect your outer persona, they are intrinsic quirks and traits directly associated with your real self. The rising sign can be identified from your natal chart, and after reading the birth chart guide chapter, there should be a straightforward interpretation of your chart, ascendant and ruling planets.

Each chapter looked deeply into the traits, patterns, and themes associated with the rising signs. So, there should be no confusion about the characteristics of each rising sign, whether it's Aries, Taurus, Gemini, Cancer, Leo, Virgo, Libra, Scorpio, Sagittarius, Capricorn, Aquarius, or Pisces. The best part about these chapters? They go into detail about the rising sign's personality, mindset, work behavior, how they deal with relationships, love, and friendships, and how they treat their family.

This in-depth explanation makes it easy for you to understand your ascendant and also makes it easier for you to embrace it. Once you understand your strengths and weaknesses, nothing can stop you from loving yourself and changing yourself for the better.

Here's another book by Silvia Hill that you might like

Free Bonus from Silvia Hill available for limited time

Hi Spirituality Lovers!

My name is Silvia Hill, and first off, I want to THANK YOU for reading my book.

Now you have a chance to join my exclusive spirituality email list so you can get the ebooks below for free as well as the potential to get more spirituality ebooks for free! Simply click the link below to join.

P.S. Remember that it's 100% free to join the list.

~~$27~~ **FREE BONUSES**

 9 Types of Spirit Guides and How to Connect to Them

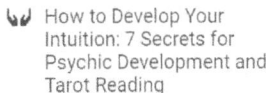 How to Develop Your Intuition: 7 Secrets for Psychic Development and Tarot Reading

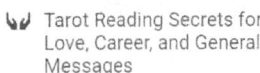 Tarot Reading Secrets for Love, Career, and General Messages

Access your free bonuses here
https://livetolearn.lpages.co/moon-sun-and-rising-signs-paperback/

References

Kelly, A. (2018, April 23). What your moon sign says about your emotional personality. Allure. https://www.allure.com/story/zodiac-moon-sign-emotional-personality

Miller, K., & Levitan, H. (2018, March 16). Your Moon sign has A huge impact on how you react to difficult situations. Women's Health. https://www.womenshealthmag.com/life/g19448039/what-is-my-moon-sign/

Moon sign dates: What are my sun and moon signs? (2022, July 5). The Sun. https://www.thesun.co.uk/fabulous/horoscopes/9307789/sun-moon-sign-compatible/

Stardust, L. (2021, February 24). Are you passionate? Impulsive? This is what your moon sign says about your emotional personality. Vogue India. https://www.vogue.in/culture-and-living/content/what-your-moon-sign-says-about-your-emotional-personality-zodiac-signs

Ward, K. (2019, April 8). Moon sign: How do you find yours, and what does it mean? Cosmopolitan. https://www.cosmopolitan.com/uk/horoscopes/a27071450/moon-sign/

Watt, R. (2021, September 8). This is your most powerful psychic ability, according to your moon sign. Yahoo Life. https://www.yahoo.com/lifestyle/most-powerful-psychic-ability-according-160100683.html

Your moon sign is the last piece of the astrology puzzle, so here's what it means. (2021, October 20). ELLE. https://www.elle.com.au/culture/moon-sign-meaning-26111

Rose, E. (2022, May 2). Sun Sign Meaning: What It Says About You & Who You're Destined To Become. StyleCaster. https://stylecaster.com/sun-sign-meaning/

Blanchfield, T. (2022, February 15). The psychology behind why we care about astrology. Verywell Mind. https://www.verywellmind.com/the-psychology-behind-why-we-care-about-astrology-5217929

Brown, M. (2021, August 11). What is astrology? A beginners' guide to the language of the sky. InStyle. https://www.instyle.com/lifestyle/astrology/what-is-astrology

Coughlin, S. (2022, May 3). How to make sense of your birth chart. Refinery29. https://www.refinery29.com/en-us/2016/11/129929/birth-chart-analysis-natal-astrology-reading

Definition of ASTROLOGY. (n.d.). Merriam-Webster.Com. https://www.merriam-webster.com/dictionary/astrology

Delgado, C. (2021, August 24). Why are people so into astrology right now? Discover Magazine. https://www.discovermagazine.com/mind/why-are-people-so-into-astrology-all-of-a-sudden

Grabianowski, E. (2005, May 26). What is astrology? HowStuffWorks. https://entertainment.howstuffworks.com/horoscopes-astrology/question749.htm

How to interpret your Birth Chart. (n.d.). Tree of Life. https://treeoflife.com.au/blogs/news/how-to-interpret-your-birth-chart

Mahtani, N. (2020, March 31). Your astrology birth chart reveals more than you might expect. Nylon. https://www.nylon.com/astrology-birth-chart

Sloan, E. (2021, July 13). Here's What Each Planet Actually Means in Astrology—So You Can Understand Your Chart in More Depth. Well+Good. https://www.wellandgood.com/meanings-of-planets-in-astrology/

Astrology Planets and their Meanings, Planet Symbols and Cheat Sheet. (2018, January 27). Labyrinthos. https://labyrinthos.co/blogs/astrology-horoscope-zodiac-signs/astrology-planets-and-their-meanings-planet-symbols-and-cheat-sheet

Thomas, K. (2021, November 5). A guide to the planets in astrology and what they each represent. New York Post. https://nypost.com/article/astrology-planets-meaning/

Solar System Symbols. (n.d.). NASA Solar System Exploration. https://solarsystem.nasa.gov/resources/680/solar-system-symbols

Atkinson, N. (2015, November 25). Order Of the Planets From The Sun. Universe Today. https://www.universetoday.com/72305/order-of-the-planets-from-the-sun/

Brown, M., & Kassel, G. (2021, January 22). The Need-to-Know Traits and Qualities of Every Single Zodiac Sign. Shape. https://www.shape.com/lifestyle/mind-and-body/zodiac-signs-meanings-dates

Stapleton, D. (2020, April 2). Aries Zodiac Sign: Characteristics, Dates, & More. Astrology.Com. https://www.astrology.com/zodiac-signs/aries

Stapleton, D. (2020, April 29). Taurus Zodiac Sign: Characteristics, Dates, & More. Astrology.Com. https://www.astrology.com/zodiac-signs/taurus

Stapleton, D. (2020, April 13). Gemini Zodiac Sign: Characteristics, Dates, & More. Astrology.Com. https://www.astrology.com/zodiac-signs/gemini

Stapleton, D. (2020, March 11). Cancer Zodiac Sign: Characteristics, Dates, & More. Astrology.Com. https://www.astrology.com/zodiac-signs/cancer

Stapleton, D. (2020, April 6). Leo Zodiac Sign: Characteristics, Dates, & More. Astrology.Com. https://www.astrology.com/zodiac-signs/leo

Stapleton, D. (2020, April 30). Virgo Zodiac Sign: Characteristics, Dates, & More. Astrology.Com. https://www.astrology.com/zodiac-signs/virgo

Stapleton, D. (2020, April 14). Libra Zodiac Sign: Characteristics, Dates, & More. Astrology.Com. https://www.astrology.com/zodiac-signs/libra

Stapleton, D. (2020, May 14). Scorpio Zodiac Sign: Characteristics, Dates, & More. Astrology.Com. https://www.astrology.com/zodiac-signs/scorpio

Stapleton, D. (2020, April 6). Sagittarius Zodiac Sign: Characteristics, Dates, & More. Astrology.Com. https://www.astrology.com/zodiac-signs/sagittarius

Stapleton, D. (2020, February 29). Capricorn Zodiac Sign: Characteristics, Dates, & More. Astrology.Com. https://www.astrology.com/zodiac-signs/capricorn

Stapleton, D. (2020, April 16). Aquarius Zodiac Sign: Characteristics, Dates, & More. Astrology.Com. https://www.astrology.com/zodiac-signs/aquarius

Houses. (n.d.). Astrology.com. https://www.astrology.com/houses

The 12 houses of astrology - the astrological houses and your natal chart. (2020, August 14). Labyrinthos. https://labyrinthos.co/blogs/astrology-horoscope-zodiac-signs/the-12-houses-of-astrology-the-astrological-houses-

and-your-natal-chart

Alicia. (2015, March 18). 7 challenging Taurus traits and how to overcome them. All Women's Talk. https://inspiration.allwomenstalk.com/challenging-taurus-traits-and-how-to-overcome-them/

Aries 101: Everything you need to know about the Kickstarter of the zodiac. (2021, March 26). Mindbodygreen. https://www.mindbodygreen.com/articles/aries-sign-101

Astrology Zodiac Signs. (n.d.-a). Aquarius Zodiac Sign: Horoscope, dates, Traits & personality. Astrology-Zodiac-Signs.Com. https://www.astrology-zodiac-signs.com/zodiac-signs/aquarius/

Astrology Zodiac Signs. (n.d.-b). Leo Zodiac Sign: Horoscope, dates, Traits & personality. Astrology-Zodiac-Signs.Com. https://www.astrology-zodiac-signs.com/zodiac-signs/leo/

Astrology Zodiac Signs. (n.d.-c). Libra Zodiac Sign: Horoscope, dates, Traits & personality. Astrology-Zodiac-Signs.Com. https://www.astrology-zodiac-signs.com/zodiac-signs/libra/

Astrology Zodiac Signs. (n.d.-d). Pisces Zodiac Sign: Horoscope, dates, Traits & personality. Astrology-Zodiac-Signs.Com. http://astrology-zodiac-signs.com/zodiac-signs/pisces/

Astrology Zodiac Signs. (n.d.-e). Scorpio Zodiac Sign: Horoscope, dates, Traits & personality. Astrology-Zodiac-Signs.Com. https://www.astrology-zodiac-signs.com/zodiac-signs/scorpio/

Astrology Zodiac Signs. (n.d.-f). Virgo Zodiac Sign: Horoscope, dates, traits & personality. Astrology-Zodiac-Signs.Com. https://www.astrology-zodiac-signs.com/zodiac-signs/virgo/

Brown, M. (2020a, March 13). Your Aries zodiac sign guide: Everything to know about the fierce fire sign. InStyle. https://www.instyle.com/lifestyle/astrology/aries-zodiac-sign

Brown, M. (2020b, April 3). Your Taurus zodiac sign guide: Everything to know about the sensual earth sign. InStyle. https://www.instyle.com/lifestyle/taurus-zodiac-sign

Brown, M. (2020c, April 17). Your Gemini zodiac sign guide: Everything to know about the curious air sign. InStyle. https://www.instyle.com/lifestyle/gemini-zodiac-sign

Brown, M. (2020d, May 11). Your Cancer zodiac sign guide: Everything to know about the heartfelt water sign. InStyle. https://www.instyle.com/lifestyle/cancer-zodiac-sign

Brown, M. (2020e, May 28). Your Leo zodiac sign guide: Everything to know about the spotlight-loving fire sign. InStyle.

https://www.instyle.com/lifestyle/leo-zodiac-sign

Brown, M. (2020f, June 19). Your Virgo zodiac sign guide: Everything to know about the detail-oriented earth sign. InStyle. https://www.instyle.com/lifestyle/virgo-zodiac-sign

Brown, M. (2020g, June 30). Your Libra zodiac sign guide: Everything to know about the social butterfly air sign. InStyle. https://www.instyle.com/lifestyle/libra-zodiac-sign

Brown, M. (2020h, July 23). Scorpio zodiac sign: Everything to know about the magnetic water sign. InStyle. https://www.instyle.com/lifestyle/scorpio-zodiac-sign

Brown, M. (2020i, August 3). Your Sagittarius zodiac sign guide: Everything to know about the adventurous fire sign. InStyle. https://www.instyle.com/lifestyle/sagittarius-zodiac-sign

Brown, M. (2020j, August 20). Your Capricorn zodiac sign guide: Everything to know about the motivated earth sign. InStyle. https://www.instyle.com/lifestyle/capricorn-zodiac-sign

Brown, M. (2020k, August 28). Your Aquarius zodiac sign guide: Everything to know about the quirky air sign. InStyle. https://www.instyle.com/lifestyle/aquarius-zodiac-sign

Brown, M. (2020l, September 8). Your Pisces zodiac sign guide: Everything to know about the dreamy water sign. InStyle. https://www.instyle.com/lifestyle/pisces-zodiac-sign

Crowley, R. (2018, July 28). If you have something to say about "B*tchy" Virgos, read this first. POPSUGAR. https://www.popsugar.com/love/Best-Qualities-Virgos-45069076

Everything to know about Taurus, the zodiac's stubborn-but-loving sign. (2021, May 4). Mindbodygreen. https://www.mindbodygreen.com/articles/taurus-101-personality-traits-compatability-and-more

Everything you need to know about the zodiac's most eclectic sign. (2022, January 17). Mindbodygreen. https://www.mindbodygreen.com/articles/aquarius

Garis, M. G. (2022, March 17). 6 Aries personality traits that sum up what it means to live life horns-first. Well+Good. https://www.wellandgood.com/aries-personality-traits/

Hrdlitschka, S. (2005). Sun Signs. Orca Book. https://www.astroyogi.com/zodiac-signs/sunsigns

Iwegbue, A., & Smith, E. W. (2020, April 9). 40 celeb Cancers who do their zodiac sign proud. Cosmopolitan. https://www.cosmopolitan.com/entertainment/celebs/g32086359/famous-cancer-celebrities/

Kelly, A. (2018a, February 2). Libra zodiac sign: Personality traits and sign dates. Allure. https://www.allure.com/story/libra-zodiac-sign-personality-traits

Kelly, A. (2018b, February 2). Pisces zodiac sign: Personality traits and sign dates. Allure. https://www.allure.com/story/pisces-zodiac-sign-personality-traits

Kelly, A. (2018c, February 2). Scorpio zodiac sign: Personality traits and sign dates. Allure. https://www.allure.com/story/scorpio-zodiac-sign-personality-traits

Kelly, A. (2018d, February 2). The personality of a Cancer, explained. Allure. https://www.allure.com/story/cancer-zodiac-sign-personality-traits

Kelly, A. (2018e, February 2). The personality of a Capricorn, explained. Allure. https://www.allure.com/story/capricorn-zodiac-sign-personality-traits

Kelly, A. (2018f, February 2). The personality of a Gemini, explained. Allure. https://www.allure.com/story/gemini-zodiac-sign-personality-traits

Kelly, A. (2018g, February 2). The personality of a Leo, explained. Allure. https://www.allure.com/story/leo-zodiac-sign-personality-traits

Kelly, A. (2018h, February 2). The personality of a Taurus, explained. Allure. https://www.allure.com/story/taurus-zodiac-sign-personality-traits

Kelly, A. (2018i, February 2). The personality of a Virgo, explained. Allure. https://www.allure.com/story/virgo-zodiac-sign-personality-traits

Kelly, A. (2018j, February 2). The personality of an Aries, explained. Allure. https://www.allure.com/story/aries-zodiac-sign-personality-traits

Kelly, A. (2018k, February 2). The personality traits of a Sagittarius, including their compatibility with other signs. Allure. https://www.allure.com/story/sagittarius-zodiac-sign-personality-traits

Lapik, E. (2020a, April 13). 25 positive & Negative Virgo Personality Traits and characteristics. Astromix.Net / Blog. https://astromix.net/blog/virgo-traits/

Lapik, E. (2020b, April 16). 19 positive & negative Aquarius personality traits and characteristics. Astromix.Net / Blog. https://astromix.net/blog/aquarius-traits/

Lapik, E. (2020c, May 7). Positive & negative Sagittarius personality traits and characteristics. Astromix.Net / Blog. https://astromix.net/blog/sagittarius-traits/

Lapik, E. (2020d, May 10). 20 positive & negative Gemini personality traits and characteristics. Astromix.Net / Blog.

https://astromix.net/blog/gemini-traits/

Lapik, E. (2020e, May 13). 20 positive & negative Aries personality traits and characteristics. Astromix.Net / Blog. https://astromix.net/blog/aries-traits/

Lapik, E. (2020f, May 13). 20 positive & negative Cancer personality traits and characteristics. Astromix.Net / Blog. https://astromix.net/blog/cancer-traits/

Lapik, E. (2020g, May 13). 22 positive & negative Taurus personality traits and characteristics. Astromix.Net / Blog. https://astromix.net/blog/taurus-traits/

Lapik, E. (2020h, June 12). 20 positive & negative Capricorn personality traits and characteristics. Astromix.Net / Blog. https://astromix.net/blog/capricorn-traits/

Lapik, E. (2020i, June 12). 20 positive & negative Pisces personality traits and characteristics. Astromix.Net / Blog. https://astromix.net/blog/pisces-traits/

Lapik, E. (2020j, June 14). 20 positive & negative Libra personality traits and characteristics. Astromix.Net / Blog. https://astromix.net/blog/libra-traits/

Lapik, E. (2020k, June 14). 25 positive & negative Leo personality traits and characteristics. Astromix.Net / Blog. https://astromix.net/blog/leo-traits/

Leo compatibility: What to know about dating or befriending this sign. (2021, July 23). Mindbodygreen. https://www.mindbodygreen.com/articles/leo-sign-101

Meet Cancer: The nurturing & emotional water sign of the zodiac. (2021, June 22). Mindbodygreen. https://www.mindbodygreen.com/articles/cancer-sign-101

Meet Gemini: The wise & witty air sign of the zodiac. (2021, June 2). Mindbodygreen. https://www.mindbodygreen.com/articles/gemini-sign-101

Meet Pisces: The go-with-the-flow psychic of the zodiac. (2021, March 12). Mindbodygreen. https://www.mindbodygreen.com/articles/pisces-sign-101

Meet Virgo: The zodiac's most dependable & detail-oriented sign. (2021, August 24). Mindbodygreen. https://www.mindbodygreen.com/articles/virgo-sign-101

Merinuk, M. (2022, May 26). Gemini celebrities: Which of your favorite stars are born under the sign of the twins? TODAY. https://www.today.com/life/astrology/gemini-celebrities-rcna23436

Mulroy, C. (2022, April 21). Taurus celebrities: Which of your favorite stars are born under the sign of the bull? TODAY. https://www.today.com/life/astrology/taurus-celebrities-rcna24439

Pai, R. (2021, September 22). 15 bad traits and characteristics of A Sagittarius (man & woman). MomJunction. https://www.momjunction.com/articles/negative-traits-of-a-sagittarius_00771750/

Scorpio sign 101: Personality traits, compatibility & more. (2021, October 24). Mindbodygreen. https://www.mindbodygreen.com/articles/scorpio

Smith, E. W. (2020a, May 26). 40 celebs who prove Leos belong in the spotlight. Cosmopolitan. https://www.cosmopolitan.com/lifestyle/g32671448/famous-leo-celebrities/

Smith, E. W. (2020b, June 10). These famous Virgos will make you wish you were one too. Cosmopolitan. https://www.cosmopolitan.com/entertainment/celebs/g32803997/famous-virgo-celebrities/

Smith, E. W. (2020c, July 28). 40 celebs who prove Libras were born to be famous. Cosmopolitan. https://www.cosmopolitan.com/entertainment/g33445883/famous-libra-celebrities/

Smith, E. W. (2020d, August 17). 40 Scorpio celebrities who prove they're the most intense sign. Cosmopolitan. https://www.cosmopolitan.com/lifestyle/g33627026/famous-scorpio-celebrities/

Smith, E. W. (2020e, September 10). 40 celebrities who are total Sagittariuses. Cosmopolitan. https://www.cosmopolitan.com/entertainment/celebs/g33983622/famous-sagittarius-celebrities/

Smith, E. W. (2020f, October 7). 40 celebs who prove Capricorns really are the greatest. Cosmopolitan. https://www.cosmopolitan.com/entertainment/celebs/g34303556/famous-capricorn-celebrities/

Smith, E. W. (2020g, November 23). 25 Aquarius celebrities who are just like their sun sign. Cosmopolitan. https://www.cosmopolitan.com/entertainment/celebs/g34759491/famous-aquarius-celebrities/

Sullivan, C., & Smith, E. W. (2021, January 21). These 31 celebrities are total Aries. Cosmopolitan. https://www.cosmopolitan.com/entertainment/celebs/g35217933/famous-aries-celebrities/

Tenorio, I. (2020, September 21). Why Are Aries so difficult? YourTango. https://www.yourtango.com/2020336922/why-are-aries-so-difficult

The Editors of Encyclopedia Britannica. (2021). zodiac. In Encyclopedia Britannica.

The zodiac's most thrill-seeking sign—and the secret to winning them over. (2021, November 21). Mindbodygreen. https://www.mindbodygreen.com/articles/sagittarius

This sign is the "boss" of the zodiac—but it's often misunderstood. (2021, December 20). Mindbodygreen. https://www.mindbodygreen.com/articles/capricorn

Thomas, K. (2022, March 18). Aries celebrities: 25 famous people born under the sign of the ram. New York Post. https://nypost.com/article/aries-celebrities-25-famous-people-born-under-zodiac-sign/

TIMESOFINDIA.COM. (2021, February 3). Your core purpose in life, according to all zodiac signs. Times of India. https://timesofindia.indiatimes.com/life-style/relationships/love-sex/your-core-purpose-in-life-according-to-all-zodiac-signs/photostory/80650045.cms?picid=80650200

What does your sun, moon, and rising sign really mean? (n.d.). Mindbody. https://explore.mindbodyonline.com/blog/wellness/what-does-your-sun-moon-and-rising-sign-really-mean

Your ultimate guide to zodiac's most ethical & equitable sign. (2021, September 22). Mindbodygreen. https://www.mindbodygreen.com/articles/libra-sign-101

(N.d.). Symbolspy.Com. https://www.symbolspy.com/zodiac-symbols-text.html

Angel, J. (2015, April 6). What's your emotional mode of operation? Harper's BAZAAR. https://www.harpersbazaar.com/horoscopes/a10491/whats-your-emotional-mode-of-operation/

Astrology: Moon in the signs. (2015, April 18). Cafeastrology.Com; Cafe Astrology .com. https://cafeastrology.com/articles/mooninsigns_pg2.html

Brown, M. (2020, September 25). What your moon sign means about your personality and life path. Shape. https://www.shape.com/lifestyle/mind-and-body/moon-sign-meaning

Daruwalla, C. B. (2022, May 17). Sun Sign Vs Moon Sign: What is it and which is better? India TV. https://www.indiatvnews.com/astrology/sun-sign-vs-moon-sign-which-is-better-zodiac-signs-latest-astrology-news-2022-05-17-777252

DeVille, A. (2019, June 10). Your natal moon: A powerful asset in workplace relationships. Llewellyn Worldwide. https://www.llewellyn.com/journal/article/2760

Douglas, M. (n.d.). Cancer moon sign: Personality and relationships. Prepscholar.Com. https://blog.prepscholar.com/cancer-moon-sign

Elara, L. (n.d.). Moon in Aries: 6 strengths & 5 weaknesses of the Natal moon in Aries. https://popularastrology.com/aries-moon

Gemsyogi, W. by. (2019, August 5). Taurus moon sign - personality, positive & negative traits. GemsYogi. https://gemsyogi.com/taurus-moon-sign/

Hall, M. (2007a, February 26). Personality traits of an Aries moon sign. LiveAbout. https://www.liveabout.com/moon-in-aries-moon-signs-206981

Hall, M. (2007b, March 4). Scorpio moon sign: Personality and characteristics. LiveAbout. https://www.liveabout.com/scorpio-moon-moon-signs-206988

Hall, M. (2007c, March 4). What are Traits of the Libra Moon Person? LiveAbout. https://www.liveabout.com/moon-in-libra-moon-signs-206985

Hall, M. (2007d, March 13). Pisces moon sign: Personality and characteristics. LiveAbout. https://www.liveabout.com/moon-in-pisces-206986

Kelly, Alice. (2022a, March 4). What it means if you were born under A Gemini moon sign. YourTango. https://www.yourtango.com/zodiac/gemini-moon-sign

Kelly, Alice. (2022b, March 9). What it means if you were born under A Capricorn moon. YourTango. https://www.yourtango.com/zodiac/capricorn-moon-sign

Kelly, Alice. (2022c, March 9). What it means if you were born under A Sagittarius Moon. YourTango. https://www.yourtango.com/zodiac/sagittarius-moon-sign

Kelly, Alice. (2022d, March 10). What it means if you were born under A Cancer moon. YourTango. https://www.yourtango.com/zodiac/cancer-moon-sign

Kelly, Alice. (2022e, March 11). What it means if you were born under A Scorpio moon. YourTango. https://www.yourtango.com/zodiac/scorpio-moon-sign

Kelly, Aliza. (2018, April 23). What your moon sign says about your emotional personality. Allure. https://www.allure.com/story/zodiac-moon-sign-emotional-personality

Montúfar, N. (2022a, March 21). Everything you need to know about that Aries Moon in your birth chart. Cosmopolitan. https://www.cosmopolitan.com/lifestyle/a39490505/aries-moon-meaning/

Montúfar, N. (2022b, May 20). If your moon sign is cancer, here's what astrology says about you. Cosmopolitan. https://www.cosmopolitan.com/lifestyle/a40061764/cancer-moon-meaning/

Moon in Gemini. (2021, March 23). MyPandit. https://www.mypandit.com/zodiac-signs/gemini/moon-in-gemini/

Moon in Scorpio celebrities who live intensely. (n.d.). Horoscope.Com https://www.horoscope.com/us/editorial/editorial-news.aspx?UniqueID=1952&CRC=CCC6EFE73F6169A915ECD36BBD17E2E7

Moon in Taurus. (2021, March 19). MyPandit. https://www.mypandit.com/zodiac-signs/taurus/moon-in-taurus/

Moon in the signs: Astrology. (2015, April 18). Cafeastrology.Com; Cafe Astrology .com. https://cafeastrology.com/articles/mooninsigns.html

Moon signs - know your moon sign/Rashi according to your birth time - Surat Diamond. (n.d.). Suratdiamond.Com https://www.suratdiamond.com/moonsigns.aspx

Painter, S., & More, R. (n.d.). Moon in Gemini signs show bright, engaging personality traits. LoveToKnow. https://horoscopes.lovetoknow.com/astrology-signs-personality/moon-gemini-signs-show-bright-engaging-personality-traits

Punarvasu, P. (n.d.). For Libra moon signs, is banking and finance a wise career option. Indastro. from https://www.indastro.com/astrology-articles/career-in-banking-and-finance-for-libra-moon-sign.html

Robinson, A. (n.d.). Capricorn moon sign: What you should know. Prepscholar.Com. https://blog.prepscholar.com/capricorn-moon-sign

Rose, K. (2022, March 16). What it means if you were born under an Aries Moon. YourTango. https://www.yourtango.com/zodiac/aries-moon-sign

Ruby, M. (2021a, October 28). Celebrities with Virgo moon. Ranker. https://www.ranker.com/list/virgo-moon-celebrities/madame-ruby?page=2

Ruby, M. (2021b, November 8). Celebrities with Capricorn moon. Ranker. https://www.ranker.com/list/celebrities-with-capricorn-moon/madame-ruby

Ruby, M. (2021c, November 12). Taurus moon celebrities. Ranker. https://www.ranker.com/list/taurus-moon-celebrities/madame-ruby

Ruby, M. (2021d, November 15). Gemini moon celebrities. Ranker. https://www.ranker.com/list/gemini-moon-celebrities/madame-ruby

Ruby, M. (2021e, December 6). Celebrities with Leo moon. Ranker. https://www.ranker.com/list/leo-moon-celebrities/madame-ruby

Ruby, M. (2021f, December 6). Moon in Sagittarius celebrities. Ranker. http://ranker.com/list/moon-in-sagittarius-celebrities/madame-ruby

Stardust, L. (2021, February 24). Are you passionate? Impulsive? This is what your moon sign says about your emotional personality. Vogue India. https://www.vogue.in/culture-and-living/content/what-your-moon-sign-says-about-your-emotional-personality-zodiac-signs

The best profession for energetic Aries. (n.d.). Indastro. https://www.indastro.com/aries/best-profession-aries.html

Your moon sign is the last piece of the astrology puzzle, so here's what it means. (2021, October 20). ELLE. https://www.elle.com.au/culture/moon-sign-meaning-26111

Denise. (2018a, September 3). Capricorn Sun Capricorn Moon: A venturesome personality. I.TheHoroscope.Co. https://i.thehoroscope.co/capricorn-sun-capricorn-moon-a-venturesome-personality/

Denise. (2018b, September 3). Capricorn Sun Taurus Moon: A stoic personality. I.TheHoroscope.Co. https://i.thehoroscope.co/capricorn-sun-taurus-moon-a-stoic-personality/

Denise. (2018c, September 25). Virgo Sun Capricorn Moon: A rational personality. I.Tthe horoscope.Co. https://i.thehoroscope.co/virgo-sun-capricorn-moon-a-rational-personality/

Denise. (2018d, September 25). Virgo Sun Taurus Moon: A composed personality. I. TheHoroscope.Co. https://i.thehoroscope.co/virgo-sun-taurus-moon-a-composed-personality/

Denise. (2018e, October 14). Taurus Sun Capricorn Moon: A practical personality. I. TheHoroscope.Co. https://i.thehoroscope.co/taurus-sun-capricorn-moon-a-practical-personality/

Denise. (2018f, October 14). Taurus Sun Taurus Moon: A benevolent personality. I. TheHoroscope.Co. https://i.thehoroscope.co/taurus-sun-taurus-moon-a-benevolent-personality/

Denise. (2018g, October 14). Taurus Sun Virgo Moon: A brilliant personality. I. TheHoroscope.Co. https://i.thehoroscope.co/taurus-sun-virgo-moon-a-brilliant-personality/

Facebook, H. F., Iii. (2011, January 24). Astrology Western Sun and Moon sign combinations. Hugh Fox III. https://foxhugh.com/divination/sun-and-moon-sign-combinations/

Moon, J. (2017, November 23). Sun-Moon astrology combinations. Astroligion.com. https://astroligion.com/sun-moon-astrology-combinations/

Moon, J. (2018a, October 11). Virgo sun Taurus moon personality. Astroligion.com. https://astroligion.com/virgo-sun-taurus-moon/

Moon, J. (2018b, October 14). Virgo sun Capricorn moon personality. Astroligion.com. https://astroligion.com/virgo-sun-capricorn-moon/

Moon, J. (2018c, October 28). Capricorn sun Taurus moon personality. Astroligion.com. https://astroligion.com/capricorn-sun-taurus-moon/

Moon, J. (2018d, October 28). Capricorn sun Virgo moon personality. Astroligion.com. https://astroligion.com/capricorn-sun-virgo-moon/

Moon, J. (2019a, March 13). Taurus Sun Capricorn Moon Personality. Astroligion.com. https://astroligion.com/taurus-sun-capricorn-moon-personality/

Moon, J. (2019b, March 13). Taurus Sun Taurus Moon personality. Astroligion.com. https://astroligion.com/taurus-sun-taurus-moon-personality/

Moon, J. (2019c, March 13). Taurus Sun Virgo Moon personality. Astroligion.com. https://astroligion.com/taurus-sun-virgo-moon-personality/

Sesay, A. (2020, November 18). Balancing the light and dark: Understanding your sun and moon in astrology. Byrdie. https://www.byrdie.com/astrology-sun-and-moon-5086414

Stardust, L. (2022, March 11). Earth signs will inspire you with their groundedness. Cosmopolitan. https://www.cosmopolitan.com/lifestyle/a33588028/earth-signs-astrology

Sun in Capricorn & moon in signs. (n.d.). I. TheHoroscope.Co. https://i.thehoroscope.co/astrology/sun-moon/sun-in-capricorn/

Sun in Taurus & moon in signs. (n.d.). I. TheHoroscope.Co. https://i.thehoroscope.co/astrology/sun-moon/sun-in-taurus/

Sun in Virgo & moon in signs. (n.d.). I. TheHoroscope.Co. https://i.thehoroscope.co/astrology/sun-moon/sun-in-virgo/

Facebook, H. F., Iii. (2011, January 24). Astrology Western Sun and Moon sign combinations. Hugh Fox III. https://foxhugh.com/divination/sun-and-moon-sign-combinations/

Moon, J. (2017, November 23). Sun-Moon astrology combinations. Astroligion.com. https://astroligion.com/sun-moon-astrology-combinations/

Sesay, A. (2020, November 18). Balancing the light and dark: Understanding your sun and moon in astrology. Byrdie. https://www.byrdie.com/astrology-sun-and-moon-5086414

Stardust, L. (2021, November 11). Air signs can talk, think, and network faster than the wind. Cosmopolitan. https://www.cosmopolitan.com/lifestyle/a33314375/air-signs-astrology/

Sun & Moon Combinations: How Well do your Sun & Moon get Along? (n.d.). South Florida Astrologer - Personality & Relationship Astrology https://www.southfloridaastrologer.com/sun--moon-combinations-how-well-do-your-sun--moon-get-along.html

Sun Moon combinations. (n.d.). I. TheHoroscope.Co. https://i.thehoroscope.co/astrology/sun-moon/

Denise. (2018a, September 16). Sagittarius Sun Aries Moon: A demanding personality. I. TheHoroscope.Co. https://i.thehoroscope.co/sagittarius-sun-aries-moon-a-demanding-personality/

Denise. (2018b, September 16). Sagittarius Sun Leo Moon: An honorable personality. I. TheHoroscope.Co. https://i.thehoroscope.co/sagittarius-sun-leo-moon-an-honorable-personality/

Denise. (2018c, October 3). Leo Sun Aries Moon: A Frank personality. I. TheHoroscope.Co. https://i.thehoroscope.co/leo-sun-aries-moon-a-frank-personality/

Denise. (2018d, October 3). Leo Sun Leo Moon: A proud personality. I. TheHoroscope.Co. https://i.thehoroscope.co/leo-sun-leo-moon-a-proud-personality/

Denise. (2018e, October 3). Leo Sun Sagittarius Moon: An inspirational personality. I. TheHoroscope.Co. https://i.thehoroscope.co/leo-sun-sagittarius-moon-an-inspirational-personality/

Denise. (2018f, October 15). Aries Sun Aries Moon: An admirable personality. I. TheHoroscope.Co. https://i.thehoroscope.co/aries-sun-aries-moon-an-admirable-personality/

Denise. (2018g, October 15). Aries Sun Leo Moon: A confident personality. I. TheHoroscope.Co. https://i.thehoroscope.co/aries-sun-leo-moon-a-confident-personality/

Denise. (2018h, October 15). Aries Sun Sagittarius Moon: A decisive personality. I. TheHoroscope.Co. https://i.thehoroscope.co/aries-sun-sagittarius-moon-a-decisive-personality/

Facebook, H. F., Iii. (2011, January 24). Astrology Western Sun and Moon sign combinations. Hugh Fox III. https://foxhugh.com/divination/sun-and-moon-sign-combinations/

Moon, J. (2017, November 23). Sun-Moon astrology combinations. Astroligion.com. https://astroligion.com/sun-moon-astrology-combinations/

Moon, J. (2018a, February 23). Leo sun Aries moon personality. Astroligion.com. https://astroligion.com/leo-sun-aries-moon-personality/

Moon, J. (2018b, February 23). Leo sun Leo moon personality. Astroligion.com. https://astroligion.com/leo-sun-leo-moon-personality/

Moon, J. (2018c, February 23). Leo sun Sagittarius moon personality. Astroligion.com. https://astroligion.com/leo-sun-sagittarius-moon-personality/

Moon, J. (2018d, October 22). Sagittarius sun Aries moon personality. Astroligion.com. https://astroligion.com/sagittarius-sun-aries-moon/

Moon, J. (2018e, October 22). Sagittarius sun Leo moon personality. Astroligion.com. https://astroligion.com/sagittarius-sun-leo-moon/

Moon, J. (2019a, March 17). Aries Sun Leo Moon personality. Astroligion.com. https://astroligion.com/aries-sun-leo-moon/

Moon, J. (2019b, March 17). Aries Sun Sagittarius Moon personality. Astroligion.com. https://astroligion.com/aries-sun-sagittarius-moon/

Sun in Aries & moon in signs. (n.d.). I. TheHoroscope.Co. https://i.thehoroscope.co/astrology/sun-moon/sun-in-aries/

Sun in Leo & moon in signs. (n.d.). I. TheHoroscope.Co. https://i.thehoroscope.co/astrology/sun-moon/sun-in-leo/

Sun in Sagittarius & moon in signs. (n.d.). I. TheHoroscope.Co. https://i.thehoroscope.co/astrology/sun-moon/sun-in-sagittarius/

Sun Moon combinations. (n.d.). I. TheHoroscope.Co. https://i.thehoroscope.co/astrology/sun-moon/

Kelly, A. (2018, February 2). 12 Zodiac Signs: Dates and Personality Traits of Each Star Sign. Allure. https://www.allure.com/story/zodiac-sign-personality-traits-dates

Coffey, J. (2009, December 27). Celestial Body. Universe Today. https://www.universetoday.com/48671/celestial-body/

Farnell, K. (2020). The man behind the horoscope column: R H Naylor. Astrology Quarterly. https://www.academia.edu/49600969/The_man_behind_the_horoscope_column_R_H_Naylor

Hall, M. (2011, November 12). Chart elements: Parts of the astrological birth chart. LiveAbout. https://www.liveabout.com/chart-parts-and-points-207194

Roberts, S. (2018, October 7). Babylonian astrology: How Mesopotamian priests influenced your horoscope. Ancient Origins. https://www.ancient-origins.net/history-ancient-traditions/babylonian-astrology-0010806

The Editors of Encyclopedia Britannica. (2021). astrology summary. In Encyclopedia Britannica.

We'Moon. (n.d.). What Sign is the Moon in, What is My Moon Sign, and What Does it all Mean? We'Moon. https://wemoon.ws/blogs/journey-into-astrology/what-sign-is-the-moon-in-and-what-does-that-mean

William Lilly (Lilly, William, 1602-1681). (n.d.). Upenn.edu. http://onlinebooks.library.upenn.edu/webbin/book/lookupname?key=Lilly%2C%20William%2C%201602%2D1681

Almanac.com homepage. (n.d.). Almanac.com. https://www.almanac.com/

Astrology Zodiac Signs. (n.d.). 12 astrology zodiac signs dates, meanings, and compatibility. Astrology-zodiac-signs.com. https://www.astrology-zodiac-signs.com/

Morin, A. (2012, October 12). Find out what a glyph is in archeology, language, and typography. ThoughtCo. https://www.thoughtco.com/what-is-a-glyph-2086584

Planets. (n.d.). NASA Solar System Exploration https://solarsystem.nasa.gov/planets/overview/

Beusman, C. (2018, October 17). Astrology is hard, even if it's fake. The New York Times. https://www.nytimes.com/2018/10/17/style/astrology-exam.html

Planets. (n.d.). Astrology.com. https://www.astrology.com/planets

Thomas, K. (2021, November 5). A guide to the planets in astrology and what they each represent. New York Post. https://nypost.com/article/astrology-planets-meaning/

Aries Ascendant / Rising Sign. (2015, April 21). Cafeastrology.com. https://cafeastrology.com/aries_ascendantrisingsign.html

Denise. (2018, November 9). Aries Rising: The influence of Aries Ascendant on personality. I.TheHoroscope.Co. https://i.thehoroscope.co/aries-rising-the-influence-of-aries-ascendant-on-personality/

Hall, M. (2009, May 23). Learn the easiest way to interpret a Taurus Rising birth chart. LiveAbout. https://www.liveabout.com/taurus-rising-rising-signs-207237

Holmes, M. (2022a, January 28). All the details on what Aries risings are *really* like. Cosmopolitan. https://www.cosmopolitan.com/lifestyle/a35293409/aries-rising/

Holmes, M. (2022b, March 8). If you're a Taurus Rising, we know what you're *really* like. Cosmopolitan. https://www.cosmopolitan.com/lifestyle/a35568032/taurus-rising/

Maffucci, S. (2022, May 18). What it means if you have Taurus rising as your ascendant sign. YourTango. https://www.yourtango.com/zodiac/taurus-rising-sign-ascendant

More on Taurus Ascendant, rising sign. (2015, April 18). Cafeastrology.com; Cafe Astrology .com. https://cafeastrology.com/taurus_ascendantrisingsign.html

Nunes, D. (2022, May 12). What it means if you have Aries rising as your Ascendant sign. YourTango. https://www.yourtango.com/zodiac/aries-rising-sign-ascendant

Sylvester, M. (2022, April 16). Aries rising sign: How it affects your personality & love life. Elite Daily. https://www.elitedaily.com/lifestyle/aries-rising-sign-personality-love-life

Sylvester, M. (2022, April 16). Cancer Rising Sign: How It Affects Your Personality & Love Life. Elite Daily. https://www.elitedaily.com/lifestyle/aries-rising-sign-personality-love-life

Sylvester, M. (2022, July 9). Gemini Rising Sign: How It Affects Your Personality & Love Life. Elite Daily. https://www.elitedaily.com/lifestyle/cancer-rising-sign-personality-love-life

Denise. (2018, November 9). Gemini Rising: The Influence of Gemini Ascendant on Personality. I.TheHoroscope.Co. https://i.thehoroscope.co/gemini-rising-the-influence-of-gemini-ascendant-on-personality